A TASTE FOR GARDENING

A Taste for Gardening
Classed and Gendered Practices

LISA TAYLOR
Leeds Metropolitan University, UK

ASHGATE

Published by
Ashgate Publishing Limited
Gower House
Croft Road
Aldershot
Hampshire GU11 3HR
England

Ashgate Publishing Company
Suite 420
101 Cherry Street
Burlington, VT 05401-4405
USA

Ashgate website: http://www.ashgate.com

British Library Cataloguing in Publication Data
Taylor, Lisa, 1966-
    A taste for gardening : classed and gendered practices
    1. Gardening - Social aspects - Great Britain 2. Mass media
    - Great Britain
    I. Title
    635'.0941

Library of Congress Cataloging-in-Publication Data
Taylor, Lisa, 1966-
  A taste for gardening : classed and gendered practices / by Lisa Taylor.
      p. cm.
  Includes bibliographical references and index.
  ISBN 978-0-7546-7221-0
  1. Gardening--Great Britain. 2. Gardening--Great Britain--Sociological aspects. I. Title.

  SB451.36.G7T37 2008
  635.0941--dc22

                                                              2008011918

ISBN 978-0-7546-7221-0

Mixed Sources
Product group from well-managed
forests and other controlled sources
www.fsc.org Cert no. SGS-COC-2482
© 1996 Forest Stewardship Council
FSC

Printed and bound in Great Britain by
TJ International Ltd, Padstow, Cornwall

Contents

List of Figures and Tables

Acknowledgements

Lots of people helped me to write this book. Thanks to all the gardeners who toured me around their gardens, welcomed me into their homes, took me to the *Spen Valley Flower Club* and shared their knowledge. For finding and introducing me, the embarrassed researcher, to many of the gardeners of the study, thanks to Jim Taylor. For sharing her memories of gardens on the Stoney Lane council estate, thanks to Nancie Taylor. I also owe a huge debt of gratitude to Kevin Hetherington and Paul Willis. For listening to my ideas, offering advice, reading drafts and recognising that ordinary gardeners and their gardens are worth writing about I'd like to thank Mark Dooley, Nick Cox, Marci Green, Gordon Hobson, Paul Lewis, Emma Robertson and Helen Wood. For encouragement thanks to Penny Botting, Martin Brady, Sarah Doonican, Michael Elson, Joanne Llewellyn, Kate O'Neill and Jane Shaw. Special thanks for particularly good advice at key points in the project must go to Kristyn Gorton, Ann Gray, Dorothy Hobson, Joanne Hollows, and Beverley Skeggs. For loving encouragement thank you Myles. And for beauty, love and joy my thanks to Alice and Freddie.

Chapter 1

Introduction: Towards an Ethnography of Ordinary Gardening

About the Book

Picture the scene. It is 1992 and I've just become a first-time homeowner with my partner somewhere in Cheshire. The house was built in 1904 and there is work to be done. It has a long back garden and a medium sized front, but the truth is that we don't really know what to do with it. At the same time, because we teach media studies in higher education we watch quite a lot of terrestrial television, where the garden is enjoying some popularity, and I'm partial to the lifestyle section of the weekend broadsheet press. We settle in, the garden slides over to me on the ledger of domestic responsibilities and then as I start to think about 'what to put in', the whole idea of the garden as media representation, as space and as a cultural practise starts to make me think.

And that is where the seed of this book really began. Faced with the question of what to do with a ready-made ordinary[1] domestic garden, a host of personal considerations about home-making began to meld together with some of my long-held interests. At this time the garden was receiving an enormous increase in media coverage, gardening magazines, such as *Gardeners' World*, which was launched in 1991, had a circulation of 272, 000 and a 1.5 million readership by 1994, and there were a number of other successful titles such as *Practical Gardening* (Bhatti 1999, 188). The garden was also a prominent facet of 'lifestyle' television, the genre which has been labelled, 'the genre of the nineties' (Medhurst 1999). Television scholars had begun to notice a definite shift in the UK 1990s terrestrial schedules from the 'hard' programming of current affairs and documentaries to softer, hobbyist lifestyle programming of home interiors, cookery and gardening (Brunsdon et. al. 2001; Moseley 2000). Makeover popularity was at its height in the late 1990s, indeed the schedules were subject to what Brunsdon has called a, 'day for night makeover takeover' (2003, 7). Wider socio-political trends inform why lifestyle television was so popular during the period: the expansion in home-ownership in the UK (Bhatti 1999) alongside a general trend towards increased lifestyling in British culture were set against the backcloth of an aspirational atmosphere of New Labour's 'things can only get better' campaign. Concomitantly, Brunsdon argues that factors such as women's continued contribution to the work force; the deferral of the first child in

---

1   My use of the term 'ordinary' is not necessarily synonymous with aspects of working-class culture; I want to use 'ordinary' to mean the non-spectacular, the mundane and the everyday in a way which is not owned by a particular class or social group.

families in higher social groups; and the appeal of independent lifestyle productions made by women for women prepared them to appreciate, the 'multi-layered feminization of the 8-9 slot' (Brunsdon 2003, 8). Actually, Brunsdon's descriptions of women at the time aptly described me: I was watching and enjoying the rather more cultured makeover programmes of the minority channels such as *Homefront in the Garden* (BBC2, 1997-), and looking at the BBC books that were tied to television series, such as Gay Search's *Instant Gardening* (1995) and magazines like *New Eden* that were aimed at helping relatively new gardeners to make a start. And while lifestyling the garden became a central trope in what Gripsrud calls the 'shared cultural menu' (2004, 213) of terrestrial television in the mid to late 1990s, people were also doing what the consumer address of lifestyle programmes was urging them to do: hungrily consuming gardening products in retailing. The garden industry's political economy expanded and diversified during the period. Specialist nurseries became retail chains such as Wyevale and Hillier which sold not just plants, but a host of other products such as books, gifts, barbecues and outdoor garden furniture. Indeed, MINTEL (1997) reported a rise in sales of 27 per cent between 1988 and 1993 and spending of £3 billion in 1996 (Bhatti 1999, 188). No wonder *Vogue* called gardening 'the new sex' in Spring 1998.

But there were other things occupying my approach to my new garden, which troubled my thinking about the media images I was looking at during the mid to late 1990s. I began to think back to the garden I had grown up in, back in Yorkshire in the early 1970s and when I stopped to consider contemporary garden images, from television and magazines and at the goods that one could buy at the garden centre, it struck me that council estate gardening in Yorkshire had held something quite specific. It represented a set of aesthetic ideas, in terms of its plants, how they were arranged and the garden's landscaping, that simply had no positive place in the mid-1990s garden culture I had begun to encounter. To pay homage to those aesthetics in the context of my own garden, I realised, would have been inappropriate, tasteless, a bad set of cultural choices. Why was this so, I wondered? Where did that lack of fit between the images I encountered and my own family garden come from? I began to realise that having access to middle-class images of the garden in the 1990s had revealed a gap between what had been desirable in Yorkshire in the 1970s and the culture I now inhabited. In this way, the impetus for the book started from my life experience of gardens and from the questions which emanated from the comparisons I made through my own class travelling form working-class origins to 'becoming', through education, middle-class. Indeed all the central questions addressed in this book come from an autobiographical root, for my own garden learning had come from affective female familial ties, from my grandmother, my aunt and from my mother. Did the tastes, preferences and knowledges I had about me in the 1990s have a specifically female edge? Why did I know about some plants and not others? How had my own location of class and gender positioned me in relation to garden culture? Effectively, it was these autobiographical questions which structured the pivotal questions around the research for the study.

This book is an empirical study about gardeners and gardening in late 1990s Britain. It records a specific moment in television, media and cultural history: it is about the ordinary cultural practise of gardening and its relationship with mediated images of the garden. The questions it asks and answers tell us something about the periodicity of classed and gendered relations in the garden and in television and media culture. And if there is to be a continuingly productive study of socio-cultural practises in relation to mediated culture, then it must learn from accounts of the past.

The book is organised around a number of key concerns which emanate from textual and ethnographic data gathered between 1998 and 1999; in this way, its findings detail a finite historical moment. Essentially it offers an analysis of the garden in television and media culture. Then using ethnographic data, it explores classed and gendered gardening practises as well as the relationship between media culture and gardening. Below, I sketch out the questions I pose in relation to these key concerns.

As a means of investigating the wider discursive regimes which play their part in the construction of ordinary classed and gendered identities, the book examines late 1990s images of the garden and gardening in the national and local lifestyle media. Using lifestyle programming and garden journalism, I ask if ordinary aesthetics were given legitimation in those representations of the garden. The book recognises the increased role of ordinary people as both 'experts' and lifestyle subjects. Arguing that this trend was indicative of a wider social shift in our culture, it asks whether the increase in ordinary subjects led to a concomitant embrace of previously marginalised representations of class and gender.

There are profound differences between how middle and working-class people have been socially, culturally and economically positioned in Britain since the nineteenth century. Domestic gardening has historically been conceived as a form of working-class regulation, while the middle-class have been positioned by urban planning as the group with the power to survey how the working-class live. I argue that working-class values have been systematically undermined by the institutional imposition of middle-class cultural values. And working-class people have more limited access to economic, social and cultural resources than members of the middle-class. This book shows how gardening has been used as a form of social class control. The chapters which follow unravel by what methods cultural values have been imposed on working-class people. Through an analysis of the varying distribution of resource assets, I ask if their equity bestows power on their owners and how such power is manifest in the context of the everyday practise of gardening. Arguing that gardening relies on taste as a symbolic mode of communication, which is closely imbricated with questions of identity, it asks whether different modes of classed and gendered being translate into how people practise gardening. And if there is a classed and gendered aesthetic, what factors comprise its visual look?

Since the book asks if gardening forms part of class identity, I ask what locations of gender bring to classed modes of gardening. The construction of gender is predicated on its proximity to class locations. Working-class women, for example, have historically been denied the right to be ladies, because of their distance from middle-classness. I question what gendered proximities to class bring to gardening practises: I ask, for example, what differences reside in the kinds of masculine and feminine gardening working- and middle-class people do. Recognising that gender is always classed, the book also questions what differences exist between men and women's gardening: can gardening be understood historically as a gendered practise?; do men and women practise different types of gardening?; are cultural resources gendered?; and is there a specifically gendered collection of aesthetic practises forged out of a specific set of socio-cultural factors?

Turning to the relationship between the media and its gardening audience, I explore how class, gender and age impinged on lifestyle media consumption during the period. I investigate whether gardeners felt incited to use or interpret lifestyle ideas or projects and, using the garden makeover genre in particular, I ask gardeners about their relationship with garden 'experts'. Were local gardening competences, which reside in dimensions of ordinariness, preferable to lifestyle ideas mediated at the national level? And finally, I ask whether ordinary gardening as a traditional way of life was preferable to lifestyling: might these practises enable people an imaginative means to cope with rapid social change?

This section has placed the book's historical perspective on the garden as a specific moment in late 1990s British television, media and culture. In what follows I discuss how the people of the study were contacted and recruited, their brief biographies, how they were 'classed' and how the interviews in domestic settings took shape.

Towards an Ethnography of Ordinary Gardening

Why ethnography?: key traditions in cultural studies and feminism

Cultural studies has always sustained a steady stream of ethnographic work (Moores 1996; Murdock 1997; Turner 1990) and the two traditions share common concerns. Historically, as a mode of enquiry, ethnography has links with the ethos of how culture was theorised by early writers in British cultural studies (Van Loon 2001). In the historiographical accounts of early culturalists (Hoggart 1957; Williams 1989) for example, the historical continuity of the English working-class, (outlined in more detail in chapter 2), operated at the mundane level of ordinary, everyday life experience. Research in the culturalist tradition centred on the generation of shared meanings by members of groups or societies in the midst of particular cultural phenomena. For them, ordinary people were theorised as active agents, responsible for generating their own sense of world-being. These emphases show the intrinsic connections between culturalism and how ethnography can be deployed:[2] both underline the pivotal role of everyday life and its meaningfulness for members as they define it 'from below'; both place an emphasis on charting specific examples of sense-making in lived culture; both are committed to uncovering and valuing local knowledges; and both are concerned to chart these meanings on their own terms.

For thinkers who align themselves with the culturalist strand of thought in cultural studies, the act of deriving meanings from sustained social contact with agents and recording and representing them on their own terms impacts on how theory

---

2   It is important to stress that ethnographic methods are not essentially linked to either cultural politics or feminism. As Skeggs (2001) argues, ethnographic methods have been used as tools for government agencies and for justifying colonialism, in other words ethnography, in some hands has been used for 'highly dubious ends' (2001, 5). It can, however, as I argue here, be used in politically empowering ways.

is positioned in ethnographic projects. In their opening manifesto to the first issue of *Ethnography* (2000) for example, Willis and Trondman argue for '"theoretically informed" ethnographic study' (2000, 6), but for them the knowledge produced by ethnography should never be 'pre-figured' by theory. Rather, as Willis argued in 1980, ethnography, 'has directed its followers towards a profoundly important methodological possibility – that of *being 'surprised'*, of reaching knowledge not prefigured in one's starting paradigm' (Willis 1996, 90). Ideally for Trondman and Willis (2000), ethnographic evidence should actually modify and refine theory: 'ethnographic writing,' they argue, 'has a crucial role to play in reshaping "theory" and in finding accommodations between, as well as forging new lines and directions from, social theorists' (Willis and Trondman 2000, 8). Some ethnographic work demonstrates how agency can contribute to the production of structure. In *Learning to Labour* (1977) for example, Willis demonstrates how the agency of 'the lads', their decisions and strategies for coping with the British class system, partially helped to structure the reproduction of class divisions. In this way, ethnographic methods enable the researcher to reconstruct a perspective from below in a way which shows the link between subjective micro-politics of everyday life and the macro-power structures which inhere within culture.

While I have so far sought to trace the mutual connections between cultural studies and ethnographic methods, there are also intellectual affinities between cultural studies and feminism. Both are concerned with the oppressed and with the role of lived experience (Gray 1997). Both have valorised the aim to represent the lives, voices and experiences of the silenced and the subaltern and both have fought a mutual antagonistic battle with academe as a consequence.[3] There have been a number of feminists working within media, film and cultural studies who have also been influenced by audience-reception studies, whose work focuses specifically on women's uses of the media. Studies such as Hermes's (1995) *Reading Women's Magazines* examines women's reading repertoires and everyday modes of consumption of magazines; Stacey's (1994) *Star Gazing* investigates acts of spectatorship and the role of female film stars in women's memories of wartime and post-war Britain; and Gray's (1992) *Video Playtime* examines class and taste in relation to women's use of VCR technology in the context of the gendered power dynamics of the household.

I want to place my own research within these traditions: the culturalist strand of cultural studies and feminism. I draw on its techniques because its methods are suitable for the kind of knowledge about ordinary gardening my book aims to produce. This study shares the early culturalist mission to value peoples' lived experience at the level of ordinary, everyday culture. It seeks to uncover the shared meanings and collective activities which inhere in gardening and it relates them to the wider cultural context in which experience is located. It envisions people as active agents, capable of creating their own sense of being-in-the-world. And it aspires to develop and represent local knowledge – as far as possible, on its own terms – about the

---

3   I do not mean to deny that while the two disciplines are affined in some ways, the relationship has been without problems. For an account of the tensions at BCCCS during the 1970s and 1980s see Brunsdon (1996) and Gray (1997).

experience of gardening in the context of people's own private gardens. In chapter 3, I argue that ordinariness has largely been vilified and that both women and the working-class have been the prime casualties of exclusion from the official annuls of academia: this project aims to give voice to such previously unheard voices as a means to value, legitimate and take them seriously. And sentient of the call to allow the ethnographic evidence to modify or at least temper the certainties of theory, I hope to allow the data in chapters which follow to surprise the reader with new, hitherto uncovered knowledge about ordinary gardening.

Why ethnography?: the garden as a new consumption site

While the home as setting has already been the subject of academic scrutiny, the garden offers new terrain to the cultural analyst. There is an established body of ethnographic work which examines the construction of class and gender in relation to domestic media consumption, utilising a variety of popular media genres and forms such as romance novels (Radway 1987), soap opera (Hobson 1982), the VCR (Gray 1992), television (Morley 1986), satellite television (Moores 1996), women's magazines (Hermes 1995), talk shows (Wood 2008) and reality television (Wood et al. 2008). Part of the political project of this body of cultural studies and feminist work was to conduct analysis of subjective locations, using the media, within the lived and familial power nexus of the home. While my book shares the need to examine the domestic setting in pursuit of similar political objectives, it also makes a spatial departure from this previous work. My analysis calls for the need to attend to the particular specificity of *the garden* as a different type of consumption space. Gardens are spaces about which one can make a range of general assumptions. Gardens are peculiar, hybrid spaces: part private, part public. In one sense they appear to exist as part of the private realm: decisions about them are often made inside the privacy of the home between family members and they are conceived and constructed as partially private extensions of the home dwelling (Bhatti 1999; Chevalier 1998; Sime 1993). Gardens are also located close to spaces within the home which have been conceived as private, domestic, 'feminine' zones – the kitchen and the dining area for example. On the other hand, the garden is an interface between the privacy of the house and the civic property of the street. It is a space onto which others can look, examine and judge. The sign-bearing garden offers an appearance that is public property; it acts as a character map of the people within the home. It is also one of the most profound and tangible manifestations of the class location of the breadwinner/s inside. Like the domestic spaces to which it is linked, it too generates work, but because it is at least partially public, that work can be seen and is on display. And just as the garden is located near to the feminine and the domestic, the garden is also attached to 'masculine' zones: for example the garden/tool shed and the garage. In these ways gardens are complex spaces which offer a new kind of window through which to investigate ordinary gender and class relations. Yet to date the assertions I discuss here remain at the level of assumption without the evidence of asking people, in the context of their own gardens, about how the garden as a space with a particular, yet specific tie to the familial, domestic setting is actually managed. There is a dearth of British, cultural studies empirical work on the garden as a material spatial entity; and there is, as I establish in chapter 3, no study which addresses the particular questions about class and gender in relation to the private small town garden addressed in this book. I argue therefore that in order to find out whether gardens as spaces where dichotomies such as professional/domestic, public/ private, masculine/feminine, work/leisure, exterior/interior remain staunchly intact or whether those boundaries can be eschewed as some navigate different ways of constructing their class and gender locations, one needs participant centred research methods. The garden as a new consumption space with its own specificities, requires ethnographic enquiry: this method has the potential to reveal whether the ideas and assumptions about the garden as a specific nexus of classed and gendered power relations have any material grounding in peoples' homes.

Finding Out …: Towards an Ethnography of Gardening

This book is based on a small-scale empirical study of a group of gardeners based in the North of England. I lived, for an eight month period, in the same small town community of the gardeners on which this study is based (for a resume of how the respondents were accessed, their personal details and how they are 'classified' by the study see Appendix 1). I draw on Bourdieu to argue that gardening is a field; a social sphere where struggles occur over access to its particular resources (for a more detailed definition of Bourdieu's terms see chapter 2). The practises in the empirical data illustrate the types of habitus as well as the strategies which are deployed and produced by the opportunities and inhibitors determined by the shape of the field. In this way, my empirical mapping acts to highlight the struggles which my respondents used for accruing, deploying and trading their various capitals in order to vie for improved positions in the field.

In order to gather the data, I used a number of qualitative ethnographic techniques. I engaged in participant observation: that is, I conducted semi-structured and informal conversational interviews in the living rooms, gardens, conservatories and greenhouses of the participants of the study (see Appendix 3 for details of the interviews). I helped respondents to garden (see Figure 1.1). The photograph shows Doris, with hoe and trowel, at the other end of the grass verge at the front of her house that I am helping to weed. I also became familiar with their gardens, either by helping them to garden, observing their gardening or by being 'toured' around them. I used what Ball and Smith call 'Camera-Supported Ethnographic Work' (2001, 313); I took photographs, which offer supporting visual evidence of the gardens on which this study is based. And on invitation from my chief informant, I joined the *Spen Valley Flower Club*, which arranged lunches, garden visits, and flower arranging events at the local church and secondary school. I also attempted, through participant observation, to glean some of the life history of the participants (see Appendix 2 for personal biographies of the people of the study). In these ways, I used ethnographic techniques as a means of gathering data which would build a 'picture' of gardening as an ordinary aspect of everyday familial life, as an activity which generated interaction between the participants and as a cultural entity in a typical small town community.

A Taste for Gardening

However, like a number of other media and cultural studies researchers, I would wish to qualify my specific use of the term 'ethnography'. Many researchers claim

Figure 1.1   Helping Doris to Garden the Front Verge, 1999

their work constitutes ethnography, even though there are wide discrepancies between the scope and breadth of the methods employed. For example, some studies are based on correspondence and questionnaires alone – see Stacey's (1994) work on cinema audiences; while others have relied upon a far deeper immersion in 'the field' which involves living in the homes and the communities of subjects for long time-periods – see Scheper-Hughes's (1982) exposure of farm parents in rural Ireland who through customary 'psychological violence' managed to 'break' a 'sacrificial child' who could inherit and manage the farm and care for the parents in old age (see also Scheper-Hughes's (2000) subsequent reflections on ethnographic methods and ethics). These kinds of differences, which focus on both the time spent and the level of intensity that the researcher can achieve with participants, have fuelled debate in media and cultural studies. For example, the claim that the in-depth, informal semi-structured interview, which characterised media reception ethnographies by researchers like Morley (1986), actually constituted genuine ethnographic work, was attacked by critics for its lack of anthropological long-term immersion in the field (Gillespie 1995; Nightingale 1993).

Already careful about making the full-blown claim to ethnography, media and cultural studies researchers have described their work in particular terms. Hermes (1995), for example, argues that her study of magazine consumption is 'ethnographic in orientation' (Hermes 1995, 178) and Gray (1992) describes her study of gendered VCR use as 'having ethnographic intentions' (Gray 1992, 32). Moreover, media researchers have mounted valid objections to the charge wrought by those who call for more anthropologically centred media studies. Gray (1997, 100) for example, argues that in making a comparison between cultural studies and anthropology, the focus – so crucial in media and cultural studies – on the analysis of the link between the textual negotiation of meaning and the social and the construction of cultural identities, is ignored. Spending longer periods of time with respondents, she asserts, would not necessarily make for a more productive analysis, if such questions are bypassed. And Moores (1996) raising practical objections, argues that it is difficult enough to cross the doorstep when researching daily domestic life, but 'to expect us to then live alongside these informants, "immersed" in the routines of a family or household group, is in most cases unrealistic. Such intrusions would not be tolerated' (Moores 1996, 31). Moores argues that interviews alone do allow for the possibility that the researcher can glean 'patterns of meaning and power' about the familial domestic setting and uncover the interpretative experiences of media consumption for respondents. Moreover, he asserts that qualitative audience research has, by bringing cultural politics to everyday practises, 'sharpened the critical edge' of ethnography (ibid.).

In the light of these commentaries, I set my own work in the tradition of media and cultural studies work that is ethnographic in intention. I cannot claim the anthropological use of the method which involves living with the subjects of the research over a considerable period of time, and nor, for the reasons given by Gray and others, do I believe such immersion was necessary. This book, centred as it is on questions of meaning, cultural identity and on the interpretative use of the lifestyle media, uses 'ethnography' as a descriptor because of the types of questions it poses and the analysis it draws upon, as much as it relies on the term ethnography to describe its theory of method.

Ethnography, Emotion and the Self

I form an important part of this study; like all writers, I am the researcher and producer of the text. In this study, however, the self in relation to my authorship is more visible: aspects of my life are interwoven at various points through the study; the research is located in a place I still call 'home'; my 'self' was known to respondents before the research process began and vice versa; and my family is connected to the place, the issues and the methods of this study. In this section I explore the issues my personal proximity to the study raises: I explore my positionality in relation to the research; I discuss how my autobiographical location and experience might act as a resource; and I consider how my emotional, subjective and personal feelings impact on the research.

The focus of this study centres on how a group of *other* people are located by class and gender. Yet I too have a particular (classed and gendered) location which I believe can be used to foreground themes that are central to this study. Class was centrally important at the early inception of cultural studies (Barker and Beezer 1992; Milner

1999) and the question of how to deal with the difficult contradictions of being in-between class locations is at the heart of the early texts which built cultural studies as a discipline (Hoggart 1957; Williams 1979). These authors used autobiography as a mode of cultural analysis through which to explore first hand experience of working-class life through the privileged lens offered by their university education. What one gleans from reading both Hoggart and Williams is sentient observation and respect for the details and nuances of working-class ordinariness. Though Williams portrays a more emotionally guarded stance than Hoggart, they were both concerned to document their personal histories of class and they wrote about their feelings. Both writers have been attacked – Hoggart perhaps more scurrilously than Williams – for their humanism and for their lack of attention to the systematic rigour of critical theory (see for example Easthope 1997). Yet as Medhurst (2000) argues, the turn to theory in the late 1980s and the relegation of class to the margins of the social science agenda tended to de-politicise cultural studies. In the process, facets of working-class culture, so key to autobiographical writing about class – 'expressivity, locality, communality, class … [became] the real casualties in the hyper-theorising which have marked the recent trajectory of Cultural Studies' (Medhurst, 2000, 23). Indeed, autobiography – such as the mode adopted by Hoggart, which is interwoven into his account of working-class culture, brings an important dimension to cultural analysis: it offers a means through which to understand lived culture; it potentially counters the de-politicisation of cultural studies and it insists categorically that the experiential be included. For these reasons I set this book within the tradition of culturalism which draws on autobiography: my own life experience of the garden offers a means to extend my analysis to how the personal, the political and the lived are experienced by others.

It is therefore necessary for me to place the location of myself under some kind of spot-light. I was born into a working-class household, though I cannot claim to be working-class now. If I use the aesthetic criteria that I show in later chapters pervades middle-class gardening practises, I too must accept, at least a partial, middle-class 'arrival'. While I once had a taste for the tight buds of hybrid tea roses and a love of bedding plants, today I have only the large, loosely formed, scented Gallica, Musk and English roses, which are prized by middle-class consumers. As an academic, I pursue, at least culturally, a middle-class profession which has a middle-class income attached. But like many academics who have been working-class, I occupy a curious, 'in-between' type of location (Hoggart 1957; Mahony and Zmroczek 1997; Medhurst 2000; Skeggs 1997). For one's class location is never just about where one stands in the present; to label myself 'working-class' would not fit, yet to be seen as 'middle-class' would not be entirely 'right' either. Class, as Medhurst argues is, 'a question of identifications, perceptions, feelings' and I can only agree with the feeling he describes in announcing his own class identity as, 'uncertain, torn and oscillating – caught on a cultural cusp' (Medhurst 2000, 20).

Being 'in-between' is a strange location, but it offers certain kinds of insights for the cultural analyst conducting this type of study. Gripsrud (1989) argues that previously-working-class academics have 'double-access' to both high and popular forms of culture. Academic training means that they have the competence to be able to consume both high and low cultural forms, even though the relationship with popular culture is no longer what it was. Double access, for Gripsrud, can only be an advantage, for previously-working-class academics have a type of lived access to popular texts which middle-class academics can never have. Similarly, Medhurst argues that his status as a 'once-working-class' academic affords him 'an understanding of how culture works' and, as a result, what he calls 'experiential literacy' in relation to popular media texts (Medhurst 2000, 33). In similar vein, my marginal, once-working-class location affords its own insights: the theoretical tools garnered in academic life can enable an understanding of a long-standing personal history of working-class everyday practises and aesthetics. However, I have come to middle-class aesthetics along a rather more complex route: while academic study of English literature, art history and so on affords a particular type of access to high culture, I have had to learn afresh the rules governing lived middle-class garden aesthetics in the field. The researcher may bring experiential knowledge of certain class locations, but the researcher may also feel a lack of confidence, ignorance and perhaps even a measure of incompetence in the social field.

Yet the experiential is connected to things that scholarly academic writing in the social sciences has traditionally been uneasy about, or at least has fought hard to underplay: feelings and emotion (Hetherington 1998). Yet when I look at the photograph of the garden where I spent those early years (see Figure 2.1) I feel the jolt of a clutch of emotions which remind me of the gendered dimension of my autobiography. The garden reminds me of an (almost) lost female family line who all made some investment in the garden: grandmother brought her nursery knowledge and tastes to bear on the look of the garden, my aunt Ella brought cuttings and plants from the places she rented in as a textile worker during the war. And the garden reminds me of passed down preferences and forms of ordinary gardening knowledge that have passed from grandmother, through to my mother and down to me. So predominantly, I feel a sense of loss in relation to locality, community and belonging – aspects of working-class culture, which I am convinced once left can never be fully re-imbursed. For when my mother married in 1979 and we packed my step father's car with belongings, I remember a street of people waved us off – and I was never to experience a sense of local community of that kind again. So what I really feel when I look at those early photographs of the garden are those emotions for which Hoggart and others who have written about their own personal histories of working-class life have been reproached: nostalgia and sentimentality. Yet these emotions are in part about valuing working-class life. Hoggart himself knew that his autobiographical work was open to attack for 'sentimental over-valuing', but as he argues, sentimentality is an emotional risk one must take if, 'we are to get away from the … attitude which thinks of working-class people as almost blank slates, with none of the rich and elaborate manners of the middle and upper classes' (Hoggart 1958, 132). These kinds of emotions are also important for keeping the motivation for the politics of class and gender alive. I return to sentimentality and the garden more fully in the final chapter of the book.

But most significantly, the location of the emotional self has an important impact on the type of research that one can produce. So that some of the strong feelings that I have had in the ethnographic research process – sentimentality and sympathy for working-class respondents and feelings of irritation and even anger at middle-class interviewees – need to be taken on board with regard to the analysis of my data, recognising emotion provides an insight in its own right. For as Walkerdine (1997) argues: 'it is an impossible task to avoid the place of the subjective in research … instead of making futile attempts to avoid something which cannot be avoided, we should think more carefully about how to utilise our subjectivity as a feature of the research process' (1997, 59). Increasingly however, the emotions of the researcher are being acknowledged in current discussions about qualitative methodology (Coffey 2002, 313). In some respects, the role of the ethnographer is to be a biographer. On the whole, one thinks of ethnography as being about writing up the experiences of *other* people. But as Coffey (2002) argues, 'the qualitative researcher or ethnographer are simultaneously involved in auto/biographical work of their own' (2002, 314). While this is generally true of ethnography, this study is especially intimately connected to my own personal history: I have a long-standing historical familiarity with the types of gardens this study analyses and I have felt the symbolic violence of others who have disdained aspects of my (previously) working-class gardening taste; the subjects and gardens at the heart of my empirical work are located only three miles from the small industrial town in which I grew up; my step father set up almost all the interviews; and several of the subjects of this study know me (one of them taught me at the local grammar school, some are my parents' neighbours, others have worked alongside my parents since before I was born) and my life development – they also know 'the story', if you will, of the relationships between my mother, my biological father and my step father. These factors render this a study which is shot through with intensely personal issues. My personal self simply cannot be separated from the methodological and representational processes of the project. I can only hope, as Coffey (2002) argues that: 'in recognising the 'self-work' that is part of both research and representational processes, there is greater scope for understanding and making sense of social settings and cultural processes' (2002, 327).

Outline

Chapter 2 contextualises and sets up the framework of the book. It begins with autobiographical moments from the council estate where my family lived and gardened in the 1950s. Setting the house and garden in the historical context of the socio-political changes which structured post-war reconstruction, I show that while ordinary people were urged in the 1950s to adopt the middle-class values of 'good' design taste, working-class people have their own locally generated aesthetic language which acts as a form of dissension against such values. Charting a general history of working-class surveillance through town and city planning (Savage and Miles 1994), I outline how domestic gardening acted as a form of working-class regulation. Using early left culturalism and culturalist feminism, I construct a framework which values working-class culture. Dedicated to understanding culture through ordinary practises, I use Felski's (2000) phenomenological approach to ordinariness and the everyday. Asserting that these dimensions are central to how people replenish their sense of identity, I make a commitment to examine the intrigue which resides in the ordinary enthusiasm of gardening. However, while everybody shares ordinary life dimensions, one of the main arguments of the book is that people are always subjectively located by class and gender. Chapter 3 turns to the theoretical framework of the book. Arguing that Bourdieu's theoretical concepts and theories hold 'explanatory power' for understanding social class, I draw on his notion of habitus, field and forms of capital (1977, 1986), his approach to taste and aesthetics (1986, 1990b) and his theory of symbolic violence (1990a). Despite the charge that class is losing its credence as a social category of identification in contemporary culture (Chaney 1996), I discuss recent empirical literature on lifestyle and class difference, classed boundaries of belonging and identification and on taste, working-class (dis) identification and the inequality of lived subjective relations of class and gender, which show the continued salience of class as a concept. Turning to questions of gender, I outline why Bourdieu's theory is inadequate for an understanding of gender, arguing that Butler's (1990) theory of performativity has more to offer my analysis of modes of gendered gardening. Chapter 4 discusses inter-disciplinary literature, with a view to historicise and geographically locate my ethnographic study of ordinary gardens in a small semi-industrial town in West Yorkshire. I argue that while much has been written about the garden – from liberal humanist, Marxist and feminist perspectives – it is recent work on the social history of the private domestic garden which offers the most productive contextual backdrop for the insights about gardening produced by this book. Drawing on contemporary social theory, Chapter 5 analyses the textually mediated images of gardens, gardeners and 'personality-interpreters' provided by the local and national media at the time the ethnographic data was gathered in the late 1990s. I investigate the importance of lifestyle for the media and culture industries. Using examples, I look at the predominant themes and aesthetic concerns of the then contemporary garden. Using both the role of the 'personality-interpreter' and examples of ordinary people in lifestyle programming, I examine the increased significance of 'ordinariness' in contemporary culture. Chapters 6, 7 and 8 reveal my ethnographic findings on class, gender and lifestyle media consumption. Using a Bourdieusian theoretical framework in chapter 6, I analyse the differences between middle- and working-class gardeners in relation to what gardening means and the differences in aesthetic disposition of each. Chapter 7 uses ethnographic data to show gardening practises are used to try on (classed) gendered identities. Using Butler's (1990) notion that gender is a masquerade, and as a means to examine how the men and women of my study inhabit gendered modes of being, I ask what tasks men and women perform in the garden. Using a case study of floristry and flower arranging I ask whether there is a gendered gardening aesthetic. Using cultural studies literature on media audiences and focusing on the socio-variables of class, gender and age, I examine the mode of consumption garden lifestyle takes in chapter 8. By analysing my respondents' approach to the action of their garden projects, I explore how/ if they imaginatively interpret/ execute mediated lifestyle ideas. Using Chaney's (2001) work on the contemporary cultural transition from 'ways of life' to 'lifestyle' I examine what the investment in ordinary gardening practises meant to the people of the study. Chapter 9 concludes the book by arguing that a new kind of capital, 'sentimental capital', is required for attempting to understand how forms of emotional valuing become fastened to everyday routine gardening practises – especially amongst the working-class people of the study. I argue that mapping the making, deployment and exchange of sentimental capital allows an understanding of the nostalgic recurrence of particular gardening aesthetics as an authentic 'way of life' which remain virtually unchanged in particular enclaves of British working-class culture.

Chapter 2

Histories and Context

My First Garden: A Case Study of Ordinary Classed and Gendered Aesthetics

The photograph (see Figure 2.1) shows a back garden on a council estate in West Yorkshire in the mid-1950s. If you look closely, in the borders there are carnations

Figure 2.1   The Thornton Garden, Stoney Lane Council Estate, 1954

and some orange hybrid tea roses, the kind bred and aggressively marketed for working-class consumers in the 1950s (Harkness 1978). A mop-head hydrangea resides in the far corner. The parameters, set in place by the council estate planners – concrete posts and green chicken wire – act as an early fencing system until the ubiquitous privet hedge was to grow up to the desired height. But the central feature of this garden is the rectangle of nemesias in the centre of the lawn. Drawing on a design reminiscent of municipal park planting schemes, the idea of a central bed in the middle of the lawn is a typically working-class aesthetic trope. The lawn acts as a frame for the summer pride of the working-class garden: the bedding plants that create a riot of colour at its centre. Subsequent summers would see the same bed full of roses and edged by bedding plants – precisely the planting scheme that the contemporary garden journalist Christopher Lloyd[1] (1984) warns the would-be gardener against. Yet the garden in the photograph, the garden where I spent my early childhood with my mother and grandparents, was admired and valued by local people in the community. Indeed my mother told me that a neighbour 'couldn't resist' taking the slide because, 'he thought the garden looked so colourful'.

In this way, the garden where I grew up was expressive of a distinctive set of classed garden aesthetics. It drew on the ordinary language of gardening specific to the north of Britain in the mid-1950s. My grandparents used their own classed, historical knowledge of gardening passed down from their parents; they looked to the plants they had seen as council tenants in other peoples' gardens; they used the local municipal park as a reference point for some of their planting schemes; grandma brought ideas back from Wells's plant nursery where she had worked since the 1940s and they watched Percy Thrower's *Gardening Club* (BBC, 1956-), on the television set they had newly purchased in 1953 for the Queen's coronation. Their gardening allusions were not drawn from the language of modernism lauded at the time by the middle-class design establishment – like, for example, Sir Frederick

Figure 2.2   Standing in Front of the Hydrangeas, 1969

---

1   Christopher Lloyd has written a number of influential books about how to select tasteful plants for the garden, see for example, *The Well-Chosen Garden* (1984). Lloyd owns the celebrated house and garden 'Great Dixter' in Surrey, and describes himself as a 'plantsman'. He has a long-standing career as a gardening journalist in middle-class quarters of the British press such as *The Guardian*.

Gibberd's Garden 'Marsh End' in Harlow.[2] Rather, their gardening was drawn from what most families in the post-war period could access: largely commonplace plants set into creative local aesthetic arrangements. From photographs and from what I have managed to learn from my mother, grandma loved hybrid tea roses, in particular the famous apricot yellow 'Masquerade' and the lilac pink 'Blue Moon'. She also enjoyed hydrangeas (mop-head as opposed to the less frequently seen lace-cap variety – now prized by middle-class gardeners), 'pinks' and spring bulbs. The garden had cheap and cheerful 'bushes' such as forsythia. And bedding plants played an absolutely key role, in particular nemesias, night-scented stock, alyssum and blue lobelia were brought back from Wells's and were enjoyed every summer. But while my grandmother brought back bedding plants during the summer months, the shrubs at Bentley Avenue had either been moved from the gardens of family or friends or they grew from cuttings. The bank of mop-head hydrangeas, the ones I am standing in front of in Figure 2.2, came from cuttings placed straight into the ground. Resources, for working-class families, have always been an issue. For as my mother was keen to stress, the family never visited garden centres – they simply 'didn't have 'em in those days'. The lack of economic resources had some bearing on what the family could 'have' in terms of trees, flowering shrubs and plants; in some instances the garden was about 'making do'. But while council houses and gardens were designed to a template, the garden at Bentley Avenue was not simply the sum of commonplace parts. As mother was keen to tell me, grandma liked to have a few things that were: 'a bit showy, for people going past, to show you had a knowledge. My mother liked to have things that were classy, upmarket. She was the only person on that estate that 'ad a magnolia tree.'

Yet while class was central to the visual look of the Thornton garden, gender had an equally important bearing on aesthetics. The garden seen in Figure 2.1 was mostly the product of grandma's choice and management. Grandad had no involvement in the garden's look, nor, my mother told me, did he have very much to do with the labour that kept it maintained. Employed as a master-plumber until his early seventies, grandad worked for six days a week. Consequently, it was my mother and her older sister Ella who 'put plants in, did the lawn and kept up to it', since grandma was too frail to labour. Consequently, the aesthetics at Bentley Avenue were centred around the plants and planting designs grandma liked. While Stoney Lane council estate was comprised of standardised houses and gardens, there were important differences in how individual gardens were planted and arranged. Grandma's choice of aesthetics could be distinguished from Mr. Moore's garden next door. His use of the garden rested entirely on re-creating the tightly patterned bedding arrangements found in municipal park designs. He had carefully manicured lawns and beds filled in summer with low level impatiens, marigolds and white alyssum that would be cleared out and left bare each autumn. In this way, Mr Moore brought a specifically public aesthetic to his garden. By contrast, grandma liked showy, ornamental, feminine plants and flowers. While the tiny detailed frailty of

---

2   Marsh End, Harlow, Essex is, 'generally regarded as one of the finest examples of late twentieth century modern design' (Brown 1999). It was made for Sir Frederick Gibberd (1908–1984), architect, landscape architect and town planner.

certain bedding plants were important, she prized flowers that traditionally signify femininity through their form, colour and perfume and she loved flowers that could be cut and taken indoors. For example, she loved the dainty shapes of double lilac and the elegance of magnolia; the perfume of lily of the valley and roses and she grew anemones because they could be cut and taken in to the house. According to my mother's account, grandma's garden tastes were hardly surprising, given that she liked the things that women have historically been constructed to desire (Coward 1984; Sparke 1995). She liked delicate jewellery, English perfume such as Yardley's 'Bond Street', good clothes and fine fabrics of lace and silk and she was fond of prints typical of the period – such as, to use my mother's words – 'big rose-blown designs'. Figure 2.3, which shows grandma and grandad in the lounge in 1966, illustrates my

Figure 2.3   Grandma and Grandad, 1966

point. The photograph shows grandma in a silk floral dress and she wears a jewelled necklace. She also had a small collection of china, including 'ornaments' decorated with porcelain roses, carnations and pansies. My grandmother, an ordinary, middle-aged woman in the 1950s, enjoyed the look, feel and fragrance of women's things;

and she took that sensuous relationship with traditionally feminine objects out to the garden.

In these ways, the garden where I grew up was expressive of an ordinary, yet distinctive collection of classed and gendered garden aesthetics[3] which contravened the legitimised modernist principles of the 1950s design establishment.

My First Garden in Context: Ordinary People's Appropriation of 1950s Establishment Aesthetics

Grandma and grandad moved to their council house, which had been built in 1947, in 1951; in this way, they lived in the context of the 1945 Labour government's post-war reconstruction plan to provide minimum housing standards for all citizens (MacDonald and Porter 1990). During this period, the government renewed its subsidies to local authority house-building programmes. Post-war re-building began with the 1946 New Towns Act which gave towns and cities 'expanded town' development: this amounted to new estates – like the Stoney Lane estate my grandparents lived at – on the town edges (Clapson 2000). The design establishment in this period was heavily influenced by the tenets of modernism and the reconstruction plan aimed to make modernity accessible to all citizens (Attfield 1999). For modernists, urban planning could bring order and rationality to the built environment and it was believed that 'good design' was under-girded by functional, utilitarian values. For modernists the *form* of housing determined its use. Modernism has been identified as a 'classed and gendered practice' (Hollows 2000, 125), reflecting masculine rationalism and upper-class privilege by valuing form over function. Its aims were to encourage the public to reject traditional decor and superfluous 'feminine' ornament, and take up a minimalist aesthetic. For example, domestic interiors were designed to reflect the embrace of modernism through the use of 'open plan', which was based on the removal of walls to reveal 'open' democratic living spaces with an emphasis on ease and use of maintenance (Attfield 1999; MacDonald and Porter 1990). In similar vein, modernist landscape architects Geoffrey Jellicoe, Russell Page and John Brookes used geometric, modern art to influence their garden designs that utilised modernist sculpture in minimalist setting. More specifically however, post-war housing was also shot through with ideas about family life and women's role in it (Hollows 2000). Feminist research on architecture explores the ways in which the physical layout of post-war housing served to organise and mediate familial gender roles (Madigan and Monroe 1990), in ways which acted to legitimate an image of 'appropriate' working-class family life (Boys 1995). Yet while urban planning and material culture might be produced with class and gender 'written-in' (Kirkham 1997), this does not necessarily hold sway over their consumption.

In 1944 the Council of Industrial Design was established by the Board of Trade. Its aims were principally to re-stimulate the growth of British industry by the promotion of 'good design'. Using 'propaganda strategies the Government had used in wartime'

---

3   I am aware that garden aesthetics are also raced. Another rich possibility for further work might be concerned to trace how the racial category of 'whiteness' (Dyer 1997) impacts on aesthetic choices.

(MacDonald and Porter 1990, 38), the CoID mobilised the media to 'democratise' design. *House and Garden* and *Ideal Home* advocated modernist design, but in order to out-reach a working-class audience the CoID enlisted the agency of *Woman,* a publication which claimed by the 1950s to reach half the female population. The design establishment created a project aimed at both manufacturers and consumers and publications, exhibitions and events were designed with the specific aim of educating women about the 'correct' principles of home layout, gardens and the means to consume home durables in ways that signified 'good taste'. For example, the Festival of Britain exhibition in 1951 showcased 'open plan' room sets as a means of advocating modernism; it also featured garden designs that drew on the geometric abstract modernism of painters and sculptors such as Mondrian, Burra, Moore and Hepworth. In this way, the gardens lauded by the design establishment drew on the ideas of gardeners excited by the aesthetics of modernist painting. Note, for example, the following description of a design by Jellicoe, who: 'designed an abstract rose garden for Cliveden adapted from Paul Klee's *The Fruit,* expressing enclosure and fecundity in a womb-like way' (Brown 1999, 235). The esoteric intellectualism encased in these kinds of descriptions, illustrates the inaccessibility of modernist aesthetics for working-class people: no wonder a gap appeared between what the establishment wanted people to do and what people could actually achieve.

In this way, while the design establishment tried to train the working-class to adopt modernist principles of 'good taste' and working-class women to make their living rooms open plan, ordinary working-class people – as my portrait of my grandparents' everyday gardening aesthetics illustrates – had their own means of making land-plots into gardens and houses into homes. Judy Attfield's (1995) study of Harlow 'New Town' in the 1950s shows how architects' ideas about family life, which were built into Harlow, were flouted by women who refused to consume domestic space in the way in which the planners intended. Since the architects built houses which had no relation to the residents' conception of what constituted 'home', residents took aesthetic purchase of them and invested them with their own meanings. For example, the Harlow women used furniture as a means to compartmentalise the open plan living room back to the traditional parlour and private back room; and windows, designed by planners to let in light, were shielded by nets and bedecked with feminine ornaments (Attfield 1995, 228). In a similar way, as Figure 2.4 shows, the windows at Bentley Avenue refused plain open glass because grandma had them leaded, and the open-plan living room was divided by the use of the sofa. What Attfield's work shows and what my grandparents' consumption of their home illustrates was that, 'many chose to take possession ... invest their own values, often knowingly in contravention of the official line' (1995, 228). In the 1950s, the working-class – most specifically women – consumed their homes as sites through which to articulate classed and gendered identities.

Indeed, I believe that the will to impose middle-class tastes on to the working-class[4] is still in stark evidence. The working-class aesthetic trope in Figure 2.1, featured in the opening lines of this chapter, so valued by my family, neighbours and

---

4   Bourdieu (1990) terms this kind of cultural imposition 'symbolic violence'. The terms of his theory will be dealt with in more detail in chapter 3.

passers-by back on a council estate in the late 1950s, and which exists to this day in ordinary British gardens, certainly had no positive place in late 1990s lifestyle media. A working-class image, so redolent of what middle-class audiences knew

Figure 2.4   Refusing Establishment Aesthetics: the Leaded Windows at Bentley Avenue, 1955

to be 'vulgar taste' was denigrated by lifestyle garden designers. In an episode of *Gardening Neighbours* (BBC2, 1998-) for example, Ali Ward and Andy Sturgeon makeover an older couple's back garden in a row of terraced houses in Sheffield. The garden they treasure, one that virtually repeats the design of my grandparents' back-garden, a concretised space with a raised central bed of multi-coloured impatiens, is bulldozed in favour of a French formal garden of topiaried bay trees. Designer-presenters Ali Ward and Andy Sturgeon are proud to have swept away a tasteless and dated design. But the reaction shot shows that meaning and personal recollection have been lost for Terry and Joan – 'it was beautiful before you changed it' remarks Terry. Working-class aesthetics, at that moment in television history, were simply not valued beyond the confines of the local; it was middle-class gardening tastes which the lifestyle media lauded and legitimated.[5] Indeed, when I began to garden

---

5   Using Bauman (1987) I argue that the lifestyle media interprets ideas for consumers. Yet, even though as Bauman argues, institutions such as the media hold less authority as legislators in the current climate, their interpretations still laud middle-class aesthetics.

seriously myself as a first-time home owner in the mid 1990s, I began to notice a difference between the tastes and practices I had grown up with as a child and the 'desirable' practices novice gardeners were being shown in the media.

This section has drawn parallels between two historical moments in British culture where the middle-class establishment has attempted, with limited success, to define and control the aesthetic fabric of the living space of working-class subjects. The following section looks at how the working-class have historically been made visible, positioned and regulated through urban planning. It shows that gardening was historically conceived as a regulatory activity with the potential to position the working-class into a safe place: the home.

Historical Legacies: Urban Planning and Working-class Leisure Since the Nineteenth Century

Since the mid-nineteenth century the State, successive governments and upper-class commentators have demonstrated their fear of the working-class.[6] Constructed as an object of social and moral concern, the working-class have been regarded as a degenerate, savage, irresponsible and fecund mass. Seen as a threat to bourgeois liberal democracy (Walkerdine 1997), they have been conceived as potentially threatening on two counts: as a dangerous revolutionary collective and as a debased threat to civilisation and respectability (Skeggs 1997). Examples from social history show how the middle-class, as a result of these negative assumptions, acted to regulate, survey and control the living-spaces and recreational activities of working-class subjects. Savage and Miles (1994) for example, argue that what was significant about the planning of British new towns and cities in the mid-1800s, 'was the extent to which the middle-class claimed the right to survey – in the name of health, education and morality – vast swathes of working-class residence' (Savage and Miles 1994, 58). Philanthropic public health observers, such as Henry Mayhew and Charles Booth, researched the geography of new cities to position and examine the working-class to render them discernible to the middle-class. Similarly, 'factory colonies', such as Saltaire near Leeds, offered Titus Salt the opportunity to regulate his entire workforce by building houses and facilities for his workers. Often leading employers funded local churches or schools and played a key role in managing them, 'which would, in turn, tend to forestall working-class organisation and activity' (Savage and Miles 1994, 61–62). Similarly, Yeo and Yeo (1981) evidence how social movements in the north of England in the 1830s, such as the Friendly Societies, which were devoted to the organisation of financial mutual aid for working-class people, were systematically denied the right to use so called 'public' buildings as collective meeting places. The same period saw open middle-class hostility, especially to group or community types of working-class leisure: 'Temperance reformers, capitalists and local authorities attacked rowdy styles of celebration …in the interests of salvation,

---

6   Matthew Arnold, for example, advocated that 'Culture' with a capital 'C' should be used to enlighten the 'populace' (working-class) precisely as a means to quieten growing social unrest in the 1840s. Arnold's anxieties about the working-class are illustrated in _Culture and Anarchy_ (Arnold 1993).

of labour discipline and of social order' (Yeo and Yeo 1981, 172). Leisure historians illustrate that the middle-class took a very negative view of public, community based popular recreation during this period. Many of their objections were focused on the fact that activities such as 'low-grade theatre, music hall or riotous street outing; wakes, fairs and violent sporting activities; and the ubiquitous public house and associated games and gambling' (Constantine 1981, 390) distracted the working-class from family, home and the domestic. Later in the century football attracted men towards organised commercial recreation – but again this was not home-centred. As a result, growing middle-class dismay and alarm led to a series of campaigns to discipline the working-class in their leisure consumption. Indeed, it was these circumstances which led to attempts to encourage gardening as a civilising agent for the urban and rural working-class. As the following extract from an editorial in an edition of *Amateur Gardening* illustrates:

> All that concerns us here to do is to direct the attention of our readers, and especially the philanthropists among them, to the possibility of accomplishing much good among the poor classes by directing their attention to the beauty of flowers … that will not tempt them to drink, or gamble, or fight, or slander …One of the safest means of improving the labouring population is to provide them with innocent recreations (Constantine 1981, 391).

Indeed some of these 'philanthropic' wishes to encourage popular gardening were realised. For example, the *Society for Promoting Window Gardening Amongst the Working-Classes of Westminster* organised flower shows in the 1860s and 1870s; and several of the industrialists who built factory colonies, such as Lever at Port Sunlight, built gardens for their workers and encouraged gardening as a recreation by setting up yearly prizes for the best plots (Constantine 1981). In these ways, gardening offered what the middle-class perceived as a deficient working-class some kind of ameliorative potential: 'private gardens were expected to lead to healthier, more contented, more efficient, and more respectable employees and citizens' (Constantine 1981, 392). Unfortunately however, statistics show that while there were more gardens available to working-class people in rural areas, there was a dearth of private gardens in urban areas. The Rowntree survey of York conducted in 1901, for example, showed that only 12 per cent of working-class families occupied class 1 houses, and of those only a handful had, 'a sad apology for a garden' (Constantine 1981, 393). Land proved costly, the working-class wage was low, high density of building was unavoidable in towns and the population, as a result of industrialisation, was drawn to urban centres: there were simply too many urban detractions to make gardening a practical possibility in the nineteenth century.

By stark contrast, social change in the twentieth century meant that gardening flourished as a working-class leisure activity. Several factors made home-centred leisure more practically possible for ordinary people: the manual worker's nine hour day was reduced to eight in 1919 and was further reduced by 1940 and the introduction of British Summer Time in 1916 gave the gardener extra time in the evenings; urban poverty decreased – wage increases were 30 per cent higher in 1938 than they had been in 1913; and family size fell, which meant that people had more income to spend on gardening (Constantine 1981). But the singularly most important factor which contributed to the popularity of gardening was the growth of house-building in the inter-war years. Between 1919 and 1939, four million new homes were built in Britain (Clapson 2000), and significantly, most had private gardens. Moreover, the standard house design which had already proved successful on new private estates, modelled on places such as Port Sunlight, which was low-density, semi-detached and with private gardens to the front and rear, was extended to new working-class housing. Clearly, planners were sentient of the arguments promulgated by urban reformers such as Lever and Rowntree: sub-standard housing, they argued, led to an ineffectual workforce, poor health, moral decline and class unrest. To these ends, gardens were a key feature of the new houses: they produced estates with a visual appeal, they offered sunlight and fresh air to occupants and, most significantly, they provided the residents with the opportunity to occupy themselves with home-centred recreation: gardening. As a result, many working-class people enjoyed the rising standard of living provided by suburban and council-estate housing – as this oral testimony of a man who moved to an inter-war London County Council cottage estate reveals: 'Before we moved in we came to the house quite a few times. It was semi-detached and had a small front garden and not a very big back garden. We would sit on the stairs and have our picnic and then wander around. I thought it was smashing really' (Clapson 2000, 155). In these ways, twentieth century urban planning gave working-class people domestic frameworks which attempted to urge them to take up morally respectable positions without the need to resort to visible, rule-bound and punitive power. Skeggs (1997) uses Foucault (1977) to argue that the 'civilising' inducements that working-class women have experienced to enjoy domestic work and child care, 'shows how pleasure was used as a form of productive power. By trying to teach working-class women to take pleasure from bourgeois domesticity they could be induced to do it without direct, obvious control' (Skeggs 1997, 46). Similarly, providing recreational activities which people enjoy means that the compliance of working-class subjects is achieved amenably and with gratification on the part of the subjects themselves: gardening gave the middle-class precisely this kind of positive power over the lower orders.

However, not everyone enjoyed gardening and not everyone was as willing to offer their social compliance as conveniently as middle-class commentators would have liked. As one historian, describing photographs from the period observed: 'the newly built estate could appear bleak and forbidding ... gardens grew willy-nilly, and war with the incipient wilderness fore and aft of the house was perhaps accepted as a necessary evil' (Constantine 1981, 397). By way of an attempt at more direct social regulation, council estate tenants were given handbooks which gave firm aesthetic stipulations on how the front garden should be tended. For example, the 1933 east London Becontree Council Estate handbook:

> Neglect of the garden spoils the appearance of any house. It is of special importance that the front garden should be neat and tidy throughout the year ...strive to obtain a natural look rather than an artificial effect. Bordered edging and concrete paths do not give the restful effect of turf with neatly trimmed edges (Preston 1995, 86).

Although my family were not as conscientious as Mr. Moore next door, who my mother told me was 'regimented, tidy – cut his lawn with scissors', I was told that they 'kept up to it'. My family were no more immune to the incitement to keep the garden tidy, and by implication respectable, than any other working-class family on the Stoney Lane estate. Preston's (1995) evidence of council stipulations cited above on council estates in both east and south-west London in the 1930s was clearly extended to north England counties. When the Thorntons moved into their house in 1951 they were given a tenant's handbook which stipulated regulations on house occupancy, regulations on pets and there were rules about the garden. From memory my mother was able to recall local council rules that insisted on clipped hedges and a regularly mown lawn with neat edges. But beyond what was written down, my family and the other working people who lived there understood that a discourse of respectability, held dear as a model of 'how to be' by most working-class tenants, pervaded the atmosphere of the estate. And it was these expectations that made the front garden – the space which the critical gaze of passers-by could so easily judge – the focus of respectability for these working-class gardeners. 'You're more concerned with the front in a way,' my mother told me.

But while estate regulations testify to some working-class dissent, evidence suggests that most people wanted gardens (Clapson 2000, 157) and social investigators found in a pre-Second World War survey that 85 per cent of people kept their gardens in a good to fair condition. There are various views on why gardening became increasingly popular. Preston (1995) argues – with some credence – that gardening is linked to English national identity and that it offered a link with an old and specifically English rural idyll, so that gardens became representative of, 'England and its historic tradition as a whole, linking modern lifestyles with the past through the ancient English landscape, a mythical 'green and pleasant land' with values deeply rooted in the national soil' (Preston 1995, 69). Constantine (1981) argues that socially aspirational working-class gardeners welcomed the opportunity to 'emulate' higher social groups. This book, however, argues that working-class people have been far more concerned with developing their own aesthetics in relation to popular enthusiasms. Bourke's (1994) exploration of working-class autobiography, offers perhaps the most useful means of understanding the social changes that 'positioned', in particular, working-class men to enjoy gardening. She argues that improvements in inter-war housing had a significant impact on the investment husbands were prepared to make in domestic labour. Travelling to and from work encouraged the view of the home as, 'a secluded, self-contained domain … a respectable domestic front had to be maintained because "there's more pass by than comes in"' (Bourke 1994, 84). Everyday life on housing estates made for fundamental changes in the division of domestic labour – investigators reported that husbands on housing estates were more co-operative than many working-class men. They were more prepared to help around the house with cleaning and childcare, but more significantly, 'manly housework' became increasingly centred on gardening and do-it-yourself. As the following oral account from a man on the Dagenham estate illustrates: 'Down here a man makes an art of having something to do in his home when he gets back from work' (Bourke 1994, 85). Bourke extends her point further, arguing that men simply, '*had* to do housework to maintain acceptable standards of housing production on which good credit levels with the local shopkeeper, the pawnbroker, and the neighbours depended' (Bourke 1994, 89). As a result, Bourke suggests that working-class men did develop creativity in relation to masculine housework, 'Creativity cannot be ignored: men maintained standards of beauty, they enjoyed the touch of plants and wood' (Bourke 1994, 89). Gardening and DIY or 'Creative manly housework' offered a means of competing with other men on the estate, of winning love and esteem from loved ones and of providing a respectable front to the working-class domestic domain.

In these ways, by the late 1930s, the nineteenth century social reformers' wish to alter working-class leisure had largely been delivered: while recreation outside the home had not altogether diminished, a large shift had taken place from community to home-centred activities. By the 1950s, working-class community ties had become far weaker than they had been in the nineteenth century: working-class men were far less interested in street leisure – most especially pub recreation. Rather, people were interested in activities which made investments in the home and family: gardening, D-I-Y and television became the most popular working-class pursuits.

In the following section I trace the growth and popularity of gardening since the 1930s, charting its continued development as part of contemporary consumer culture.

From National Recreation to Lifestyle Consumer Culture: Gardening Since the 1930s

Even as early as the 1930s, the historical antecedents of home-centred consumer culture were being set in place by marketers, publishers and small horticultural businesses, who recognised the market possibilities in home-based leisure. By the 1930s, gardening had become a national working-class pursuit and the publishers of the day sought to capitalise on its growing popularity. Gardening magazines grew in number. Securely middle-class magazines like *Amateur Gardening* began to popularise their appeal by using colour on the front cover, including straightforward gardening instructions and by carrying much more advertising (Constantine 1981, 398). Similarly, the most popular magazine of the day *Home Gardening*, appealed to people using comic conventions, gave away seeds as free gifts, gave simple instructions illustrated with photographs, was packed with advertisements and embraced the complete novice. Moreover, as the following editorial shows, the publishers clearly recognised the context and conditions in which ordinary people were setting up home and garden:

> a *real home-garden paper*, a paper which caters for the needs of those who not knowing very much – knowing, maybe, nothing at all – about gardening, would yet make their gardens beautiful. ...Are there not gardens to most of the new homes on the Council Housing Estates? (Constantine 1981, 398)

Continued media growth followed: the national press started gardening columns, part-works and popular comprehensive guidebooks appeared and gardening talks were broadcast on BBC radio. And the popularity of gardening continued: two-thirds of Britons had gardens by the 1950s and four fifths by the late 1960s, and by 1969 a government survey found that for men, gardening followed television as their favourite form of leisure (Constantine 1981, 401). Concomitantly, the consumption of home-centred leisure products grew: by 1970 for example, £100 million was being spent on garden products per year. Since then, gardening has played a key role as part of the contemporary consumer lifestyle package; in fact according to MINTEL (2001a) 'Gardening Review' report it was 'still the number one hobby in the UK'. Garden lifestyle television began to burgeon in the mid-1990s and this led to a steady growth in the gardening retail sector. For example, the total garden market was worth £2.75 billion in 1996, but had risen to £3.35 billion by 2000 (MINTEL 2001b). The number of garden centre outlets rose by 17 per cent between 1998 and 2001 and total retail sales were 25 per cent higher in 2000 compared to 1995 (MINTEL 2001a). Changes to the primetime schedule highlight the popularity of lifestyle gardening television in the mid to late 1990s (Brunsdon et al. 2001) and there was a concomitant rise in the popularity and spending on garden magazines. By the late 1990s – at the time when the research for this book was being conducted – gardening was a phenomenally popular leisure pursuit and the garden lifestyle consumer circuit was beneficial to both the media and garden retailing.

So far this chapter shows that while the middle-class have historically acted to frame the working-class both in terms of the spaces they inhabit and the aesthetic choices they might make, ordinary people create their own meanings and creative aesthetics in relation to their surroundings. However, it also shows that there is a history of the excoriation of working-class culture and aesthetics. Because this book is about ordinariness and working-class culture I now turn to thinkers who provide a means to value working-class culture and aesthetics on their own terms. In the following section, I turn to the founders of the early left-culturalist strand of cultural studies, in order to frame my own ethnographic study within a tradition of thought which values working-class lived experience and ordinary culture. However, early culturalism tends to offer a gender blind approach to class. I therefore also turn to contemporary feminist work which continues the culturalist project of valuing ordinary culture and working-class lived experience, while insisting that gender is central to cultural analysis. In *Formations of Class and Gender* (1997), Skeggs uses ethnography to examine how the subjective locations of class *and* gender are lived out in contemporary culture.

Frameworks for Valuing Working-class Culture, Gender and Lived Experience

'Culture is ordinary' argued Raymond Williams (1989, 4), one of the founders of British cultural studies. William's definition provided a direct challenge to earlier writers on 'culture'. Matthew Arnold in the mid-nineteenth century defined culture as the 'best that has been thought and known in the world' and the pathway to 'sweetness and light' (Arnold 1993, 79). Arnold embraced the political philosophy of liberal humanism. Liberal humanist values, which arguably still under-gird British cultural institutions (Jordan and Weedon 1997), assert that the individual can develop their potential as a human being by valuing culture and by cultivating personal creative skills. Arnold, the foundational thinker behind the liberal humanist tradition, had an elitist approach to culture: culture for him was synonymous with high culture. An upper-class commentator, who like the nineteenth century philanthropists already discussed earlier in this chapter, had an interest in regulating the working-class he feared, argued that high culture offered an unruly proto-revolutionary mass the ameliorative potential for enlightenment. This could be achieved, he argued, by teaching high culture in the general school curriculum. Well-intentioned but naïve, Arnold thought that culturally enriching forms such as poetry, painting and classical music could erase class barriers. Arnold's myopic view of the role of culture can be appreciated when one considers both the deeply ingrained class divisions of the Victorian age in which he wrote and his failure to recognise the relationship of culture to class and the obstacles to an appreciation of the high arts that lower class positions imposed.

However, Arnold's ideas were foundational for the culturalist paradigm that later emerged in British cultural studies. Culturalism has an ancestry from Arnold to F.R Leavis to key thinkers allied with cultural studies, Raymond Williams and Richard Hoggart.[7] It conceives of culture as a 'lived experience' and as a repository of artistic value. Arnold was a culturalist and a liberal humanist and Leavis a culturalist influenced by both conservative and liberal humanism. The poet T.S. Eliot was a modern culturalist located by conservative humanism. In *Notes Towards a Definition of Culture* (1948) he associates culture with social practice, identifying culture as 'a way of feeling and acting' handed down through generations, so that culture is constituted by everyday life experience. Eliot's conservatism is revealed however, through his belief that society is structured by a natural order in which people are ranked. Although he argues that a number of ordinary activities constitute culture, such as: beetroot in vinegar, the dog races, boiled cabbage cut into sections – he conceived everyday culture as remaining segregated from the fine arts of elite culture. Eliot harboured an Arnoldian view of the arts but was equivocal about extending the arts to all social classes. For him, the arts are intrinsically elite – of interest only to a select, elite minority. Indeed, Eliot argued that the cultural elite should act as the vanguard of the artistic canon and ensure its continued nurturance.

Raymond William's book *Culture and Society, 1780–1950* (1958) contested Eliot's conservative culturalism. Indeed, Williams' book and Richard Hoggart's *The Uses of Literacy* (1957), marked the rise of left-culturalism, a position which augmented the institutional inception of cultural studies at the University of Birmingham in 1964. Both of these texts emphasise the essential bond between politics and culture, the value of working-class culture and the importance of the inclusion of working-class culture in cultural analysis. For early culturalists, for example, the analysis of ordinary garden practices in the context of working-class communities would be theorised as an intellectually rich and valid pursuit. Hoggart's alignment with left-culturalism is filtered through a social democratic type of humanism, while Williams is positioned more radically as a socialist influenced by Marxism. Both authors were

---

7   I must thank John Hughson for his lectures at the University of Wolverhampton on left-culturalism.

from working-class backgrounds and this was crucial to their contributions to cultural studies. Indeed, they developed a specifically British approach to the connection between class and capitalism (Savage 2000a, 31). For example, while contemporary intellectuals in other capitalist nations highlighted working-class vulnerability to the damaging tenets of mass society as a result of commercial capitalism, Hoggart and Williams argued that '"traditional" working-class values might constitute some kind of critical bulwark against "massification"' (Savage 2000a, 31). As a means to show this, both authors constructed the working-class as both the likely victim of widespread commercialism and as a countervailing force against it. Drawing on autobiographical material, Williams and Hoggart chart a historical and nostalgic account of the working-class in which working-class collectivism offers a positive impetus against competitive, individualistic middle-class society.

Hoggart's *The Uses of Literacy* (1957) is a book of two parts. In the first, he writes of the 'older order', in effect his impression of working-class community life in pre-war Britain – a community under threat of being eroded by commercial imperatives. The cultural life he describes is drawn from memories of his own life growing up in Leeds in the 1930s. Hoggart offers a unique and finely detailed account of the 'rich full life' of the working-class; indeed his analysis offers an account of the region where my own study is set. He sympathetically sketches aspects of working-class sociability to be found in the neighbourhood, family bonds and, drawing on his educational training, he applies literary concepts to a variety of popular culture artefacts – from popular song to popular fiction. Most especially however, critics have lauded his sensitivity to the 'interconnections' between the public and private aspects of the typical working-class neighbourhood: 'what is revealed is the network of shared cultural meanings which sustains relationships between different facets of the culture' (Critcher 1979, 19). In these ways, Hoggart's work is invaluable for my study of the working-class garden; for I argue that the garden as a site is characterised by its position as an interface between public and private connections within a community. Yet, while Hoggart's conception of the working-class mourns the loss of authentic, organic forms of culture of the 1930s, his important contribution to cultural studies is to value the lived experience of working-class culture. His view that working-class culture is both ordinary and 'intrinsically interesting' (Hoggart 1957, 120) became inspirational to the ongoing academic study of the cultural activities of ordinary people. The garden, for Hoggart, was precisely the kind of ordinary site that would merit cultural analysis.

Raymond Williams was from a Welsh working-class background. In his book *Culture and Society, 1780–1950* (1958), he charts the history of British 'culture and civilisation' writers within the culturalist tradition, citing F.R Leavis and T.S. Eliot within its twentieth century lineage. He argues that both Leavis and Eliot work with a selective, yet obsolete notion of culture because it segregates culture from the structural developments of contemporary society. Leavis and Eliot create a chasm between cultural values and the cultural experience of everyday life. Williams rebuffs this position, arguing that culture is ordinary; it emanates from lived experience and represents 'a whole way of life'. The study of culture, for Williams, should not imply a closed tradition but rather the possibilities of openness and democracy. The high arts should not be elevated to a higher quarter of cultural life than other cultural activities. Further, culture should not float above politics but should be embedded within political activity. In these ways, Williams' approach not only embraces the garden as a valid site for cultural politics, it also extends the notion that the garden is an everyday space which is potentially saturated by cultural politics.

To this end, Williams proposed a moral basis for a socialist approach to the analysis of culture through his conception of what he termed a 'common culture': 'collectively made, continuously remade and redefined by the collective practice of its members' (Williams 1993, 334). This marked a difference from figures like Eliot who used the term common culture to denote a passive form of cultural life. For Williams, 'the distinction of a culture in common is that…selection is freely and commonly made and remade. The tending is a common process based on common decision' (Williams 1993, 337). For him the idea of a common culture is progressive, it holds 'the idea of solidarity' which is 'the real basis of society' (Williams 1993, 332). Common culture comes about through the process of long revolution where all cultural groups have equal access to and actively engage in the rich and varied cultural life of a society. Williams also refused the cultural pessimism, harboured by Leavis and Eliot, of an emergent mass culture. Williams shunned the word 'mass' on the grounds that it was no different to 'mob', a term used by conservative critics to denounce collective activism. He recognised the term 'masses' as an ideological category as opposed to a social descriptor. Such an approach justifies the privileged place for elite culture and a cultural elite. Yet Williams was also critical of conventional Marxist positions on culture which he felt also served to denigrate mass culture. By envisaging the working-class as cultural dopes who passively consume popular culture produced by the capitalist media, Marxist critics reduce the working-class to an inert docile mass. For Williams, Marxist theory suffered from economic determinism, thus he argued for a position where culture could be perceived as relatively autonomous to the economy. As both culturalist and humanist Williams could never accept deterministic versions of culture – hence his need to rework Marxism. For him culture is always about lived experience: 'culture is ordinary, in every society and every mind' (Williams 1989, 4). These tenets became influential as cultural studies emerged as an academic field.

However, early cultural studies had come under attack by the late 1970s. Savage (2000a) argues that despite the enormous influence of left-culturalism, it had never had a 'real' or empirically evidenced working-class culture on which to make its case. The intellectual influence of Hoggart and Williams came from the 'formulation of class cultures as historical residues, as nostalgic figures whose lingering presence could help explain current concerns' (Savage 2000a, 33). And while this explanatory mould summarised here by Savage – 'the break up of the nostalgic 'working-class community' led to attempts to symbolically reclaim the integrity of these old imagined spaces, but in displaced, even 'debased' forms' (Savage 2000a, 33) – was used to investigate a diverse range of cultural forms at CCCS, its demise came alongside its critical re-evaluation. The import of feminism, new critical work on race and ethnicity, the turn to structuralist theory and the new focus on individualised cultures by writers such as Giddens (1990) and Beck (1992) meant that early cultural studies work, with its defined emphasis on the collective nature of class culture, waned in influence. According to Savage (2000a), it was not until Bourdieu's work, with its different perspective on the connection between class and culture, began to enjoy popularity in the 1980s, that class reappeared on the socio-cultural agenda.

Yet while Hoggart and Williams have been criticised even beyond the charges levelled by Savage (2000a) for over-sentimentalising working-class life and for romanticising the collectivism of working-class community (Bourke 1994), aspects of this book on the cultural practice of gardening rest on tenets of the legacy of left-culturalism. Firstly, their cultural critique provided a challenge to both liberal and conservative brands of humanism, political philosophies which have no real interest in the value of working-class culture. Liberal humanist values continue to under-pin dominant British national cultural institutions which promote, fund and disseminate ideas about gardening. As a result, facets of the media, funding bodies, local councils and historic houses and gardens tend to prescribe cultural messages about the 'right' garden aesthetics, about 'great' gardens and gardeners and such messages tend to marginalise the ordinary and the working-class. Left-culturalism insists that the working-class be included and valued in questions of what constitutes culture. Secondly, they argued for the recognition that cultural analysis should widen to include ordinary things, activities and artefacts of everyday culture; the focus of this study – lifestyle gardening television, gardening practices, gardeners and the aesthetics of domestic gardens – is an analytical investigation about what is interesting about the mundane. Thirdly, their work emphasises the value of lived experience of peoples' 'whole way of life' as a worthwhile addition to the agenda of the culturally valuable. And finally, they believed that common people have the collective capacity to actively generate creative practices and shared meanings.

However, while I am indebted to early cultural studies work in terms of aspects of its principles on class, my work is also concerned with dynamics of both class *and* gender. Unfortunately, as feminist critics have argued, early cultural studies work has been attacked by feminists for charting historical accounts on class which ignore the lived experience of working-class women's lives:

> That "full sense of a way of life"…from Williams lies at the root of the problem. As a version of "society" it belongs firmly to the cultural sphere, where, as we shall show, it invokes both the private and the domestic, but then for historical reasons, it excludes women as subjects (Jardine and Swindells 1989, 129).

Similarly, Nava (1992: 9) argues that in Williams's autobiographical work on his own intellectual history in *Politics and Letters* (1979), there are no references to the female forms of labour which made his intellectual and academic life possible, for example, the parenting of his children or to domestic labour in his household. In these ways, one can see how the humanist element of left-culturalism, as feminists have claimed (Weedon 1987), tends to figure as an ungendered category, in which speaking for humankind produces accounts which tend to reproduce men's accounts of the lived experience of cultural history. It is for these reasons that I now turn to Skeggs (1997), who manages to blend the valuable tenets of early cultural studies mentioned above, with a Bourdieusian perspective on class, but whose commitment to feminist theory provides an ethnographic study of ordinary working-class lives to produce a classed and gendered account of subjective identity.

Formations of Class and Gender (1997) is an ethnographic study of white working-class female consciousness. Set in the north of England, Skeggs conducted ethnographic research over an eleven year period and studied the lives of over eighty women. Structured by the terms offered by Bourdieu's concept of capitals, the book has a mission to 'provide a space for the articulations of the marginalised' (Skeggs 1997, 23). Skegg's project was to interrogate how the women of her study occupied and identified with locations of both class and gender. This involved an investigation of her subjects' whole way of life, from their employment in the caring professions, to their cultural constructions of self in terms of their homes, bodies and relationship to fashion and beauty, to how they inhabit or identify with locations of class, gender and sexuality.

In order to produce an understanding of the construction of contemporary classed and gendered locations, Skeggs looked at the textual emergence of femininity since the eighteenth century. The ideal concept of the 'lady' appeared in magazines and conduct manuals of the day and was produced in conjunction with the habitus of the upper classes and signified 'ease, restraint, calm and luxurious decoration' (1997, 99). Being a lady meant the cultivation of particular practices of both appearance and conduct, and by the nineteenth century, femininity had become established as a middle-class entity. As a classed sign, femininity could be infused with varying degrees of status and value. Middle-class women already had access to the distinctive moral superiority of femininity, it gave them a vantage point from which to judge the femininity, and therefore the respectability, of others. Working-class women on the other hand, who were already defined negatively as physically strong and sturdy against the frailty of middle-class women, were denied access to femininity. Working-class women's labour, 'prevented femininity from ever being a possibility' (1997, 99).

Skegg's argues that contemporary constructions of working-class femininity are framed by these historical antecedents. Working-class women have been historically denied access to respectability, yet its acquisition respectability a means by which they can dis-identify with the pejorative associations of working-class femininity as worthless and sexually lascivious. Investments in femininity offer a way of providing distance from, 'being positioned by the vulgar, pathological, tasteless and sexual' (1997, 100). But their performances are produced in order that they be taken seriously, Skeggs's subjects have no access to forms of knowledge which might enable them to play with identities with post-modern irony. Rather, their attempts to 'pass' as feminine, through acts of glamour and dressing up, are always constructed out of an affective context of fear and anxiety that they might not 'get it right'.

Drawing on post-modern theory (Butler 1990) Skeggs views femininity as a masquerade; the women of her study become, try on, practice and do feminine performances. For Skeggs, femininity is an unfixed category, historically and discursively constructed and always relative to the cross-cutting categories of class and race, which are themselves contingent and open to change. Female subjectivity is produced by discourse and disseminated within representational systems. The women use the textually mediated forms of ideal femininity found in popular mediums to inform and legitimate their constructions of a feminine appearance. Yet while the women were conscious of doing the 'right' kinds of feminine performance in order to secure respectability, the act of feminine construction was both a site of pleasure and an opportunity to collectively enjoy their own forms of female competence. Dressing up was a chance to validate locally generated feminine capital – it was one site where middle-class approval could be excluded: 'Style is not seen to be something that middle-class women know anything about. It is seen as a working-class competence' (Skeggs 1997, 104). Generating and creating shared meanings around looking good was also about enjoying collectivity. Producing femininity, is a site of contradiction: it is a process of anxiety where 'passing' as feminine induces anxiety; yet it is also a pleasurable arena for displaying local competencies in the context of supportive friendship groups.

While post-modern feminism has been attacked for showing scant regard for questions of lived agency (see Weedon's discussion, 1999), Skeggs's analysis offers a wider position: while she argues that the subject positions these women are able to occupy are the effects of institutional structures and discourse, her analysis holds on to lived experience, 'as a way of understanding how women occupy the category "woman"' (Skeggs 1997, 27). Her choice to produce an ethnography acts as a means to value, legitimate and take seriously the voices and experiences of those previously relegated to the margins. And, while her work is about the discursive limits of subjective locations, her ethnography insists that questions about lived subjectivity and agency be addressed; as a result, discursive locations are always anchored by materiality.

In these ways, *Formations of Class and Gender* (1997) draws together a set of theoretical concepts, ideas and methods which are politically empowering for my analysis of the ways in which classed and gendered subjectivities are lived out in the humdrum practices of gardening. Her work generates interesting questions in relation to class and gender for my own study. Skeggs highlights the profound class differences between the lived locations occupied by middle- and working-class women in terms of their access to respectability. Her work provides a means of understanding why respectability has historically been such an important facet of working-class life for both men and women and shows why investments in femininity – such as my own grandmother's use of feminine aesthetics of both the self and the home – have enabled women to dis-identify with working-classness. Skeggs's work enables an understanding of why the 'sign-laden'[8] garden, a site fastened between the private and the visible public realm, is a key space where attempts at respectability are made and differently expressed. Yet Skeggs' study is about more than working-class anxiety and the search for approbation; it is also about the value and pleasures of local competencies and about exploring the gap between approved national aesthetics and those which fight shy of compliance. In this way, her work helps to provide an explanation for the creative, specific local language of creative shared gardening practices.

---

8   The women of Skeggs' (1997) study were extremely self-conscious about how their bodies communicated meaning to (potentially judgemental) others; she refers to it as the 'sign-laden body'. Here I borrow the phrase: the garden as also a site which signifies meaning about those indoors.

This section has focused on thinkers who have argued both for the cultural validity of ordinary culture and for the importance of the inclusion of ordinariness in cultural analysis. The following section defines what 'ordinariness' means for this book at both micro and macro levels.

Ordinariness, Identity and Everyday Life

Gronow and Warde note in their introduction to *Ordinary Consumption* that, 'the sociology of consumption has concentrated unduly on the more spectacular visual aspects of consumer behaviour' (1999, 3–4). By contrast, this book is about ordinariness. Firstly, it is about ordinary micro-entities which are fastened to practices of everyday living: it is about gardening which is seen as profoundly mundane; it is about the home as a setting – often seen as everybody's everyday 'base', the fundamental grounding of ordinary living; it is about television and magazines – ordinary media forms embedded within everyday life; it is about lifestyle media programmes, characterised by their 'lack of anything special, their very triviality, their ordinariness' (Bonner 2003, 2), programmes which use everyday life as a primary resource 'not just as topics but as guides to style, appearance and behaviour' (Bonner 2003, 32); it is about ordinary places – thought of as too unremarkable for anyone to consider or write about; it is about ordinary, unknown people – the subjects of this study – whose voices have never before been officially recorded; and it is about giving both history and place to the ordinary practices and life-worlds of unremarkable people in humdrum settings.

And secondly, these micro-entities are set against macro-changes, experienced as a wider cultural shift in which everyday life and processes of 'ordinari-ization' (Brunsdon et al. 2001, 53) which became increasingly significant in the 1990s. Chaney (2002) argues that this shift can be understood as a result of two processes: what he terms 'radical democratisation' and 'cultural fragmentation' (Chaney 2002, 5). In relation to the first, Chaney holds that public discourse has become increasingly dominated by forms of populism. In relation to public media discourse for example, news and current affairs programmes have been subject to increased tabloidization (Turner 1999); and as I explore in depth in chapter 5, television has changed historically to become more 'ordinary': it simply contains more ordinary people and its concerns embrace the quotidian (Bonner 2003; Taylor 2002). In relation to the latter, Chaney argues that traditional forms of cultural authority are becoming 'increasingly dissipated and discredited'; in this way, 'cultural fragmentation' has led to a 'broader process of informalisation' (Chaney 2002, 5). This is culturally manifest in forms of televisual discourse where forms of civic knowledge, hitherto imparted by legislators, are being replaced in the contemporary climate by interpreters conveying forms of consumer knowledge. As a result, as I argue in chapter 5, expertise has been levelled down and democratised and is increasingly represented in more ordinary forms. In these ways, ordinariness and everyday life are central to both the micro- and the macro-concerns of this study.

Ordinariness is a term which is always in need of qualification. Felski's (2000) discussion of ordinariness and everyday life however, provides a detailed definition as well as a positive counter to the Marxist tradition of writers who theorise the everyday as a sphere of alienation (Lefebvre 1984). Felski gives the ordinary a temporal dimension through 'repetition'; she grounds it by suggesting ordinariness is staged at 'home'; and she catches at the rhythms of ordinariness by examining 'habit'. And for Felski, ordinariness is fastened to the backdrop of everyday life: we are all somehow anchored to routine, to a place called home and to the sheer mundanity of daily habit. In this way, Felski takes a phenomenological stance on ordinariness and the everyday. She charts both as modes of experience which belong to everyone's lives, as opposed to theorising them as the authentic preserve of particular groups, such as women or the working-class. 'Everyday life', Felski argues, 'is not simply interchangeable with the popular: it is not the exclusive property of a particular class or grouping, Bismarck had an everyday life and so does Madonna' (2000, 16). In this way, by separating everyday life from issues of class and gender, Felski's discussion prevents ordinariness from being idealised as the authentic locus of class heroism or demonised as a dehumanising sphere where women are enslaved; rather her approach allows one to take seriously everyone's lived experience of the micro-spheres of ordinariness. This is not to argue that mundane practices, such as garden-making or watching television, float-free of class and gender: gardening is a symbolic practice which is drenched with classed and gendered meanings. However, I argue that ordinary practices – doing everyday things in ordinary settings – are shared by everybody *and* they are located in class and gender terms. For example, both working- and middle-class people garden in repetitive cycles, they may plant at particular times within the larger repetitive seasonal cycles and this constitutes a shared ordinary practice, but what they plant to generate symbolic meaning is inflected by their class location. In similar vein, while both men and women reside in a taken-for-granted, ordinary place called 'home', gender impacts on how the home and garden are staged. In these ways, ordinariness is a shared ground, inflected, as I explore in chapters 6 and 7, by the subjective locations of class and gender. What this book sets out to do is to lay the shared ground of ordinariness bare, to expose its aspects of intrigue and to argue that there is something interesting and valuable about ordinary enthusiasms like gardening.

I want to draw on Felski's argument in relation to the creative potential of the ordinariness of everyday life. Felski argues against critics who regard everyday life as problematic or alienating. For example, Lefebvre's thesis is that everyday life is at odds with the dynamic potential of modernity. The structural repetition of everyday life, for Lefebvre (1987), is problematic because its cycles are antithetical to modern accumulation and progress. Lefebvre (1961) makes a distinction between linear and cyclical time: linear time, the temporal system of modern industrial society, propels forward; conversely, everyday life, unchanged by centuries, has natural, diurnal rhythms. According to Lefebvre, daily cycles drag against progress: everyday life detains the momentum of the historical progress implied by modernity. Another critic of repetition, but on behalf of women in relation to everyday life, is de Beauvoir (1988). For her repetition is symbolic of women's captivity within the dull compulsion of the ordinary. Beset by routine, everyday life can never offer women a space for newness or creativity. Forever trapped within the rhythms of the mundane, the future merely re-presents the past, acting to stunt women's inventive capabilities.

Felski refuses these definitions, emphasising instead the necessity of routine and continuity for human development. Repetition is a sense-making mechanism which helps people to organise their lives. And routines are crucial to the accumulative process of identity formation: 'Quite simply, we become who we are through acts of repetition' (Felski 2000, 21). More significantly, rather than theorising routine as a cycle of domination which circumvents progress or creativity, Felski sees repetition as a potentially innovative, resistant force. Challenging the view that newness is by necessity superior, Felski argues the contemporary period is characterised by social change which is often imposed on subjects, against their will. Under these circumstances repetition within the ordinary cycles of the everyday can serve as a coping device:

> everyday rituals may help to safeguard a sense of personal autonomy and dignity, or to preserve the distinctive qualities of a threatened way of life. In other words, repetition is not simply a sign of human subordination to external forces but also one of the ways in which individuals engage with and respond to their environment. Repetition can signal resistance as well as enslavement (Felski 2000, 21).

Dimensions of ordinariness – time-based repetition, the rhythm of habit and the home as site where these entities are performed – are stabilising cognitive mechanisms which are central to how people forge and replenish their sense of identity. Indeed Savage et. al.'s (1999) empirical work on the ordinary consumption of radio, found that people were not concerned to impress through distinctive consumption practices or by claiming a firm class identity. Rather, the middle-class people of the study wanted to be thought of as 'ordinary' – as though ordinariness allowed them a way of being real and authentic people as opposed to being fixed by class signifiers. Savage et. al argue that both being and consuming ordinarily offers comfort and reassurance at a time of accelerated social change (1999, 140). I argue in this book that rapid social change has potentially incited people to tighten their grip on dimensions of ordinariness. It is through the micro-practices of ordinary activities like gardening, forms of leisure that bear the marks of their locations of class and gender, that people find ways to cope with the travails of everyday life in the context of wider and potentially de-stabilising forms of cultural change.

Chapter 3

Gardening Taste: Theoretical Concepts and Framework

Introduction

One of the central questions underpinning this book is: is the garden a site where identities of class and gender are played out? This chapter sets up the main theoretical framework for my empirical findings around questions of class and gender. The theories and concepts laid out here inform the whole book, but most especially they under-gird the analysis of my empirical findings in chapters 6 and 7 which examine class, gender and gardening, sections of my argument about the lifestyle gardening media in chapter 5 and my empirical findings on lifestyle consumption in chapter 8.

I begin with a discussion of the continued efficacy of Bourdieu's concepts for thinking about contemporary social class. In particular, I draw on Bourdieu's theories of habitus, field and forms of capital (1977, 1986), his approach to taste and aesthetics (1986, 1990b) and his theory of symbolic violence (1990a). Arguing that Bourdieu's theories hold 'explanatory power' (Skeggs 1997; Fowler 1994) for understanding contemporary class relations, I discuss the kinds of insights Bourdieu's concepts generate for my analysis of ordinary gardening. The predictive power of Bourdieu's work mitigates against current claims that the 'consumption as social distinction' approach is waning and that class is a less relevant social division for studies of consumption (Warde 2002, 12). Rather, I argue for the continued explanatory power of Bourdieu's metaphors of capital in relation to practices of cultural distinction.

Some theorists argue however, that class is no longer a stable and singular site of identification in contemporary culture. Rather, it is argued, the present climate is characterised by shifting forms of identification (Chaney 1996). While I accept that class can never describe identity without other crosscutting variables such as gender, race or sexuality, I want to argue for the continued importance of class both as a descriptor of subjective relations and as a relevant tool for cultural analysis. The chapter then turns to review selected examples of literature, many of which are empirical studies, which argue for the continued salience of class. This section examines lifestyle and class difference (Savage et al. 1992; Walkerdine et al. 2001, Wynne 1990); work on classed boundaries of belonging and identification (Savage et al. 2000; Southerton 2002); and work on identity, taste, (dis) identification and the inequality of lived subjective locations of class and gender (Skeggs 1997). I take the findings from these research projects to my own analysis of class, ordinary gardening and the media of the late 1990s.

Bourdieu's model has less to say about other social variables which cross-cut class and he has faced up to criticism for situating gender and race as secondary to his analysis of class (Frow 1995; Moi 1991; Reay 1995). Bourdieu's concept of habitus – a relatively fixed conceptual tool, faces limitations in relation to gender (Lovell 2000; McCall 1992). Here I explore why Bourdieu's concept of habitus has been attacked by poststructuralist and post-modern feminists. Turning to Butler's (1990) theory of performativity, I explore what her theory might offer an understanding of how and why subjects make investments in the practice and performance of masculinity and femininity. However, both Bourdieu and Butler (1997) have opposing theories about the status of performatives, especially in relation to their institutional limits and social possibilities. Focusing on the debate between Butler (1990, 1997) and Bourdieu, I ask what the terms of their arguments have to offer my analysis of gendered garden practices.

Bourdieu, Class and Social Distinction

Bourdieu argues that taste is socially constructed and that the hierarchies of taste which govern the acquisition and consumption of goods are inextricably linked to class divisions within a society. In his analysis of French 1960s culture, *Distinction: A Social Critique of the Judgement of Taste* (1986), Bourdieu argues that goods possess symbolic significance within the social order and that taste operates as a central organising principle for how resources are distributed both through and across it. In this way taste has a central role in reproducing and maintaining the dominant order, the effects of which are at least as significant as the political and economic factors which might serve to maintain the unequal distribution of a culture's assets. It is through the consumption of taste that people, themselves part of class groups, struggle and vie to gain social status within the 'cultural field'. The dominant groups in society maintain the eminence of their positions by conferring superiority on their tastes and by dismissing working-class tastes as vulgar and base. In doing so, they affirm their lifestyle choices as distant from others who occupy a hierarchically lower position in the cultural field. By contrast, the stigmatised working-class suffers the affective pain of what Bourdieu describes as a kind of 'class racism' (Bourdieu 1986, 179). 'For Bourdieu,' Fowler argues, 'the game of culture which is at stake in relations to consumption, always has the working-class as its negative classificatory foil' (Fowler 2000, 11).

Class, according to Bourdieu's thesis, is not simply defined by the amount of economic capital one has – it is also determined by one's cultural, social and symbolic capital. Economic capital refers to financial assets: inherited wealth, the monetary status derived from occupational income, investments in the form of stocks and shares and so on. Cultural capital or 'informational capital' (Bourdieu and Waquant 1992, 119), acts as a form of symbolic wealth in the realm of culture. It exists in three states: embodied, resulting in durable dispositions of both body and mind; institutionalised, in the form of educational qualifications and antiquated forms of knowledge; and objectified, existing as cultural objects and goods. Social capital is predicated on access to resources acquired through social connections and society or group affiliation. And finally, symbolic capital is, as Bourdieu describes, 'the form that one or another of these species takes when it is grasped through categories of perception that *recognise* its specific logic' (Bourdieu and Waquant 1992, 119). Symbolic capital is the form that other forms take once they have been recognised and ordained as consecrated, legitimate forms of culture.

Bourdieu's 'economistic metaphors' (Skeggs 1997, 9) offer a dynamic model of class based on the acquisition and subsequent distribution of capital endowments across social space. Individuals are born with historically generated capital assets: these might, for example, exist in an objectified state as cultural goods or in an embodied state within the habitus as competencies or dispositions. Agents then engage in a lifelong trajectory of struggle to sustain or improve their location in the field by pursuing methods of reconversion, in which one form of capital is traded for another. To that end, individuals strive to make investments in a bid to accrue forms of capital with the highest symbolic returns. As Bourdieu argues, he understands, 'all practices, including those purporting to be disinterested or gratuitous, and hence non-economic, as economic practices directed towards the maximising of material or symbolic profit' (Bourdieu 1977, 183). The conversion rates between capitals however, are set to some extent by institutions, for instance the media, the labour market or the education system; these bodies can work to confer value and power on types of capital or they can de-legitimate or place a ceiling on its tradeability.

Habitus is the term Bourdieu (1977, 1986) uses to describe the system of competencies and dispositions which govern the movement of the individual through social space. Central to his theory of taste and social distinction, he describes it as:

> the strategy-generating principle enabling agents to cope with unforeseen and ever-changing situations ... a system of lasting, transposable dispositions which, integrating past experiences, functions at every moment as a matrix of perceptions, appreciations and actions and makes possible the achievement of infinitely diversified tasks, thanks to the analogical transfer of schemes permitting the solution of similarly shaped problems (Bourdieu 1977, 82-83).

Acquired in childhood, built upon through the education system and within the context of the family, habitus is primarily determined by one's class position. It is revealed through the cultural value of the unconscious, yet seemingly naturalised everyday tastes of the individual's choices of food, fashion and cosmetics, sport, music, art – and, though Bourdieu is silent on them, garden design and horticultural preferences. It is also actually lived out through bodily social practice: one's gestures, facial expression, accent and speech patterns, the amount of space one feels one has the right to absorb in social encounters – all these physical encounters reveal one's habitus (Bourdieu 1986, 190). Habitus is embodied: indeed some have argued that his theory of habitus emphasises the 'corporeal sedimentation' of social practice (Lovell 2000, 14). Bourdieu's account of the construction of subjectivity through habitus is deeply engrained, so rigidly is it bound to the social processes through which it is formed. Throughout life in the cultural field individuals use the 'transposable dispositions' of habitus in their everyday encounters; the commonplace familiarity with one's cultural milieu creates a seemingly 'natural' context for existence, or what Bourdieu calls a 'doxa' (Bourdieu 1977, 164; 1986, 471). It is one's habitus which enables agents to make consumer choices which in the wider culture are subject to classifications. For example, those with a bourgeoisie habitus would be able to distinguish between dominant and popular aesthetics. The ability to make certain choices through consumption, for example purchasing goods where form takes precedence over function, indicates that one has the powers to discriminate between legitimate (or elite), middlebrow or popular tastes.

If for Bourdieu the unthinking habituation of routines in the habitus is akin to agency, then one also requires his concept of field, akin to structure, as a means of understanding how agents are organised across social space. A field is a social sphere where it is possible to map the struggles which agents undertake as a means of securing access to resources or capitals; in effect it is, 'a structured system of social positions ... the nature of which defines the situation for their occupants' (Jenkins 1992, 85). Historically contingent, the borders of fields are fuzzy and indeterminate – indeed for Bourdieu it is only through the acquisition of empirical data that their boundaries can be understood. Fields are determined by the specificity of their content, whether it be education, lifestyle goods or gardening, and each field produces a habitus which in turn is germane to the field in question. Here I define gardening as a field which operates according to its own specific logic, but which is productive of the kinds of classed habitus(es) which are described empirically in some detail in chapter 6.

Bourdieu argues that the root cause of taste distinctions is directly related to the material conditions of people's experience of social class in contemporary society. Legitimate taste is the privilege of the bourgeoisie, since this is the only group which is economically able to cultivate a 'distance from necessity' or an aesthetic of disinterested contemplation. Legitimate taste for Bourdieu is based on Kantian aesthetics: for Kant, pure art had to be separated from the 'coarse pleasure' of sensual response, rather it must be enjoyed by privileging the 'pure pleasure' of intellectual faculties above any other. Elite taste, for Bourdieu, is premised on the ability to appreciate the representational form of an artwork over its function. The capacity to privilege mode over matter in virtually every area of life, to wear clothes that are fashionable as opposed to warm and serviceable, for example, or to seek leisure pursuits with no practical purpose, is to cultivate desires which are distanced from the urgent, physical needs of the working-class. Indeed, bourgeoisie taste defines itself against the 'taste of necessity' of working-class people. Popular taste, by contrast, is described by Bourdieu in terms of a reversal of the Kantian aesthetic. In fact the working-class, according to Bourdieu, possess what Kant had called 'barbarous taste'. The popular aesthetic is characterised by the expectation that, 'every image explicitly ... fulfil a *function*' (Bourdieu 1990b, 86). In *Photography* (1990b) Bourdieu illustrates that the working-class '"functional" aesthetic' is comprised of an inability to be able to make judgements based on the universal attributes of form. Asked to comment, his respondents were unable to see that images of a dead soldier and a pregnant women might constitute what others in the field might describe as 'beautiful photographs'. Rather, they were reduced to their ethical or moral functions, for them the picture of the soldier, '"could be used to show the horror and uselessness of war"' (ibid.) In short, the working-class are unable to separate the representational from that being represented; for them taking photographs has nothing to do with the celebration of art, rather, the camera is used to celebrate working-class life.

The middle-brow taste of the petty bourgeoisie is characterised by what Bourdieu describes as 'cultural goodwill': they recognise legitimate goods, but they lack the competence to consume them with the insouciance of those rich in cultural capital. It is this class who, according to Bourdieu, hungrily seek the advice of the new cultural intermediaries working in the media, whose task is to judge the value of the latest positional goods (Leiss 1983) and proffer befitting ways of how they should be consumed. There are a whole swathe of lifestyle garden media products which cater for a petty bourgeoisie audience, texts which are designed to help assuage any anxieties about revealing their reader's middling position. *Gardens Illustrated* (March 2001, 35) for example, shows the reader a set of plant tags which ape the patina of 'authentic' labels. The feature also carefully demonstrates ways in which the 'verdigris copper tag' from The Conran Shop, or the 'steel "tournefort" label' from Botanique Editions should be displayed in relation to the plants.

Bourdieu's work offers an analysis that insists on the social dimension of taste. Objects and goods are not intrinsically imbued with value; rather, taste is historically and socially constructed. And the classifying systems through which taste is regulated are not fixed, they too are historically contingent and changeable. In this way, his work provides an historically flexible model for understanding the significance of taste in the context of societies that are divided by class inequalities.

Symbolic violence

In order to define Bourdieu's theory of symbolic violence, it is necessary to turn to his empirical work on the French education system, in particular the text he jointly authored with Passeron, *Reproduction in Education, Society and Culture* (1990a). Central to their theory, is the idea that all societies exercise power through discrete cultural processes, rather than by punitive and coercive prohibition.

Symbolic violence is the subjection of symbolic systems of meaning on to classes or groups using methods which appear inevitable and are experienced as legitimate. Successful subjection occurs, he argues, because the felt legitimacy of symbolic violence works to mask its power relations. This is brought about by the process of misrecognition; rather than seeing power relations objectively as a constructed set of interests, classes perceive them as rightfully sanctioned (Bourdieu and Passeron 1990a, 12). Hence, symbolic violence is exercised upon the social agent with his or her complicity, a process which continually works to re-inscribe their domination. Yet as Bourdieu argues, culture is itself arbitrary – there is nothing intrinsically valuable about either the contents or the subjection of what any society deems as 'Culture'; this is what is implied by Bourdieu's term the 'cultural arbitrary'.

Much of the work of symbolic violence occurs through 'pedagogic action', or the process by which the imposition of the cultural arbitrary upon social agents is achieved. Symbolic meaning systems are transmitted through three types of pedagogic action: 'family education' and 'institutionalised education' – both of which are self explanatory – and 'diffuse education' (Bourdieu and Passeron 1977, 64). Diffuse education, works casually through inter-personal contexts as those with cultural competence interact and educate less competent members of the social order, for example, among one's work or friendship groups. It is also possible to envisage diffuse education occurring through the informal consumption of artefacts which trade in cultural capital, for example, aspects of the media. In these ways, pedagogic action works both to reproduce the cultural formation in which it operates and the power relations which under-pin its own system. It acts to uphold the ideological interests of the dominant classes and re-inscribes the unequal distribution of cultural capital in any social formation. The ideas of pedagogic action are carefully monitored: it 'involves the exclusion of ideas as unthinkable, as well as their positive inculcation (depending, of course on the nature of the ideas). Exclusion or censorship may in fact be the most effective mode of pedagogic action' (Jenkins 2002, 105). Misrecognised by both its promulgators and its receivers, the authority of pedagogic action is either willingly embraced or thought of as at least impartial. Furthermore, pedagogic action has a cumulative effect on the social agent: family education prepares the individual for institutionalised education, which in turn acts as preparation for a lifelong trajectory of diffuse education in the form of cultural messages. In these ways, pedagogic work acts to sediment durable intellectual and cultural dispositions through the habitus. It is through these processes that legitimate culture becomes consecrated and, according to Bourdieu, is deemed irreversible.

Importantly however, the results of pedagogic authority are not immutable either within or between classes; pedagogic action is received with varying degrees of success. This is because different classes have dissimilar dispositions towards pedagogy or as Bourdieu terms it, each class holds its own 'pedagogic ethos' (Bourdieu and Passeron 1990a, 87). These dispositions vary depending on a group's perception of the tradeable value of educational credentials. Middle-class secondary school pupils, for example, are likely to regard qualifications as assets which are worth the investment because their high tradeable potential will equip them for possible futures in the professions. Further, Bourdieu argues that pedagogic action is administered in different ways, on a scale which moves from the 'implicit' to the 'explicit' (Bourdieu and Passeron 1990a, 47). These need to be distinguished, for they impact on how different classes receive them. Implicit pedagogy is transmitted unconsciously, is suited to 'traditional' forms of knowledge and is most effectively conveyed through a learning channel such as that experienced between student and tutor or craftsman and apprentice. Explicit pedagogy, on the other hand, is 'articulated', rationally structured and formalised and best serves 'specialised' forms of elite knowledge.

In all senses, Bourdieu argues that the working-class are disadvantaged in relation to both forms of pedagogic action. For example, whereas the working-class are left to contend with the practical urgencies of daily life, the dominant class are released from ordinary necessities and are therefore in a better position to receive explicit forms of pedagogic work. Furthermore, in the context of post-industrial societies where 'symbolic mastery' is favoured by the dominant and is restricted to the elite, those marginalised are confined to 'practical mastery'. Most pedagogic work in schools relies on the implicit transmission of symbolic mastery, so that yet again, the dominant are privileged because they already possess, through family education, the prerequisite competencies of symbolic mastery. Thus the working-class are doubly disadvantaged: unable to take advantage of explicit pedagogic work, they are excluded from elite forms of knowledge; and insidious, discrete symbolic mastery,

...is rendered remote and mysterious because it is only ever implicitly communicated to them. By virtue of their upbringing they lack the necessary practical mastery which is required to recognise it without recognising it, hence they cannot acquire it competently or authentically (Jenkins 2002, 108-09).

In these ways, the practice of symbolic violence, or the ways access to forms to educational skills in a culture are governed, act to reproduce class differences from generation to generation.

This section has outlined the mainframe theoretical concepts which I take up in subsequent chapters of the book. In what follows, I discuss a collection of studies as a means to show why class still matters as a social descriptor and as an analytical tool.

Class, Difference, Lifestyle and the Everyday

Whether social class still holds credence as a category in contemporary social life has been the focus of intense debate. Some critics suggest that the present period is characterised – not by the singular category of class identification – but rather by, 'changing forms of identification' (Chaney 1996, 95). A consideration of the processes of social change offers one way to understand why the solidity of social class has recently undergone challenge from social theorists. Chaney (1996) for example, argues that contemporary culture is undergoing a shift from ways of life to lifestyle in which privatised forms of leisure are replacing public, communal forms of cultural participation.[1] For Chaney lifestyles epitomise the 'privatisation of communal life' (Chaney 1996, 95). As a consequence, Chaney suggests that the 'language of social description and explanation' (ibid.) are also undergoing change: traditional assumptions about the solidity of collective phenomena, such as social classes and communities, and how they affect or shape individual action and identity, are de-stabilised. As Chaney further illustrates:

> This is not because this type of entity has become less 'real' or powerful in processes of cultural change; they were always metaphorical fictions or analytic devices, but they seemed more persuasive when the terms of social identity were less malleable (Chaney 1996, 95).

Chaney's argument shows that in the contemporary climate social class can never be a monolithic concept, capable of describing an agent's sole sense of identity. Nor as the literature below illustrates, is class still thought of as a collective identity in the way in which the early culturalists conceived it.

However, some critics emphasise the continued structural salience of class, stressing both the continuity of class inequality and its continued impact on how people choose to announce and establish class location. For example, in Walkerdine et al.'s (2001) twenty year empirical study on young women, they argue, 'it is class

---

1   One can set the development of gardening as a leisure activity against the backcloth of Chaney's argument, since gardening – as I show in chapter 2 – signalled a shift from communal and collective recreation to privatised, home-centred leisure.

that massively divides girls and young women in terms of their educational attainment and life trajectories' (Walkerdine et al. 2001, 4). Others stress the continued power of class to determine lifestyle and differences between class factions. Wynne (1990) for example, uses Bourdieu's concepts of economic and cultural capital in his ethnographic investigation of the differences in lifestyle between two contiguous factions of the 'new middle-class'. Similarly, Savage et al. (1992) use empirical work to modify Bourdieu's (1986) claims about French class and culture, arguing that the British middle-class is made up of three factions that must also be set against variables of gender, age and region. In these studies, all of which in some way account for the specificity of dramatic social and cultural change, class continues to be the key determinant in the differences between peoples' lifestyle and life chances.

Others offer a more robust dialogue with contemporary social theory, in an attempt to engage with the conceptual approaches which map social change, while holding on to class as a category. Savage (2000) and Southerton (2002) both bring contemporary social theory to bear on their analysis of class. Their work is not wholly incompatible with Chaney's (1996) claim about the shifting nature of forms of social identity. For them, class still matters, but its form of salience has changed: 'ordinariness' has become a central identity motif, replacing collective class identities with individualised class identities (Savage 2000b); and while class is still central, it is not the only factor at play in social practices of identity and belonging (Southerton 2002).

The issue of whether people still feel a sense of belonging to social class is addressed in a tranche of empirical studies by Savage (1999, 2000a, 2000b, 2001, 2005). He contends for example (2000b), that people tend not to recognise the structural significance of class, and in cultural terms, class is not self-consciously acknowledged as a source of social identity. Yet as he asserts: 'structurally, in terms of the impact on people's life chances, class appears to be as important as it ever was, indeed possibly more important than it was 30 years ago' (Savage 2000a, xii). While he suggests that in contemporary Britain class is no longer a stable origin of collective identity, he argues against the 'individualization' thesis (Beck 1992; Giddens 1991) that class is a redundant concept in late modernity. Using an empirical survey with 200 middle-class men and women in Manchester, Savage analyses 'repertoires of class talk' (Savage 2000b, 110): respondents were asked if Britain was a classless society and if they identified with a social class.

Arguing for a move which no longer sees class as a collective enterprise, Savage draws on Bourdieu's notion that class groups act to *differentiate* themselves from others in the social field. For Bourdieu, class is implicitly experienced as a category which is embedded in people's sense of self-value; it affects their approach to others and, crucially, how they conceive of themselves as individuals. In this way, Bourdieu's approach gestures implicitly towards some of the useful tenets of individualisation while holding on to the category of class. Savage's data revealed that people were uncertain which class they belong to, in fact two-thirds of the sample were ambivalent about their class identity. Despite this, people did have a working knowledge of class terminology: they recognised it as a measuring device which acts to 'position' people and they were aware of the social assessments of people which inhere in class terms. Significantly, people were more ready to discuss class in structural terms as a process than as something which related to their individual identity and they eluded seeing themselves in class terms. Yet, while class is evaded at one level, it is a category which is still necessarily evoked in order to describe people's life narrative. In this way, Savage argues that his data demonstrates the 'individualization of class identity' (Savage 2000b, 113):

> class is salient in constructing an idea of difference, not in terms of defining a class which one belongs to. Very few people indicated that they had a sense of belonging to a class with a strong collective identity. Those with ambiguous class identities defined their class in terms of who they were not. Even those respondents who had a strong sense of class identity defined class membership in largely individualized terms, as a personal statement of who they were (Savage 2000b, 113).

Asking people to consider class is a way of getting people to 'place' themselves in differential terms, which is not always a comfortable process. Indeed, to widen the point, what Characterises the empirical studies undertaken by Savage on class identities is that what matters to people is that they wish to be seen as 'ordinary'; being able to regard oneself as average, 'OK', 'proper', just 'ordinary' mattered far more to people than being able to classify themselves in class terms. In this sense class was significant because it threatened to contaminate claims to being 'ordinary'. Yet since ordinariness could only be claimed as a result of relational comparison in class terms, class came back into the conversation as a necessary descriptor. Class locations, for Savage's respondents, acted as default descriptors – necessary as something people wanted to exist in between. Interestingly, even in Savage's (2005) more recent secondary reading of the Affluent Worker Study he found themes of 'ordinariness, hesitancy and individuality' in the respondents' accounts of class. Most of the workers did not think of class in terms of occupational categories, rather class was related to ideas about individuality and authenticity (2005, 938). There was no shame in working-class identity for the respondents; rather, being ordinary was a way of refuting both privileged and stigmatised positions into being 'normal', 'authentic', having 'natural attributes' without any pretensions to social distinction, in a way which afforded them the means to lead their lives as they chose (ibid.)

Narratives of class identification based on notions of 'us' and 'them', across three groups living in a Southern English town, form the basis of an empirical study conducted by Southerton (2002). Drawing on Bourdieu's (1986) metaphors of capital, Southerton measured each group's volume of economic, cultural and social resources in three geographical locations in the new town of Yate. Using these categories, he was able to examine how his subjects identified themselves as relating to class based groups according to collective lifestyle consumption practices of '"what is" and "what is not" for "Us"' (2002, 172). Southerton asserts however, that the consumption of symbolic goods is not the only medium through which people make identifications. Drawing on Jenkins (1996) he argues that collective perceptions of the contextual use of social practices, enables people to formulate boundaries between similarity and inclusion – 'Us'; and difference and exclusion – 'Them'. Boundaries relate to identification and (dis)identification because they signal the end of shared practice and the start of difference. By investigating how his subjects related 'narratives of boundaries' he was able to analyse processes of identification.

Yate proved a salient geographical location precisely because it allowed Southerton to engage with current debates which surround the changing character of social bases of identification. A feature of the town's fast development meant that many residents had geographical mobility and owned their homes – factors which potentially encourage identification with neo-tribal lifestyles whilst lowering feelings of attachment to the locality. Furthermore, Yate's 'north-south status divide' (2002, 174) gave residents a signifying tool for demarcating boundaries between class groups.

Southerton's data revealed that three groups invariably differed in terms of their hobbies, consumption practices and narratives of identification. For example, the 'Bowland Road' respondents lived in South Yate, had a paucity of economic, cultural and social resources and low levels of geographical and social mobility. This group were characterised by their valuing of the economy of their housing – 'us' – as opposed to the extravagance of the more expensive houses belonging to 'them' in north Yate. As a result of their low levels of cultural resources, they further signalled their sense of 'us' by disparaging the extravagance of 'them' through anti-cosmopolitanism and the denigration of cultural experimentation, especially in relation to food and travel. Their moral outlook was also significant: they valued 'down-to earth' people who were honest, hard-working and who lacked pretension – declarations which provided a demarcation between themselves and the people of north Yate who were described as materialistic, and labelled 'cultural snobs'. By contrast, those from 'Lonsdale Avenue' – the most affluent group identified by Southerton – had high capital levels and marked their socially superior distance through reference to their housing status, often by marking a distinction between themselves and the people of north and south Yate. These residents tended to demonstrate their success by foregrounding their material possessions and their status as 'professionals' became a pivotal point of identification. While all respondents had high rates of geographical mobility, this group was divided into long-standing residents and newcomers. Long-standing residents spoke of 'we' in relation to their refined cultural tastes, newcomers used 'I': both were concerned to display their consumption of things traditionally enjoyed by the middle-class, to quote one respondent: "'I love good food, I love good wine, I love good holidays, theatre, cinema, good books and music'" (2002, 184). Unlike Bowland Road occupants, Lonsdale residents had no staunch moral code but they were conscious of personal values and stressed community responsibilities. Largely however, this group's key form of identification was cast around professional middle-class categories which were expressed as tacit cultural preferences shared with other Lonsdale residents.

Based on the volume of capitals owned by each group and on shared themes of boundary identification, Southerton's main conclusion is that, 'class formed the most significant social basis of identification for respondents interviewed in this research' (2002, 186). In this way, Southerton's empirical work shows that diagnostic theories, propounded by critics like Chaney (1996), are at least partially premature in their sceptical predictions about collective forms of identification and social change. On the other hand, it would also be quite wrong to see social class as an all-encompassing category of belonging. For Southerton social class was not the only source of identification showed by the groups. For example, while the Lonsdale group could all be categorised as middle-class, they showed internal incoherence by differently using 'I' or 'We' in their sense of 'Us'. For Southerton, geographical mobility accounted for these differences because it impacted on respondents' relationship to cultural resources and had an effect on their senses of belonging. They had different ways of describing their cultural sense of Yate: established respondents in Lonsdale highlighted shared cultural refinement and community responsibility in reference to their sense of 'we'; whereas newcomers, who spoke in terms of 'I', placed more focus on the local frames of reference and mentioned more easily discernible criteria – such as embodied social differences – for distinguishing themselves.

There are further studies which emphasise the importance of cross-cutting variables in contemporary modes of identification. In *Formations of Class and Gender* (1997) for example, Skeggs argues for a return to class analysis, yet she insists on the importance of locations of gender and race. Structured by the terms offered by Bourdieu's concept of capitals, her book argues that we are born into, 'an inherited space from which comes access to and acquisition of differential amounts of capital assets' (1997, 8-9). We occupy designated positions of class, race, and gender and the meanings and different forms of knowledge assigned to those locations. Capitals exist across the inter-relationship of these social arenas and bring, 'access to or limitation on which capitals are available to certain positions' (Skeggs 1997, 9). For the white working-class women of Skegg's study, femininity is a form of cultural capital. However, in the context of a society where whiteness and masculinity are valued forms of cultural capital, the young women had only meagre capital assets to trade. Feminine capital could only be transformed into limited material gains through a dwindling labour market. Their chances of gaining wider institutional power were severely limited – interpersonal relationships, secured through heterosexuality and marriage were the only forms of power these women could hope to access. Providing a feminine appearance was a means to secure better chances of exchange on the marriage market, but more importantly, femininity afforded a pathway to respectability.

The women of Skegg's study did not articulate working-class identification; rather, they made 'multitudinous efforts' to dis-identify, refuse and deny being working-class. These refusals of classification are understandable, Skeggs argues, given the history of institutional representations of working-class women as dirty, valueless and pathological. Recognising that to be working-class was pejorative, the women used 'imaginings of the respectable and judgemental middle-class' (Skeggs 1997, 74) as a yardstick with which to assess themselves. Focusing on the relationship between positioning and identity, Skeggs argues that the women of her study experienced class as a form of exclusion; they simply lacked access to the capital resources to 'be anything other than working-class' (ibid.).

Skeggs examines how the women occupied the lived experience of class day-to-day. Providing a distance between themselves and working-classness could be achieved by attempts to improve the self. One route to improvement is to attempt to bolster the conversion potential of cultural capital by making it tradeable beyond the local. Educational caring courses gave them 'caring capital' to trade on the labour market and investments in femininity meant they might garner potential assets on the marriage market. In this way, the women extended improvement to every facet of their lives – their minds, bodies and relationships – as a means to distinguish themselves from members of the working-class who did not seek to improve. They worked hard to develop tastes which they hoped would enable them to escape classification and 'pass' as not working-class. Yet their limited cultural capital meant that they lacked the knowledge to be able to judge what it means to 'get it right'.

For the women of Skegg's study, the home is a 'central site' where claims to respectability and legitimacy in relation to the self are made. The women felt positioned by their aesthetic tastes in furniture and decor, to the extent that when Skeggs entered their homes, they apologised. Skeggs uses Press (1991) to argue that since the women of her study knew few middle-class people, their access to images of middle-class lifestyles came from television. In these ways, Skegg's study shows how mediated lifestyle images enact symbolic violence against the working-class. Interaction with images of middle-class aesthetics added to the doubts about tastes the women already experienced. For Skeggs, the home is therefore a site where the working-class can never feel at ease with their own aesthetic choices; rather they feel as though they stand under the judgement of the ever-present (middle-class) surveillant other. Located by anxiety, powerlessness and insecurity, their tastes are articulated from positions of doubt:

> The working-class are never free from the judgements of imaginary and real others that position them, not just as different, but as inferior, as inadequate. Homes and bodies are where respectability is displayed but where class is lived out as the most omnipresent form, engendering surveillance and constant assessment of themselves (Skeggs, 1997, 90).

This review of recent literature yields important tenets for my own research questions around gardening, identity, consumption and class. The literature shows that despite the claim that the contemporary climate is characterised by shifting forms of identity, structurally class continues to make a significant difference to peoples' life chances (Walkerdine et al. 2001; Skeggs 1997). Empirical and ethnographic studies illustrate that differential access to forms of capital determine the kind of lifestyle choices people are able to make; in this way, class is expressed symbolically through consumption practices (Savage et al. 1992; Wynne 1990). Furthermore, despite claims that people no longer experience class as a collective entity, similar features characterise forms of consumption in ways which suggest that there are shared cultural and aesthetic class practices (Southerton 2002; Skeggs 1997). However, while class is still a category of identity and belonging, it is always cross-cut by other social variables, like gender or race, which impact on identity with the same force (Savage et al. 1992; Skeggs 1997). And class must also be conceived as a flexible entity, able to withstand dialogue with the type of social theory which examines the consequences of epochal social change. For example, Southerton's (2002) work illustrates that the social changes wrought by post-industrialisation have meant that some middle-class factions have geographical mobility, which is another social factor which impinges on modes of identity and belonging. These studies also reveal that class identity continues to be the focus of debate. People are sentient that class has continued pertinence as a form of social measurement, but – depending where people reside in class terms – the labels of class are less readily claimed. Class is less about the collective valorisation of being part of a class group – 'I am working-class' – and more about being able to *differentiate* oneself from others, either by announcing one's individualisation through claims to 'ordinariness' or through tastes and consumption practices. But, for fractions of the working-class, however, the ability to differentiate is central to the dis-identification process in making claims about not being working-class. Skegg's (1997) study shows that exercising taste through consumption can be a painful process for working-class women; making aesthetic judgements in relation to lifestyle spaces – through doubt and insecurity – shores up the 'emotional politics of class' (Skeggs 1997, 90). I take up the questions posed by these findings in chapters 6 and 7.

Bourdieu and Feminism: Bourdieu In Question

Unfortunately, while Bourdieu's work has undoubtedly enlightened the study of class, his contribution to gender studies is more problematic. Some critics have accused him of simply marginalising gender in his theoretical work. Frow for example, argues that Bourdieu, 'is curiously silent about gender' (Frow 1995, 5). Others have expressed frustration at his insistence on placing gender secondary in his analysis of class (McCall 1992). And Bourdieu has also been accused of 'symbolic violence' against the women's movement, for choosing to ignore thirty years worth of 'rich and diverse' second wave feminist scholarship (Lovell 2000, 27-28). As a result, unlike other French theorists, such as Lacan, Foucault and Derrida, who have enjoyed a degree of eminence in feminist circles, Bourdieu has been poorly disseminated. However, where feminist scholars have usefully appropriated Bourdieu's work, in particular his concept of 'capitals', they have fruitfully theorised the relationship between class and gender.

Gender and Bourdieu's concept of habitus

One of the problems feminist critics have identified with Bourdieu's work centres around his concept of habitus. McCall for example, argues that Bourdieu theorises the social structure as a, 'male-gendered ... public sphere of economic and cultural life' (McCall 1992, 839). As a derivative consequence, his notion of habitus also suffers from androcentrism because it is theorised as a 'largely public' entity. This is problematic for women, because although both men and women shift between the public and personal realms, it is women who are mostly identified with family, home life and with the private and the domestic. As a result, women are only partially accommodated by habitus and are seen as the secondary, 'lesser part of the dual ordering of social life' (Yeatman 1986, 157). Bourdieu's analysis suffers from gender blindness because his conception of the public, economic sphere fails to account for the 'gender-biased and segregated sphere of official masculine production' (McCall 1992, 848). Indeed, McCall argues that Bourdieu ignores the patriarchal relations which impinge on the domains between which women often have to mediate: the masculine/public sphere of work and the feminine/private sphere of the home. Bourdieu's conception of habitus fails to 'fit' women: it is flawed because it is unable to account for the complexities of women's everyday institutional and social experiences.

Moreover, feminist critics argue that habitus is problematic because Bourdieu theorises it as a set of transposable, '*unconscious* regulating principles' (Garnham and Williams 1980, 302). Habitus is a mode of being that agents acquire as a result of socialisation – it cannot be consciously learned or imitated; rather, it is procured through what Bourdieu calls lived practice. Habitus affords agents the competence to be able to move efficiently through a given social field with what Bourdieu calls a 'feel for the game'. It releases schemes of perception and appreciation that seem and feel entirely natural to the agent. In this way, the abilities of habitus cannot necessarily be expressed as conscious forms of knowledge. From a gendered perspective however, McCall takes issue with the idea that women can ever feel a sense of unconscious 'feel for the game' in a gender-biased male-dominated culture. Just as working-class people use the slogan 'that's not for the likes of me' because they make the practical recognition that they cannot have the cultural and economic opportunities afforded to the dominant classes, so women, 'are continually entering and struggling in environments that are not for the likes of them' (McCall 1992, 849). Rather, she argues, women develop the exact opposite – they acquire self-consciousness from continually attempting to join male-dominated fields in which they cannot find a positive equal position. In this way, MacCall argues, habitus as a concept fails to fit the social realities of women's experiences.

In similar vein, Lovell takes issue with the social fixity of habitus, for her it, 'tends towards an 'overdetermined' view of subjectivity in which subjective dispositions are too tightly tied to the social practices in which they were forged' (Lovell 2000, 11). Lovell reads habitus as an over-restrictive concept, for despite the fact that its social, non-essentialist construction is underlined by Bourdieu, the literal embodiment of habitus and its natural schematic attributes tend to emphasise its 'corporeal sedimentation' (Lovell 2000, 14). She uses historical examples of gender-passing as instances through which to challenge the unconscious element in Bourdieu's account of habitus. Using Dutch research, Lovell cites 119 cases of women who successfully lived and cross-dressed as sailors and soldiers in Northern Europe between the thirteenth and nineteenth centuries (Lovell 2000, 13). Garfinkel (1987) also documents the case of 'intersexed' Agnes, who successfully passed as a woman Los Angeles in late 1950s. If it is possible for women to convincingly inhabit and perform masculine modes of being, including the ability to, 'assume the bodily hexis and *habitus* characteristic of the militia' (Lovell 2000, 13) she reasons, then the natural, unconscious 'feel for the game' characteristic of habitus is rendered untenable. What these examples show is that despite Bourdieu's thesis of the acquisition of social identity through the practical sense, a 'feel for the game' can be consciously learned: it is possible for a woman to develop a masculine habitus.

Butler, Bourdieu and the Performance of Gender

From the terms of this discussion, one can see the problem Bourdieu's concept of habitus presents for contemporary feminist thought. Poststructuralist feminism for example, is centred around the idea that subjectivity is unfixed, in process and open to potentially radical re-construction (Weedon 1987). Similarly, feminist postmodernists theorise gender as a masquerade or performance (Butler 1990; Skeggs 1997). Both these positions valorise agency and the instability of self-hood – ideas which are at odds with the corporeality and social durability of habitus in Bourdieu's account of subjectivity.

In the post-modern theory of Butler, there is no authentic self lurking beneath the masquerade of identity; there are only performative layers – behind the performance is yet another performance and so on. As Butler argues, 'There is no gender behind the expressions of gender; the identity is performatively constituted by the very "expressions" that are said to be its results' (Butler 1990, 33). Indeed, Butler's theory hinges on the idea that identity itself can be conceived as a form of passing, since there is no 'real' identity masked by the act of performance (Lovell 2000, 14). For Butler, the notion of the removal and re-casting of identity is extended to the fleshy body; the corporeality of the body is conceived as yet another tool in the act of identity performance. As Butler observes, 'Gender is the repeated stylization of the body, a set of repeated acts within a highly rigid regulatory frame that congeal over time to produce the appearance of substance, of a natural sort of being' (Butler 1990, 43-4). In this way, masculinity and femininity are cultural performances, constructed through 'discursively constrained performative acts' which generate the effect of the inevitable and the natural (Butler 1990, xxviii-xxix) . In these ways, Butler's theory offers radical political potential for feminists, for she argues that ironic performances or contradictory masquerades act to unhinge the social fixity of gendered modes of being. Butler uses drag as a means to show the assumed fictional unity of the heterosexual performance of gender. As she argues, 'In imitating gender, drag implicitly reveals the imitative structure of gender itself' (Butler 1990, 175). Yet to perform drag, in Butler's terms, is not to mimic an original 'natural' version of gender, rather it is to, 'imitate the myth of the originality itself' (Butler 1990, 176).

In fact, Bourdieu and Butler share some intellectual ground in that they both draw upon the concept, developed by Austin (1962), of performativity. Performatives are the performed utterances which secure social contracts, such as a marriage declaration. But while performatives are speech acts, they must be institutionally authorised. In this way, they are always more than just performances because they carry social authorisation. Bourdieu and Butler however, theorise performatives differently. Butler argues that transgressive acts, which seize their own authority, can alter the meaning of performatives by dislodging them from their social structure (Lovell 2000). Butler (1997) illustrates her argument using the example of the black American woman, Rosa Parks, who flouted the conventions of racial segregation in the South by sitting at the front of a bus. 'In laying the claim to the right for which she had no prior authorisation,' Butler argues, 'she endowed a certain authority on the act, and began the insurrectionary process of over throwing those established codes of legitimacy' (Butler 1997, 147). Bourdieu on the other hand, argues that performatives derive their power firstly from the institutional authority which sanctions their status, and secondly, through the habitus which honours that authority. Unlike Butler, whose view of performatives offers agency to the subject through which to transform the self, Bourdieu's habitus and doxa are too rigidly sedimented to allow for the flexibility of identity. What Bourdieu's theory offers, as Lovell argues, is a powerfully rooted sense of the 'compelling presence and effectiveness' of the social (Lovell 2000, 15). For him, Butler's post-modern performances are mere performances; too easily the signs of identity can be removed and re-cast as simply and straightforwardly as donning a new set of clothes. Social reality, for Bourdieu, remains too solidly embedded within the subject to be left behind through transformation.

There are problems with both of these positions, yet both theorists offer efficacy to the debate about performativity. Bourdieu, 'at times reads like a structuralist with an 'oversocialised' concept of the individual, who ... is destined to become what he/she 'always already' was: a mere bearer of social positions, one who comes to love and want his/her fate' (Lovell 2000, 15). Yet the value of his argument lies in the insistence that almost erasable traces of social learning escort the individual throughout life; for Bourdieu performativity is grounded by the solidity of both institutions and the social. Butler on the other hand is a voluntarist: for her social agents are free to delete or re-fashion the markers of identity at will, with an additional margin of freedom in relation to the choice of the new self. Yet Butler's strength lies in the will to effect some kind of social transformation in a bid to resist political paralysis. Both writers are guilty of choosing contexts which fit the terms of their own theoretical concerns. Bourdieu tends to fight shy of analysing areas where social reality can be exposed as manufactured and open to re-construction; whereas spaces of leisure – the sites typical of post-modern analysis of play, leisure or carnival – are precisely the spaces Butler chooses to focus down upon. In these ways, Bourdieu and Butler offer useful contributions to the debate on performativity, but they are positions which, if left whole, are irreconcilable. The answer is surely to draw on both: to identify the potential for intervention by challenging the discursive construction of gender in order to augment social transformation while recognising the tight social and material circumstances which strenuously bind men and women to their gendered roles.

Bourdieu, Butler and the Performance of Gendered Gardening

Application of the terms of the debate between Bourdieu and Butler generates an interesting set of ideas about what one might expect to find out about gender relations in the field. In particular, it poses questions about the relationship between the institutional site where modes of gendered gardening are represented and my empirical findings of gardening by men and women.

If, as Bourdieu suggests, performatives are fettered by institutional authorisation and if habitus acts to honour institutional authority, one would expect there to be some relationship between the textually mediated representations of gendered gardening in the media and how the men and women of my study take up modes of performed gendered subjectivity. Will it be the case, for example, that the men and women of my study simply take up the traditionally gendered images offered to them by the national and local media? And, since gender is always classed, might class inflect how men and women chose to become particular kinds of gendered gardening subjects? On the other hand, if as Butler argues, performatives can seize their own authority without being tied to institutional sanctions, it may be that the institutional role of the media – with its conventionally gendered images – is negligible. It might be that the men and women of my study choose *not* to perform gender in conventional ways. It may be that female gardeners might 'make like men', or that men might develop a feminine 'feel for the game' and develop feminine gardening skills. If this is so, what social circumstances in ordinary everyday contexts, produce the choice to do gendered gardening differently or subversively? And if men and women are acting to unhinge traditional modes of gender, in what ways do such 'insurrectionary acts' shake the foundations of institutions such as the media? Might ordinary insurrectionary acts set the agenda for more politically empowering images of how men and women are represented in the lifestyle gardening media? These questions are taken up in relation to my empirical findings in chapter 7.

Conclusion

This chapter argues that Pierre Bourdieu's cultural approach to class offers the most productive collection of theories and concepts for understanding gardening consumption and taste practices. Turning to a review of recent literature on class, lifestyle, difference and identity, I argue that recent claims about class in social theory carry a degree of pertinence. Ultimately however, recent empirical and ethnographic studies lead me to conclude that class is both structurally and culturally salient. I use these studies to map a further set of questions regarding class and the book thereby refining its main questions. Focusing on gender, I argue that recent post-modern theory (Butler 1990), offers the most politically empowering way of theorising gendered acts of gardening. However, I argue that out of the critical dialogue between Bourdieu and Butler, Bourdieu productively tempers Butler's ideas that identity can be re-cast at the subject's will.

Chapter 4 asks if the ordinary garden has a history or place in academic literature. Reviewing a range of inter-disciplinary sources, with class and gender at the forefront of the analysis, I ask how far the people, history, sites and spaces of ordinary gardening are accounted for. Can this literature, I ask, map an adequate geographical and historical context for my ethnographic findings on the classed and gendered dynamics of gardening?

Chapter 4

Gardening Legislators: Gardening, Ordinariness and History

Introduction

This book asks how classed and gendered identities are played out *in the ordinary garden*. Turning to sources which take the garden as its focus, this chapter critically reviews an inter-disciplinary range of literature as a means of asking how British gardens, gardeners and gardening practices are documented. The first section, 'Histories' examines what are arguably culturally dominant approaches to garden, landscape and allotment history; it then turns to the gardeners who people those histories and movements. The second, 'People', looks at the types of garden spaces and sites that are documented in garden history. The third section examines relatively new scholarship on the social history of the private home garden. And finally, arguing that gardens have been important consumption sites which communicate meaning about their owners, the third section looks at a number of case studies on gardens which perform symbolic work.

The core of this book is centred around my own ethnographic findings on class, gender, gardeners and identity, which are to be found in this study. Using a group of people from a small provincial semi-industrial town in West Yorkshire, I interviewed and gardened with the people of my study in the context of their own ordinary gardens. Yet the distinctive set of gardening practices which I found are historically produced and materially grounded. All practices in this sense are historically contingent and located. In order to understand the emergence of particular practices and what makes them distinctive and meaningful they need to be historicised and geographically located. This chapter aims to ask whether the existing literature drawn from disciplines such as garden history, women's studies, cultural geography, sociology, cultural, urban and rural landscape studies and design and social history can provide an adequate contextual backdrop for understanding the symbolic meaning of the ordinary garden practices which are manifest in private domestic gardens in a small town in the North of England.

Approaches to Garden History: Great Gardens, Allotments and Landscape

Liberal humanist approaches to garden history

Much of the extant literature on gardens is underscored by a liberal humanist approach to gardens in the past. The most comprehensive, respected and oft-mentioned histories (see for example, Clifford 1962; Hadfield 1979; and Thacker 1979) seek to establish a Leavisite great tradition or historical canon of gardens. The mission to document an Arnoldian version of the, 'best that has been thought and known' about gardens is clear in Christopher Thacker's introduction to *The History of Gardens* (1979). 'There is no end to bad gardens,' he begins, 'but we need not mention them. My task is far happier, since I may choose the best, among vanished and almost-vanished and existing gardens' (Thacker 1979, 7). In similar vein, Derek Clifford elevates his history of gardens to a survey of the garden 'as a work of art', or as a 'fine art'. The gardens that Clifford is concerned with are those which contribute to, 'the art of living'; gardens of leisure, opulence and luxury are the historical sites which construct his study. Plants hold no interest for Clifford, for him, plants are merely raw materials which warrant no further discussion, 'A history of the art of painting would be thought strange if nine-tenths of it were devoted to the introduction of new pigments' (Clifford 1962, 15). Rather, Clifford's survey, which reads like an art history of garden design, treats gardens as the traditional art historian discusses the oil-painting: complete artworks judged according to the efficacy of their internal coherence.

Clifford, Hadfield and Thacker all seek to provide a linear, cause and effect narrative trajectory of 'great' garden design movements using the internal design dynamics of Early Roman, Italian Renaissance, French Formal and English Landscape gardens. These movements constitute the garden history canon. Thacker admits to his non-European omissions, 'I have *obviously* not been able to cover all the magnificent gardens which can be seen in South Africa, Ceylon, New Zealand, much of the United States and Latin America' (Emphasis mine, 1979, 7). These gardens need not be included, he reasons, because their antecedents only lead back to the white European canon.

Liberal humanist commentators argue that the universal power of great culture has the power to educate ordinary people to appreciate the sublime beauty of high culture in ways which transcend barriers of class, race and gender. Note the emphasis on transcendence, which acts to denigrate the idea that ordinary culture itself is not an object of value. Liberal humanist values, still arguably the dominant value system in British cultural institutions, tend to ignore the structural power relations which deny some people the resources to access these forms of culture (Jordan and Weedon 1997). Moreover, canonical constructions often reflect the white bourgeoisie values of those who construct them; as a result the canon of garden history constructed by Thacker is a white, male, Western version of legitimate garden culture. The eurocentrism of Thacker's text is admonished by a plea that the reader recognise that the best culture lies innate within the art form itself; acts of choice or discrimination on the part of the critic become overpowered by the greatness of art: 'gardens' we are told, 'are greater than their historians, as poems and paintings tower over those who try to explain them' (1979, 7). But if the great tradition in these garden histories is Eurocentric, it is also unapologetically elite. The great tradition, for these writers, is produced either by royalty or the aristocracy and constitutes a pure, essentially elite order of white European style and artistic taste. In Bourdieu's (1986) terms, knowledge of these versions of garden history, constitutes a rich source of cultural capital; surely a desirable commodity for the middle-class reader.

Problematically, these histories tell the reader almost nothing about what great gardens meant, either for their owners or for those who consumed them. The patrician voices of these writers are more attuned to providing design tradition connoisseurship than they are with enabling the reader to understand the social and cultural use or meaning of gardens in the past. Thacker's drive to locate every garden into a tendency or movement leads him to categorise Biddulph Grange – the British nineteenth century garden which leads the visitor through a fantastical world tour of juxtaposed scenes – as an 'eclectic garden.' In doing so he blocks off any understanding of the garden's role as a symbolic marker for social standing and status. Yet there are arguably more useful ways of theorising garden aesthetics.

Mukerji's (1990) materialist analysis of the French formal garden, for example, insists on understanding the relationship between capitalist economic development and conspicuous plant collection and consumption. At particular historical moments traditional sources of rank are weakened by new economic and political forms of power, at those junctures, she uses Bourdieu (1986) to argue that people use consumption to lay claims to social standing. For Mukerji, seventeenth century courtly gardens are much more than examples of consistent historically specific design principles, they were also used for, 'creating, declaring, and reading claims about social station' (Mukerji 1990, 652). Biddulph Grange, a garden that marked what Geoffrey Jellicoe (1975) was to call, 'a new era of British internationalism,' was created by James Bateman and Edward Cooke in the 1830s. It comprises a rocky Scottish glen; a Wellingtonia walk; 'China' – including rhododendrons from Sikkim, Bhutan and Nepal; the 'Italianate'; and 'Egypt' which comprises sphinxes, a topiary pyramid, and the 'Ape of Troth'. This garden amounts to far more than an eclectic juxtaposition of different aesthetic styles; the presentation and arrangement of petted exotic plants, the pursuit of which explorers such as David Douglas had literally given their lives, communicated the supremacy of the British colonial empire and acted as markers of the impressive international power and reach of their owners. Seen in this context, Clifford's curt dismissal of the significance of plants to garden history, ('plant growing is not gardening' he argues (1962, 18)), seems almost risible. As Mukerji points out, orangeries and stoves (heated glass houses) were built precisely for the purpose of displaying prized exotics so that gardens could, 'be seen as collector's maps' conferring, 'God-like power to control the elements' (Mukerji 1990, 657) onto their owners. Yet in order to arrive at this kind of reading the shift in focus must move from reading the textual mechanisms of a chronology of artworks as part of art movements, to thinking about the importance of their consumption.

Interestingly, the drive towards producing a final chapter on great gardens of the twentieth century proves difficult for liberal humanist garden historians. Writing the present as though its achievements are somehow commensurate with the past is impossible given the influence of popular culture and mass consumption. While Hadfield acknowledges that 'the real feature of the twentieth century was the growth of a huge suburbia of small houses,' (1979, 428) he devotes only three paragraphs to suburban gardens in a 454 page text. He bemoans the salient feature of suburban gardens: standardisation, 'They are but of one general type … an almost invariably rectangular patch covering but a few square yards' (ibid.). The twentieth century common-law gardener becomes indistinguishable from his house, garden, and neighbours. A single paragraph covers all suburban gardens, because the description of one stands for all. The design features or the aesthetics of these gardens – even standardised characteristics – are not deemed worthy of discussion. Similarly, for Clifford, the twentieth century is characterised by the fall of the artist who creates private artworks to the rise of the professional who manages public parks or the gardens of civic buildings. Garden artists of the past from high cultural quarters conversant with poetry, painting and architecture have given way to mere professionals whose techniques for, 'needs which are principally hygienic and sociological' can be acquired through training (Clifford 1962, 213). Domestic gardens are given short shrift in a single paragraph, where Clifford bemoans the lack of space in the city garden, the lack of time for the commuting suburban gardener and the battle of competition popular culture pitches against gardening as a pastime more generally (Clifford 1962, 212). The ordinary suburban garden can never aspire to be part of the canon for liberal humanist garden writers.

The historical antecedents of the 'culture and civilisation' tradition are firmly present in liberal humanist conceptions of garden history. More recent texts demonstrate their continued popularity and dominance (see for example Brown 1999). Principally, their aim is to legislate garden taste and culture. In Bourdieusian (1986) fashion, these histories package legitimated forms of gardening knowledge which are high in cultural capital. Tradeable for middle-class readers, such knowledge - about the 'right' gardening movements and the 'best' gardens in the 'right' locations – can be reconverted in the field for high symbolic returns. Manuals for the acquisition of cultural capital, these kinds of texts show that knowledge of High garden Culture functions as a form of social distinction for its readers.

Liberal humanist garden histories also function as a form of symbolic violence (Bourdieu 1990a).[1] Often misrecognised as legitimate historical accounts, they impose bourgeoisie values about which shall be the most treasured gardens in history could be forgiven for thinking that the only gardens worthy of documentation are canonised artworks. The pedagogic action of symbolic violence, as Jenkins (2002) reminds us, often works most effectively through practices of exclusion or by treating some ideas as though they were 'unthinkable'. To be sure, these accounts leave whole swathes of garden history – for example working-class gardening, the practices of the garden labourers who built and maintained 'great' gardens and female gardeners – out of the historical picture. The message is clear: only elite garden history is of value. In these ways, liberal humanist texts serve to re-inscribe the uneven distribution of cultural capital, they reproduce the cultural formation, thereby serving the interests of the dominant group.

Gardening and its relationship with ordinariness and everyday life are also thought too trivial and inconsequential for mention in these histories. Even the quotidian practices that the aristocracy put to these sites is excluded, so that the

---

1   In this sense they join the other historical and contemporary instances of symbolic violence charted in this study. The will to educate working-class women about home taste in the 1950s (as charted in chapter 2), and the ways in which the contemporary media at the time this study was conducted, ignored local working-class gardening competencies in favour of bourgeoisie tastes.

reader is left with no clue about the role these gardens had in even the everyday lives of royalty. The researcher hoping to find a history of ordinary gardening, or even of gardening as a daily, circadian part of the travails of the life of the wealthy, need search elsewhere. The dimensions of ordinariness defined by Felski (2000), of home, habit and repetition, have no place here, in these histories it is escape from the everyday that is the *raison d'être* for creating gardens in the first place. For Clifford, the great gardens are places of spiritual solace where 'man' might feel 'a sense of awe... remote from the dulling effect of everyday experience' (1962, 19). And the domestic ordinary garden of the lower-, middle- or working-class gardener is not a place liberal humanist garden historians care to even think about: it is cursorily mentioned, invites generalised scant definition, warrants numerous complaints, but it is never analysed because it has never actually been looked at. Yet given the dominance of liberal humanist values in Britain's chief cultural institutions, without the sanction of liberal humanist approval, it has been, until relatively recently, rendered a space without a respectable history.

Gardening and alternative land movements

My concern in this study is to find a history of ordinary gardening, which includes the notion that working-class and women's gardening practices can be valued. Liberal humanist approaches thwart that possibility, so it is to alternative land movements that this chapter now turns.

Crouch and Ward's book *The Allotment: Its Landscape and Culture* (1999) is a socialist history of both British and European working-class allotments. In this sense it forms a challenge to liberal humanist conceptions of garden history and one can see the historical antecedents of early left-culturalism in its themes and concerns. The book charts the development of the allotment movement since the early 1800s, examining the economic, political and social history of the plot. Like the nineteenth century development of trade unions, friendly societies and the co-operative movement, the allotments are regarded as, 'an expression of working-class self-help and mutual aid,' formed in direct response to the impact of the industrial revolution (Crouch and Ward 1999, 11). The authors reclaim a forgotten history of working-class political activism in the struggle against establishment land policies formed by councils and local government and the capitalist aspirations of county developers to build over allotment sites. The book also focuses on the quotidian role of allotment gardening in the lives of working-class people: it is an important site for the production of food when resources are scarce; it acts as an important symbol of working-class self-sufficiency; it is a place where 'quiet calm', peace and 'therapeutic value' from the noise and oppression of everyday life can be found and it plays a role in the expression of individual and collective identities. Allotments, for Crouch and Ward, are characterised by a particular kind of social connection, one based on the 'gift relationship' within what they call a 'culture of reciprocity'. Working-class allotment holders, they argue, have historically established communal bonds based on giving away home-grown produce to needy neighbours and other community members. As a result, a set of mutual bonds which bind working-class communities also help to strengthen the political dimension of working-class community activism.

These aspects of Crouch and Ward's work demonstrate the influence of Hoggart (1957) and Williams (1958, 1989): there is a concern with re-writing and valuing a collective working-class history; ordinariness and the everyday form part of what is worthy about culture; and the writers foreground, perhaps somewhat nostalgically, the positive bonds and connections of working-class community (Bourke, 1994).

Yet while allotments have served to provide an alternative space for self-sustainability for ordinary working people, allotment sites have conversely served institutions and individuals concerned with the regulation of a potentially unruly working-class. In these ways, their organisation forms part of the history of working-class regulation charted in chapter one of this book. The authors describe the actions of educated philanthropic men, such as the clergyman John Stevens Henslow, professor of botany at Cambridge and friend to Charles Darwin, who set up an allotment scheme in Suffolk in the 1840s. His campaign for allotments, published in the local newspaper and addressed to landlords, 'on the advantages to be expected from the general establishment of a spade tenantry among the labouring classes,' (Crouch and Ward 1999, 51) was surely an inducement that landlords recognise the potential for social control that land plots would provide. Similarly, the book details examples of the rules and regulations by which allotment holders were forced to abide: 'tenants shall maintain a character for morality and sobriety, and shall not frequent a public-house on the Sabbathday' (Crouch and Ward 1999, 56) stated one set enforced in 1872 for allotment gardens near Swindon. Yet the authors underplay these kinds of philanthropic or paternalistic moves as effective mechanisms for regulating the working-class. In their concern to celebrate the radicalism of the allotment movement, Crouch and Ward tend to minimise the surveillance techniques inherent in allotment schemes which were set up by those concerned about the poor.

An important part of the movement, according to Crouch and Ward, is the aesthetic challenge allotments provide to conventional images of the landscape, 'the allotment breaks the rules: it fails to comply with the accepted image' (1999, 15). Predominantly urban spaces, allotment gardens challenge both dominant mainstream images of the rural landscape and they provide an alternative to 'supervised and controlled' municipal parks, the 'open-air leisure pursuits' of the working-class terrace garden or the 'politeness and privacy' of the Georgian square garden. Allotments, the authors assert 'provide a landscape of freedom' (1999, 31). An important aspect of the freedom of the landscape is expressed by the allotment shed: the authors describe where sheds are located, how they have been maligned by councils and middle-class onlookers and how they function for their owners. However, when the discussion moves to the question of how sheds look, how their aesthetics are organised, the authors fight shy of honest description. They fall to euphemistic statements which circumvent any real analysis of the aesthetic meaning of their construction or 'look': rather, ranking as an especially creative entity, shed construction is elevated to a 'self-builder's art' (1999, 11), sheds are unique 'expressions of individuality', indeed they act as tangible cornerstones of resistance to dominant established landscape images.

As leftist critics, Crouch and Ward are interested in weighing up the potential the allotment movement provides for *alternative* meanings in the context of a *collective* land movement. But rather than admitting that the sheds they have seen might be 'make do', ramshackle, not especially aesthetically interesting, plain ordinary, or perhaps even shabby and run-down – they are theorised, in a bid to view the working-class as potential revolutionary fodder, as art or symbols of political resistance. Crouch and Ward (1999), unlike liberal humanist writers, are at least prepared to allow the existence of mundane aspects of working-class culture into their analysis, but once faced with the mundane, they are unable to find anything interesting and intriguing about ordinary aspects of gardening culture.

Explorations of the land and landscape can be found in the work of cultural geographer and historian David Matless. *Landscape and Englishness* (1998) explores versions of English landscape from 1918 to 1950 using a vast array of materials – from British press cartoons, advertising, literature, ordinance survey maps and social commentary – to German motorway construction maps and Danish health regimes. Matless is interested in the tensions which exist between landscape and culture: he examines the social and aesthetic values ascribed to the English landscape; the 'right' and 'wrong' reasons to look at, make visits to, engage with or utilise aspects of the English countryside; and at the 'character' of both place and the social conduct of the people who choose to inhabit it. For Matless, landscape is a site of competing claims and values: if it is a site of value in terms of conservation, residence and commerce, it is also a site of acrimony against authorities, developers and unsightly buildings. In this way, he traces the competing agencies who make discriminating cultural judgements about what and who has the right to belong in the landscape.

Matless traces the emergence of the preservationist landscape movement in Britain in the early part of the twentieth century. Planning documents, newspaper cartoons, letters and diaries are just some of the materials Matless uses to show that a notion of landscape and Englishness came from a 'crisis of landscape and politics' in the 1920s (1998, 14). Matless argues that a modernist sense of order and design informed the 1920s vision of country, city and suburb. He develops these themes around landscape and citizenship, arguing that particular manners of conduct in the countryside were established as the 'right' basis of citizenship – while others, focused, for example, around litter and unruly behaviour – indicated what he calls, 'anti-citizenship, an immoral geography of leisure' (ibid.). Country leisure was embraced by the largely middle-class preservationist movement, yet as Matless shows, the leisure activities of some were regarded as forms of cultural infringement. Landscape citizenship defined its meaning against the notion of the 'anti-citizen'. Usually from the 'vulgar' working-class, Matless argues that the anti-citizen is often labelled 'Cockney', portrayed as a, 'cultural grotesque, signifying a commercial rather than industrial working-class whose leisure is centred around consumption and display' (1998, 68). And there were specific kinds of activities associated with the cultural trespass of working-class anti-citizens: the deposit of litter, noise pollution, disturbing local flora and unruly bathing and dancing. This kind of inappropriate conduct was often linked to a lack of aesthetic discernment; the working-class were conceived as people who did not know how to look at or see the countryside. As one preservationist remarked, 'man has to go through a vigorous training before he can see the country at all' (Matless 1998, 67).

Modern landscape citizenship came to depend on methods of regulation which sought to cultivate the correct ways of being and seeing in landscape. This rested on attempting to instil amongst the landscape public the right social and aesthetic distinctions. In 1928 the *Council for the Preservation of Rural England* for example, advanced its 'Anti-Litter Campaign' using a satirical postcard displaying two docile picnickers checking their litter before they leave, "Better have a look round among our litter and see we haven't left anything be'ind," reads the caption. Similarly an informal Country Code was designed, its specific aims to encourage gate closing, litter disposal and to appoint officers for the surveillance of potentially unruly countryside users. Seeing the landscape was also regulated by practices of observation, mapping and orienteering; the construction of an 'intellectual, spiritual and physical citizenship' depended on producing observant citizens via survey. Sharp observation was part of the walking code for scouts, as Matless demonstrates: 'a dibdobbery of observant walking emerges: "Remember that it is a disgrace to a Scout if, when he is with other people, they see anything big or little, near or far, high or low, that he has not already seen for himself"' (Matless 1998, 75). Only certain practices and particular kinds of people were fit for the preservationist movement's idea of the English countryside.

Several of the ideas in Matless's thesis about landscape are germane to the themes of gardening culture under discussion in this study: he demonstrates that the preservationist movement's vision of landscape was shot through with aesthetic and social class distinctions and he shows the means by which the working-class were regulated in an attempt to make them landscape citizens.

Undoubtedly, these examples from the alternative land movement offer an advance on liberal humanist garden history. Both Crouch and Ward (1999) and Matless (1998) are attentive to the power relations of class: Crouch and Ward (1999) value the working-class to the extent that they centre their account around its community, both trace historically how working-class consumption of land plots and the landscape have been subject to forms of middle-class surveillance; and Matless (1998) demonstrates how approaches to landscape are shot through with practices of social distinction.

Given these attributes it is therefore unfortunate that neither of these studies actually centres on the private, ordinary domestic *garden*. Crouch and Ward (1999) centre on a personal space that is removed from the domestic and the private and they offer no real analysis of the relationship between the allotment and the garden. And, while Matless (1998) explores a number of themes and ideas which are germane to my study – ideas around land, culture, soil, aesthetic and social distinctions, the representation and regulation of the working-class in relation to land – he makes absolutely no mention of gardens.

Nonetheless these are studies that allow admission to the ordinary. Matless' study probes the most mundane quarters of the English landscape. And *The Allotment: Its Landscape and Culture* (1999) marks an attempt to document, historicise and somehow value the quotidian gardening experiences of ordinary working people in the context of their communities. However, its analysis shows discomfort with the ordinary. In its leftist quest to establish the allotment movement as an alternative working-class subculture it tends to focus on the transformative potential of the collective working-class rather than accepting ordinary people on their own terms. This would explain its focus on an alternative site – the allotment – at the expense of the individual, private, ordinary domestic garden. The Left have been attacked for being interested only in the politically conscious working-class and cultural studies for attempting to find active and positive forms of subcultural resistance in working-class culture (Walkerdine 1997, 20). As a result the ordinariness and mundanity – the coping, living, dreaming and hoping of working-class life – is rendered invisible as a result:

> what is important to me is to be able to talk not about subcultures or resistance, or an audience making its continually resistant readings, but about the ordinary working people, who have been coping and surviving, who are formed at the intersection of these competing claims to truth, who are subjects formed in the complexities of everyday practices...I want to talk about people who cannot easily be characterised as part of a politicized working-class, nor resistant subcultures, the ordinary people that the Left seemed to forget (Walkerdine 1997, 21).

Moreover, omitting the private and the domestic in favour of the public, politicised alternative allotment movement means that although the authors strive to deny it, Crouch and Ward (1999) tend to offer a predominantly male alternative history of working-class community. Allotments and their sheds they suggest have occasionally been sites where men go precisely to *escape* the domestic – 'getting away from the wife and children' was one man's reason for holding an allotment according to the Thorpe Report (Crouch and Ward 1997, 90). While this kind of text goes much further towards offering a history of ordinary gardening than those with liberal humanist values, working-class women are only partially mentioned, and once again, the space, meaning, and aesthetic tendencies of the ordinary garden are circumvented in the drive to capture the political ethos of a land movement. The private, individual garden – a space which belies the drive to be read as a public land protest is perhaps too mundane, too conformist to be of real interest to leftist critics.

People

So far this chapter has examined how gardens have been represented in particular dominant versions of garden history. This section turns to the people of gardening. Reviewing both liberal humanist and feminist approaches to gardening, I ask: what gardeners are considered worthy of being named as the most valued and celebrated gardeners? And what are the consequences for those unnamed in official histories?

Great white men: the liberal humanist approach

The movements of innovation which characterise liberal humanist accounts of garden history are attributed to the work of 'great' gardeners or gardening genius. The histories by Thacker, Clifford, Hadfield, and Scott-James and Lancaster (1977), as well as more recent texts by Brown (1999), contain a tacit canonised agreement about the gardeners who were responsible for the main structural movements of the Great Tradition. All these texts reference key names and associate them with peak moments in garden history; for example, Addison, Pope and Lord Burlington are credited for the English Landscape movement and Charles II, Mollet and Le Notre with the French Formal tradition. As a result, the focus on great gardens and the great gardeners who constructed them results in a largely white, male, elite history of gardeners.

Unfortunately, even when some of these accounts do seek to flesh out the standard great tradition with further examples of great gardeners from more mundane quarters, the focus on male, white, middle-class privilege is never entirely dislodged. In *The Pleasure Garden* (1977) for example, Scott-James and Lancaster devote their chapter 'The Parsonage Garden' to the innovative contribution, particularly in plant breeding, of eighteenth and nineteenth century country priests. However, as they argue, priests such as Gilbert White and the Rev. the Hon. William Herbert were in a unique position to research and practice botany, 'as his property and status increased,' argues Scott-James of the typical parish priest, 'he became a natural leader in most country pursuits, having more education and a better library than any of his parishioners, and would tend to have the best garden in the village' (1977, 75). While these instances provide examples of gardeners who foray beyond royalty and the aristocracy, they still add to a middle-class version of gardeners in garden history.

In these ways the liberal humanist tradition establishes a small group of revered legislators who are white, male, elite (or at least upper middle-class) and European. These are the figures responsible for the 'great' movements and gardens that liberal humanist histories laud. In this sense, the issue of class is never mentioned or addressed; the reader is merely delivered a 'great' history of 'great' yet extremely privileged people. Ordinary people and the working-class are nowhere to be found in these histories and one could be forgiven for thinking that women have made no contribution to 'great' gardens. It is to feminist literature on gardens, in search of histories where at least gender is taken in to account, that this section now turns.

Great white women: feminist approaches

Available feminist histories of gardening tend to use the strategy of uncovering a specifically female contribution to the construction of great gardens or gardening trends. Susan Groag-Bell's (1990) essay on eighteenth century English garden history for example, argues that the 'ongoing' and 'commonplace' trends of the eighteenth century – flower and shrub gardening – often practised by female gardeners, have been obscured in traditional garden history as a result of the tendency to concentrate on the key developments of the 'Landscape Movement'. Yet as Groag-Bell argues the, 'absence of women from eighteenth-century gardens is an historical anomaly' (Groag-Bell 1990, 473). Using gardening advice books, magazines, travel accounts, letters and diaries, Groag-Bell traces 'considerable evidence' of 'women's participation in garden art' (1990, 476). In an article on gardening by the female editor of the *Female Spectator* (1745) for example, Groag-Bell notes that the author encourages female readers to be knowledgeable about gardening and to undertake gardening tasks themselves. And through an examination of the journals and letters of an upper-class gardener such as the traveller and writer Celia Fiennes, Groag-Bell identifies the specific interests of female gardeners of the time; Lady Mary Wortley Montagu, for example, was interested in incorporating natural terrain into the garden and had a passion for flowers. Other important female gardeners that people Groag-Bell's history include Lady Mary Coke, Hannah More, Sarah Ponsonby, Harriet Stratfield and Elizabeth Cottrell Dormer. In this way, she is able to construct a female history of previously hidden eighteenth century female gardening as well as evidence of female gardening as a physical activity that some of these women pursued.

Dawn MacLeod's book *Down-to-Earth-Women: Those Who Care for the Soil* (1982) is similarly devoted to the construction of a specifically female garden history. Describing the lives and achievements of mostly twentieth century female gardeners, MacLeod tells the story of early 'humble' gardeners and nuns; celebrated garden innovators such as Gertrude Jekyll; pioneering specialists, for instance, the herb farmer Margaret Brownlow; garden preservationists such as Octavia Hill, co-founder of The National Trust; and influential professionals who, with horticultural, scientific or botanic qualifications, managed to set up women-only training schools, like for example Studley College in Warwickshire (founded in 1910), in order to pave the way for new aspiring female gardeners. In this way, MacLeod's book examines the ways in which women have extended their gardening skills and knowledge for use in commerce, education and historic preservation.

What these feminist histories share is a belief that men and women garden differently in ways which produce a gendered gardening aesthetics. While all-male renowned landscape designers focused on the construction of natural terrain using lakes, hills and Greco-Roman classical motifs and statuary, Bell argues that women grew herbs and plants for medicinal use and had kept alive the female tradition of flower growing since the Middle Ages. A specifically female enjoyment of flowers, shrubs and walks characterised female aesthetic appreciation and creativity during this period.

In like manner, MacLeod also argues for the existence of female garden aesthetics, though her analysis extends male and female gardening differences out to essential gendered characteristics. In this way, the influence of radical feminism, with its belief in a fixed, transcultural and biologistic notion of gendered subjecthood can be seen to exert an influence on MacLeod's conception of gendered gardening practices (see for example, Griffin (1981), and Dworkin (1981)). 'Man,' she argues in her preface, 'likes to dominate and impose his own will upon the smaller fry of existence (at times on his own kind too), whereas woman through centuries of motherhood has learned to appreciate life in all its manifestations' (1982, ix). For MacLeod, men's gardening is tainted by their destructive and competitive nature; their desire to garden is often confined to the pursuit of money or fame. Women on the other hand, characterised by the desire to nurture and care for the soil, share one thing in common: 'a strong love of the earth and its growing plants, a devotion in which desire for personal power and prestige has had very little place' (ibid.). MacLeod extends her thesis to gardens, arguing that, 'Certain gardens could only have been made by a woman' (1982, x) – though no real rationale is given to inform the reader why this is so. One of the problems with MacLeod's book is that it tends to make assertions about female garden aesthetics without offering any analysis of the specific kind of gardening vocabulary male and female gardeners draw upon.

However, Christine Dann's (1992) work on gendered gardening in New Zealand makes a series of interesting claims about the differences between men and women's gardening practices. Dann's source material is drawn from personal observation, informal letters and interviews with fifty cottage gardeners in Christchurch. Dann argues that women gravitate towards herbs and they appreciate a wide variety of flowers; by contrast men are interested in vegetables and bedding plants and they tend towards connoisseurship or collecting. Perhaps more interestingly, Dann claims that women have a relaxed approach to garden design, whereas men, whose flowers are often placed in 'mathematical rows' possess a, 'rigid and unimaginative style of flower gardening' (1992, 239). Men, she asserts, are competent with fertilisers and sprays, are interested in public floral display (hence their love of bedding), but they face limitations in relation to garden design and philosophy. Ultimately, Dann's argument is that female aesthetics offer a more valuable contribution to the practice of gardening. However, the fact that these practices are also classed tends to escape the reach of Dann's argument. My ethnographic findings reveal similar types of practices undertaken by male and female gardeners in private gardens in West Yorkshire, but while Dann suggests that regimentation, clinical tidiness and a love of bedding plants are gendered preferences, I argue that these tendencies demonstrate a classed garden aesthetic which cross-cuts issues of gender. More usefully, Dann's work refuses the import of an essentialising radical feminist perspective on gardening differences. However, she tends to avoid any theoretical engagement, even for example with a social constructionist perspective, as to why gendered gardening practices exist.

Writers such as Groag-Bell, MacLeod and Dann offer an important contribution to existing garden scholarship: they work to reclaim a 'forgotten' history of women's gardening. They counter the tendency of historians to write women out of history and present them as either unimportant, or simple victims of historical processes. What these histories tend to leave intact however, are the fundamental assumptions of the liberal humanist tradition of celebrating 'great' individuals. As a result, feminist garden histories tend to replace the gender blind category of great people with great women. Great male legislators are merely replaced by great female legislators. In these histories 'women' is cited as a homogeneous category which claims to speak on behalf of all women – class as an analytic category is ignored. Yet as these texts reveal, the women who people these garden histories are middle-class or aristocratic women who have access to the resources which enable them to aspire to liberal definitions of greatness. As a result working-class contributions to garden history, or to the historical formation of gardening as a cultural practice are entirely missing from these accounts. Yet class as a category of identity difference is an identity which has significant impact and value in relation to gendered aesthetics of gardening.

Place

So far this chapter has analysed how gardens and gardeners are officially represented in garden history. In this section, I investigate the *where* of garden writing. I ask:

what places, sites and spaces do official forms of literature on gardens explore? In the first part, because of its focus on ordinariness, I examine writing on suburbia as a means of uncovering work on gardening and the mundane. In the second, I turn my attention to literature which explores the gardens of ordinary people, of the disenfranchised and the homeless; could it be, that studies on ordinary gardeners focus on gardens sited in ordinary locations?

Mundane places: studies of suburbia

Constructed out of a particular geography of modernisation and urbanisation in 1930s Britain, suburbia has its own particular specificity. As Roger Silverstone argues, 'the suburb is the embodiment of the same ideal ... the attempt to marry town and country, and to create for middle-classes middle cultures in middle spaces' (Silverstone 1997, 4). In this way, the material environment and architectural space of suburbia cannot provide a located cultural and geographical context for an ethnography of a small semi-industrial town. Practices and modes of identity are framed by the specificity of place and suburban gardening is different from that which is practised in the small town. However, one of the few avenues where a serious investigation of ordinariness exists is by writers who have examined suburbia.

At the start of his introduction to the edited collection *Visions of Suburbia* (1997), Roger Silverstone argues that it is through the mundanity of suburbia, as an emergent, middling third space between the country and the city that a sense of the specificity of place emerges: 'Yet it is precisely the ordinariness of suburban everyday life, the rhythms and routines of day and week, commuting and housework, that the particular character and distinctiveness of suburban culture is to be found' (1997, 9). Indeed it is the regularity of the circadian rhythms of the everyday that lead him, in a bid to encapsulate 'every-suburb', to begin his introduction with a portrait of the 'unique and typical' architectural layout and characteristic features of Bromley. In this way, Silverstone shows a readiness to explore and take seriously the aesthetic bricolage of ordinariness as embodied in the fabric of the suburban streetscape; from the haphazard, messy architecture of the shopping precinct to the noises of suburbia. Challenging the modernist attack on standardisation, Silverstone points to Levittown, as an example which has become, 'a passable model of postmodern individuality, as standardised houses have been transformed, trees and gardens planted, and the basic structure of grid and lot has been overlaid by other designs ...Spaces, both inside and outside, are redesigned, reformed into expressions of personal taste and identity' (Silverstone 1997, 6). His willingness to consider the creative personal taste inflections and aesthetic differences within ordinary lower middle-class domestic space counters the existing and extensive body of pejorative English intellectual literature bemoaning the standardisation of suburbia (see for example, Edwards 1981; Bedarida 1990; Lebeau 1997). The problem with the attack on suburban architecture as Mark Clapson argues is that, 'the lives lived within these houses are castigated as narrow-minded and trivial', such writing assumes, 'that people live a singular 'suburban' life: a privatised, repressed and banal existence behind the net curtains and the front gardens of the suburban home' (Clapson 2000, 151-152). Clapson argues that suburbs have made a positive contribution to English culture largely because the suburban home has enabled, 'popular expression in housing tastes' and because both working-class people and ethnic minorities have enjoyed a rising standard of living because of the suburbs. Suburbs have been a success according to Clapson because they have arguably enabled working-class people to 'have'.

By contrast, Sophie Chevalier's (1998) work takes the suburban garden in the 1990s as the central focus of her study. Chevalier conducted interviews with a small sample of white-collar and retired factory workers on 'Jersey Farm', a suburban estate in St. Albans. Originally, she set out to gather data on home interiors and extended her study out to include the garden; as a result, her work concentrates on the relationship between the domestic interior and the garden. But whereas in this study I define the private garden as a peculiarly hybrid interface between the private/ domestic and public/civic space, Chevalier conceptualises the garden squarely on the side of the domestic realm, the garden is, 'a British space firmly located within domesticity' (Chevalier 1998, 47).

Chevalier identifies a structuralist typology of the suburban garden. For her informants the front garden acts as, 'the presentation of the household, an identity marker' while the back is both an individual and familial space where one can express what she describes as 'being at home' (1998, 49). The most salient feature of her argument however, is that there is what she calls 'strong symmetry' between the interior decor of the house and the garden (1998, 51). The garden acts as the correlative to the lounge: just as the suburban lounge has standard elements which have a set spatial organisation – the television, three-piece suite and the woollen carpet – the garden has a lawn, flower beds and fences which are composed in a particular 'architectural disposition.' Furthermore, Chevalier also found that the content of the gardens she visited were also alike: sheds in all cases contained tools and mowers and the gardens she visited were devoted to flowers and (mostly evergreen) shrubs. Effectively, her argument is that suburban gardens are comprised of a standardised template. Chevalier extends her argument – suburbanites, even across the Atlantic, conceptualise their lounge and garden in similar ways both in their production and in the ways in which they are maintained and consumed. For example, she cites Jenkins (1994) who shows that USA post-Second World War advertising for lawn mowers were covertly compared to vacuum cleaners and explicit parallels were drawn between the carpet and the lawn.

Methodologically Chevalier's work is interesting. She uses the voices of her informants to convey the experiences and values of ordinary gardeners. She makes an important point, for example, about the distance that exists between everyday gardeners and Latin nomenclature. Using Thomas (1983), she argues that since the late eighteenth century and the introduction of Linneus's classification, the gap widened between popular and cultured ways of regarding the natural world. In common parlance the people she interviewed tended to avoid Latin terms, rather they named plants according to their view or touch, for example, '"rabbit's ears" …or the "plant-with-yellow-flowers"' (1992, 52).

The valuable contribution from writing on suburbia is its preparedness to engage with the positive nuances of ordinariness: Silverstone (1997) catches at the rhythms and aesthetics of the fabric of the ordinary suburb; and Clapson (2000) recognises that an ordinary location like the suburb allowed working-class people access to decent living standards and offered them space for their own aesthetic expression. Yet despite their willingness to engage positively with the aesthetics of suburbia and despite the endless references to the semiotic significance of the suburban front garden and lawn, neither of these writers engages in any sustained analysis of the suburban *garden*. For example, in an almost lyrical description of Bromley, which is part paean, part mocking evocation of a typical suburban landscape, gardens, for Silverstone, exist as just one component in a plethora of external ephemera. Garden space is placed on a par with dilapidated window frames: 'Gleaming doorsteps, decorated paths, polished cars, weeded gardens, the junk of ages, lopsided caravans, peeling window frames, painted brickwork, double glazing, double garages...' (1997, 7). Furthermore, none of the chapters in *Visions of Suburbia* are about gardens. In like manner, Clapson documents opinion surveys conducted in the 1940s by Mass Observation and local councils on the housing needs of the people. Often semi-detached properties were most popular, in part Clapson concedes, because of the value residents placed on having a garden (Clapson 2000, 156). Yet the role played by gardens in providing living satisfaction for working-class people is merely mentioned without any further exploration. Writing on suburbia is valuable because it is intrigued by the aesthetics of ordinariness, but it has tended to refuse to explore the garden as a significant site of study.

Indeed the only exception to date would seem to be Chevalier's (1998) study. She is one of the few academic writers who has bothered to look at and empirically examine ordinary gardens. Her work maps a typology of quotidian contemporary British garden practices – a typology which, to my knowledge has not to date been documented in academic writing. As a result, the reader has some idea of the content and spatial organisation of suburban garden aesthetics.

However, there are also problems with Chevalier's work. Her suburban garden template smacks of the well-worn English intellectual view of suburban living – that it amounts to little more than standardisation. Moreover, the argument that the suburban inhabitant can do no more to their garden than replicate their lounge, theorises the suburbanite at best as unable to break the structural mould. Moreover, Chevalier's analysis of her respondents floats free of class, gender, ethnicity, sexuality or age. In what ways, one wonders, are tastes and choices inflected by age or class? Chevalier's work makes an important contribution because her work focuses gardens in the context of an ordinary place, but her work does not address both the locations and the attendant aesthetics of class and gender.

Extraordinary places: from the transitory to the cemetery garden

The previous section looked to writing on suburbia as a means to spatially locate classed and gendered ordinary gardens. Here I turn to work that examines gardens which belong to the homeless, the disenfranchised, those living in communal dwelling places and the Second World War dead. How, I ask, are those gardens manifest and where are they located?

Tired of garden histories which marginalise, 'the under-class and women' and mindful that, 'gardens other than those of the wealthy have rarely left a trace' writer

Diana Balmori and photographer Margaret Morton set out to upset the great tradition of garden history in their photographic account of New York gardens *Transitory Gardens: Uprooted Lives* (1993). Conscious that the wealthy have the resources to establish, maintain and document gardens valued by traditional garden history, Balmori and Morton announce their interest in documenting the impermanent urban gardens made by poor people living on the edge. Their desire to examine 'ephemeral constructions – found objects arranged in found places' is about the desire to capture the momentary condition of gardens, made under circumstances which mean they might only last for a month or even a day. While the book is about 'community', 'appropriated' and 'homeless' gardens, it is also about the garden as a temporary installation sited in transitory enclaves and borrowed places.

Beautifully composed black and white photographs portray gardens such as 'Tranquilidad' a Puerto Rican community garden at 310 East Fourth Street and Spanish appropriated garden 'Jardin de la 10 B - C' at Tompkins Square Park. But it is the most temporary garden 'compositions' made by the homeless, for example 'Jimmy's Garden' made by a middle-aged, peripatetic, Afro-American man, that most interest these authors. Art photography is not out of place in a book that is devoted to gardens that most resemble the art installation. The authors celebrate the use of particular garden building materials, 'found objects or salvaged, recycled trash' (1993, 6): skids (wooden pallets), plastic milk crates, shopping carts, matting or discarded carpet and used furniture are the stock in trade materials of the homeless garden constructor. Plants, which take time to grow, are inappropriate for gardens like Jimmy's Garden, which was bulldozed only days after its completion. The garden 'composition' is more likely to utilise representational items, such as brightly painted metal flowers, which 'stand in' for plants and flowers. In these ways the authors celebrate politically resistant avant-garde gardeners who seek to, 'liberate the word *garden* from its cultural straightjacket and validate the temporal, the momentary, in landscape' (1993, 4).

Transitory Gardens: Uprooted Lives (1993) takes the garden 'compositions' of the poor, the homeless, the politically marginal and the disenfranchised and elevates them to an art form of resistance. This is also partly expressed in their admiration for gardeners who refuse to engage with government agencies and bureaucracies. By generating, 'an aesthetic element uniquely its own' the authors invest hope in the liberal humanist ideal that, 'the individual's creative expression' will go, 'beyond education, economic class, age and gender' (1993, 7). The gardens celebrated in this book are anything but ordinary: they are spectacular urban forms of resistance, and resistance is to be found, according to these authors, in extraordinary art forms. As Felski argues, 'to contemplate something as art is to remove it, at least temporarily, from the pragmatic needs and demands of the quotidian' (Felski 2000, 17). These gardens are documented precisely because they are transitory representational compositions which mimic, but never become, everyday conceptions of the garden in urban places; their political *raison d'être* is predicated on a time frame which rejects the mundane rhythms of everyday life.

Transitory Gardens: Uprooted Lives is just one example of many which illustrates that truly mundane, everyday places have been ignored in some historical accounts. But this is not just the case with regard to radicalised liberal art critics such as Balmori and Morton. Leftist writers, in a bid to chart the benefits of social activism, have focused solely on collectively constructed public places such as urban community projects. Rebecca Severson's contribution to *The Garden as Idea, Place and Action* (1990), for example, is typical of this kind of writing. 'United We Sprout: A Chicago Community Garden Story' (1990) describes the collective revamping of a derelict land site in a Hispanic neighbourhood in West Town, Chicago. The narrative trajectory of the piece takes the reader through the collective process of building the garden: from initial meetings to organise rubbish clearance and develop a site plan, to the democratic naming of the site and the organisation of a celebratory festival to which residents and local politicians were invited. The garden was possible remarks Severson, 'when residents of a decaying urban neighborhood combined the power of organisation with the power of nature' (Severson 1990, 80). For leftist critics, writing about gardening is worthy if it amounts to collective sites of resistance. And while documenting this kind of project is politically valuable, one cannot help but wonder if leftist writers are guilty of harbouring genuine fears of finding political stagnancy and revolutionary inertia in the mundanity of the private, domestic garden.

Indeed there is far more existing literature on unusual and extraordinary garden sites than there are about the ordinary and the mundane. Mandy Morris's (1997) work, with its focus on the symbolic meaning of homeland and Englishness in British First World war cemeteries further illustrates my point. Morris charts the transformation of the 'signless spaces of "No Man's Land"' which were to become, 'visual frames of reference for the war, as enclosures of national identity and grief ...to become powerfully symbolic spaces of Britain and empire' (1997, 411). Morris's cemetery gardens are fashioned out of moving oppositions where the horrors of war are covered over by greensward, but where the numbers of headstones serve to demonstrate the violence of war: 'Serene surfaces of lawn and flowerbed stood as uneasy interfaces between a sanitized landscape of national grief and the shattered bodies beneath, between the official and unofficial, the private and the public' (ibid.). Morris's work is about an exceptional interface, about gardens constructed in order to represent grief, trauma and loss. But as Felski argues, 'everyday life is typically distinguished from the exceptional moment: the battle, the catastrophe, the extraordinary deed' (Felski 2000, 17).

These instances of writing, which temper the focus on the elite and aristocracy in dominant liberal humanist histories, at least serve to academically legitimise the gardens of the marginalised and the *déclassé*. And given the poverty and disenfranchisement of the people these studies examine, one would expect the analysis of their gardens to be focused on the *über*-ordinary. Yet rather, these texts are reminiscent of the approach to class adopted by work on subcultures in cultural studies (Hall and Jefferson 1976; Hebdige 1979), which are attacked by Walkerdine (1997) for refusing an analysis of the ordinariness of working-class culture in the rush to exoticise or identify sites of political resistance. Similarly, the texts under discussion here, which push the extra-ordinariness of the garden as event or site, act to offer an apology for the ordinariness, the everyday and the mundane. And so once again, the potential and intrigue of the ordinary is eluded, by-passed and ultimately denigrated in these writings.

The historical accounts of the garden surveyed thus far offer only partial fragments of knowledge for historicising and locating a recent study of the private domestic garden as a classed and gendered site. In the following section I turn to writing in social history – work which arguably provides a rich contextual backdrop for the ethnographic details of classed and gendered gardening practices explored later in this book.

Locating a Social History of the Private Domestic Garden

Bhatti defines the home garden as 'an area of 'enclosed cultivated ground' within the boundaries of the owned or rented house, where plants are grown and other materials arranged spatially' (1999, 185). His definition conceives the garden as an ordinary everyday space, attached to the home of either middle or working-class people. In this section, I discuss a range of authors (Bhatti 1999, 2000, 2006; Bhatti and Church, 2001; Constantine 1981; Hall and Davidoff 1994; Hoyles 1991; Morris 1995; Ravetz and Turkington 1995; Wilson 1991) whose work charts both the development of the garden plot, as well as an understanding of what the aesthetics of the 'area of enclosed cultivated ground' has meant to both middle and working-class people since the 19th century. The starting point for these writers is a shared agreement that the private home garden has been neglected across the social sciences.

One way in which social historians have acted to challenge the silence on home gardens has been to map its socio-historical development. Constantine (1981), for example charts the moves made by the professional middle-class in the early 1800s out of inner city London to the Northern and Midland suburbs into homes with private gardens. He draws on early forms of gardening media, such as magazines, on sources from an emerging gardening industry and from horticultural clubs, as a means of charting middle-class enthusiasm for gardening, which became something of a social necessity during the period. Ravetz and Turkington (1995) argue that classed styles emerged at this time and that middle-class gardeners used the 'formal Victorian suburban tradition'. Their account gives colour to the reader by sketching out the aesthetic details of such gardens: roses, exotics and rockeries were popular and lawned areas and distinctive trees were used as points of interest in these spaces. And by the late 1800s the 'natural' school, valorised by William Robinson with the idea of the herbaceous border of perennials was influential.

Central to the literature is the idea that the garden is a moral space. Gardens were used during the early 1800s as pedagogical devices for children through which caring practices were taught through cultivation (Davidoff and Hall 1994, 373). Hoyles notes how Dickens thought gardening was a useful reform for prostitution (1991, 16), and working-class urban and school gardens in the late nineteenth and early twentieth century were thought to make boys employable and girls into better mothers (Morris 1995, 60). Practices of sowing, tending and reaping were made synonymous with good moral forces as children were represented metaphorically as gardens in fiction (Davidoff and Hall 1994, 373; and see also Morris 1995). And the idea of privacy was important in the suburban garden, for unlike the aristocratic gardens, which had been intended for the display of ostentation, middle-class sanctuary behind high fences away from the public gaze was seen as a space where moral family ideals could be fostered and held dear using gardening as a rational recreation (Constantine 1981, 390). So that while typically jobbing gardeners were employed in the suburban garden, the middle-class did much of the work themselves as a means of ameliorating any sense that leisure time could be tarnished by idleness. Gardening was a morally cleansing attribute for both mind and body.

Indeed moral imperatives under-girded bids in the nineteenth century to encourage gardening among rural and urban working-class people. Class analysis is central to Constantine's history of popular gardening. He argues that public forms of popular leisure such as wakes, violent sports and music halls, seasoned as they were, according to leisure historians (Bailey 1978) by drinking and gambling, reportedly 'dismayed the middle-class observer' (Constantine 1981, 390). Such dismay was underpinned during periods of industrial unrest by growing middle-class anxiety about the working-class as a potential revolutionary force. In this way, gardening was conceived as a respectable form of leisure which could steer the poor away from degrading group activities to useful home-centred recreation and political compliance. These sentiments had a real impact on new imperatives to encourage gardening, such as the moves by landowners to attach gardens to cottages in model villages, such as the Earl of Winchester and Earl Grey, followed later in the century by industrial philanthropists, for example Cadbury at Bournville in the 1850s (Constantine 1981, 392). Yet while such changes were intended to augment healthier, more serviceable and respectable employees, very few working-class people actually benefited from such schemes. Leisure time was scarce, pollution was not conducive to gardening, but most especially housing provision determined garden access – so very few working-class people had one. The garden was more common in rural and farming villages and the historical antecedents of working-class specialist expertise in plants in specific regions (for example gooseberries in Manchester) began in areas which had undergone the first phase of industrialisation (Hoyles 1991) and the use of allotments to support the income of households in rural cottage gardens was also common (Ravetz and Turkington 1995). But largely, the issue for working-class gardening was about the lack of access to the garden as a resource: many urban dwellers were simply denied a garden. And in Britain during the nineteenth century the population was becoming increasingly urban: in 1851 54 per cent of the population occupied towns, by 1911 that figure had risen to 79 per cent. Moreover, what constituted a garden was often little more than a window box or tubs over a concreted small rear yard (Constantine 1981, 393). Ravetz and Turkington (1995) name the working-class style that contributed to the development of the twentieth century garden the 'vernacular tradition'. But while attachments to flowers and specialist flower tending by the artisan – for example, growing chrysanthemums for prizes and pet-keeping characterises the working-class vernacular it would seem from most of the sources, that the lack of back garden for working-class households somewhat prevented a particular working-class planting aesthetic from developing during this period. Interestingly, by the turn of the century the front garden had more ubiquity than the back though by the inter-war period it was subject to class differentials: private sector front gardens were controlled by social pressure while working-class front gardens on council estates were subject to the 'neat and in cultivated condition' stipulations of the Tenants' Handbook (Ravetz and Turkington 1995, 181).

By contrast, the twentieth century is characterised by increased popularity in gardening for the upper working and lower middle-classes. Constantine charts the move to eight hours for manual labourers, British Summer Time (1916) and the decrease in urban poverty as factors which made gardening more possible for a greater number of people (see Chapter 2). Undoubtedly however, the most important factors were growth in housing during the inter-war period – almost 4 million new houses were built in Britain between 1919 and 1939 – and the large increase in home-centred forms of leisure. Constantine traces popular enthusiasm for gardening mirrored by burgeoning gardening journalism, books, guides and encyclopaedia. And public investigators from the period emphasise a shift from public activities like the pub to interests in DIY and gardening at home. Indeed, Constantine's conclusion is that the nineteenth century reformers' wish to locate the working-class in to the home was successfully realised.

For Ravetz and Turkington (1995) most garden developments were focused on the back garden during the twentieth century. Using council estate records the authors argue that most gardens on such estates were well kept. Note the following excerpt from Rowntree (1941) who reported that in York, summer 1936 council estate gardens were: 'ablaze with colour.' The authors note that the typical working-class council estate garden had to be a utility space with some room for aesthetics: 'in practice, people used their gardens to grow vegetables and flowers, for drying washing, keeping chickens, rabbits and dogs, children's play, relaxation and 'nothing'" (1995, 189). Sketching the development of what they call the lower middle-class 'modern garden', they argue that it increasingly became an 'open-air room', acting often to compensate for the lack of space within the home. And charting new developments, such as the introduction of concrete, the authors discuss the move to the patio garden and the influence of the garden centre.

The richest on-going work on the ordinary contemporary home garden coming out of the socio-historical tradition to date is by Mark Bhatti. He adopts empirical analysis using qualitative data from the Mass Observation Project (2006), at times blending MO data with his own supplementary survey material as a means of analysing what gardens mean to people (Bhatti and Church 2001; Bhatti 2000). Gardening, for Bhatti, carries such personal investment as an identity marker, that to label it a hobby is to seriously under-state its significance (Bhatti 1999, 184). Identifying the social, cultural and economic investments in gardening as a popular pursuit using quantitative statistics from MINTEL, Bhatti situates his data within the context of a number of contemporary trends: high levels of home and garden ownership (20.2 million private gardens in the UK in 1999); increased numbers in adult participation in gardening; the 'presence of conglomeration capital in the garden industry' in the form of the garden centre and the impact of gardening programmes on television in the UK (Bhatti and Church 2001, 372). In these ways, he builds a view of the garden as an increasingly important feature of contemporary living.

A distinctive feature of Bhatti's work is his insistence on conceptualising the garden as a central element in any conception of the home and home-making. Following a phenomenological route, he traces the relationship between the garden and the outside world as part of the construction of psycho-social life-worlds within the practices and routines of everyday life. In these ways, Bhatti's work brings a multi-layered perspective to his analysis of what gardens mean and how they work as embedded forms of cultural practice against a backcloth of wider cultural processes. Subtle thinking and attention to detailed nuance in relation to the garden informs his oeuvre on gardening in a risk society (1999); the environment and gardens as brokers of human-nature relations (Bhatti and Church 2001); gardening in relation to gender (2000) and the aging process (2006). Countering Beck (1992) in his early work on gardening in an age of risk, he argues that peoples' awareness of environmental risk acts to accelerate, 'the search for local meaning and ontological security in everyday objects' (1999, 183-4). He therefore identifies gardening as a way in which anxieties about modernity can be assuaged by returning to the everyday rhythms of making home and garden. His work on leisure, the home and human-nature relations in the garden uses data to uncover highly personalised 'practices, routines and memories' in relation to nature (2006, 275). This came through peoples' responses to their awareness of the consequences of using pest controls; their enjoyment of engaging their senses in the garden; their memories of experiences involving nature in the garden with friends and family members – often uncovering how plants and objects within the garden become imbued with emotional meanings. Bhatti argues that while the garden industry and media representations showcase instant consumerist gratification, his data reveals 'more traditional sociations' in which people still enlist their agency in to develop 'complex, sensual and personalised readings of nature' with a view to potentially re-ignite re-enchantment with nature (2006: 380). In more recent work on gardening and the ageing process he unearths the garden as a space which offers a sense of home, a site of independence and identity, a status symbol to be 'maintained' and a space through which the aging process is resisted (2006). Indeed, if as Hoyles argues there is a 'kaleidoscope of cultural meanings attached to gardening' (1991, 8) then Bhatti's detailed empirical analyses show its various infractions. Gardens are spaces where people can: till the earth; find sanctuary; connect with family history; express identities of social standing and taste; generate symbols of moral authority and respectability; utilise space as a source of conflict with neighbours; find a way to sensuously connect with nature and re-negotiate gender relations.

While Bhatti (1999) concedes that the garden is a highly gendered space, his work makes a departure from previous social historians who argue that gardens have historically been spaces with highly demarcated roles for men and women. Davidoff and Hall (1983), for example, argue that women in the mid nineteenth century became responsible for the decorative function of flowers. In Wilson's (1991) account of the North American postwar suburban garden, he argues that the shift to service industries meant that lower middle-class men used gardening as a form of remasculisation. Men presided over barbecues and mowed lawns, while women tended flowers and tilled the earth with trowels (1991, 91). In similar vein, Olechnowicz (1997) argues that it was working-class men who governed gardens on council estates during the inter-war period in Britain: gardening was men's work and parts of the garden belonged to them. Drawing on MO data and giving weight to Constantine's (1981) argument that amateur gardening located the working-class in to the home, Olechnowicz argues that the garden stood in for the decline of the pub during those years. Yet Bhatti's research complicates the idea of staunch gender boundaries in the contemporary garden. Insisting that the garden and home are inseparable and acknowledging the tradition of research which uncovers the differences in how men and women conceptualise home, he concedes that the garden is a highly gendered space, though his emphasis on the social making of gender usefully avoids the idea of biologistic gendered aesthetics. However, his empirical data also shows that gender roles are constantly being 're-negotiated'; the garden is a site of local bargaining about project decision-making and how labour is to be divided.

Social history, with its emphasis on mapping both the social trends and the mores of people in everyday life, offers a structured account 'from below' of the private domestic garden of the past, which in turn provides a contextual backdrop for understanding contemporary practice. Unravelling the narrative of the historical formation of the 'enclosed cultivated ground' attached to homes in the nineteenth and twentieth century, it charts the differential access to resources for middle and working-class people, thereby providing an understanding of the historical legacy of the classed garden of the contemporary. Such accounts provide a sense of the aesthetic development of classed gardening – from the embrace of Robinson's 'natural' herbaceous border in the middle-class garden to the prized chrysanthemums of the working-class garden – as classifiable categories. Moreover, such accounts show a clear historiography of the garden's moral dimensions: as a cleansing recreation for maintaining the balanced disposition of the middle-class mind and body; and as a corrective form of leisure to both ameliorate the atavistic tendencies of the working-class and to diffuse their potential political radicalism by locating them at home. In this sense the front garden especially, has literally been inscribed with virtue by the nature of its upkeep, acting as a moral index of the worth of the people inside.

Garden Practices and Symbolic Work

This section turns to work that recognises the cultural consumption of gardens as a means of communication. Garden practices and garden aesthetics are forms of expression which render visible the categories within a culture: they act as symbolic identity markers. For example, Wolschke-Bulmahn and Groening (1992) show the 'nature garden' was used in the early 1900s in Germany as a national symbol of fascist political ideologies; and Helphand (1997) brings together world examples of 'defiant gardens' which act as symbolic sites of assertion and resistance.

Douglas and Isherwood (1996) argue that, 'all material possessions carry social meanings and...(we must therefore)...concentrate a main part of cultural analysis upon their use as communicators' (Douglas and Isherwood 1996, 59). Used as a symbolic means to communicate with others, 'goods' they argue, 'are part of a live information system' (1996, xiv). Douglas and Isherwood argue that consumption is never related to purely economic factors; rather, it is a cultural as well as an economic practice. Consumer goods must be analysed within the specific cultural context in which they are acquired, used and exchanged. Their thesis is that people invest meaning in the most trivial everyday objects. For them, goods are far more than objects with specific uses: goods also have a cultural role as demarcators of cultural value. Goods therefore take on tremendous importance as carriers of meaning for people, because they are so closely tied to the construction of social identity. In this way, goods act as indicators of how social relations are organised at particular historical moments.

Garden aesthetics and class

While many social historians concede that there is an important relationship between gardens and class (Bhatti 2006; Hoyles 1991; Ravetz and Turkington 1995; see also Tilley 2006) there are very few existing empirical studies on garden aesthetics and class. However, empirical work on gardening and class was conducted by geographers in the late 1960s and 70s in both north and south America. For example, in 1969 Clarissa Kimber (1973) surveyed 80 Puerto Rican gardens using low-altitude photography, a plant census and interviews with 'the cultivators'.

Out of her findings, Kimber argues that there are six 'classes' of Puerto Rican gardens: there is the 'jibaro' or hut garden which acts as the lowest polar prototype; the 'manor' or great house garden which exists at the highest end of her classification system and four other garden types exist in between. Kimber's article, concerned as it is with the geographical features of her named garden types, provides quantitative, descriptive summaries of the types which feature in her taxonomy. Kimber summarises the features of each garden type. In 'Table II – Presence or Absence of Various Traits by Garden Type' however, Kimber plots the cultivators' activities in relation to each garden type. Here the cultural uses of the garden types is pulled in to focus. For example, owners of the jibaro garden engage in activities such as, 'Gossiping through windows', 'Laundering', 'Open Drains', 'Spontaneous plants tolerated or cultivated' whereas the manor garden owners engage in none of these (Kimber 1973, 21). Conversely, manor garden owners, 'Use plants for design purposes', have 'Avenues of trees planted', engage in, 'Enjoyment of the garden from the house' and have, 'Ornamentals segregated at least in part' whereas the jibaro owners have no claim to any of these activities (Kimber 1973, 21). These differences are assigned to the 'presence and persistence of two contrasting traditions': the 'vernacular' and the 'high-style' (Kimber 1973, 23). Kimber's summary offers a discussion about the class differences in these traditions, while avoiding any direct use of the term class. People practising the vernacular tradition use gardens functionally for waste disposal, gossiping and as a children's play area – they are described as having an 'unsophisticated' relationship with the garden. Interestingly however, Kimber's conclusions recognise the relatively disinterested ease with which the high-style tradition is consumed by its owners. Kimber's observation of the manor garden and its focus on the need to, 'express the esthetic taste of the owner' amounts to an admission that the garden performs at least some type of symbolic work for the household. While Kimber's article studiously avoids any mention of class as a culturally lived category, her ultimate conclusion is provided by recourse to economics. Chronic poverty explains the persistence of the vernacular tradition in Puerto Rico and the loss of aristocratic traditions has its roots in the decay of old wealth. The high-style tradition is the result of new money and the rise of the 'American suburban ideal' – 'as new money permits more people to enjoy flexibility in exercising esthetic tastes … a more modern ideal will be expressed in the manor garden' (Kimber 1973, 25).

Kimber's research was followed in 1975 by a startlingly similar study about dooryard gardens in Brushy, Texas. Gene Wilhelm (1975), who had clearly read Kimber's 1973 article, developed a six garden type classification system based on the rural black community's gardening practices. Wilhelm concludes that factors such as family life cycle, occupational demands and economic status were the factors which influenced the type of dooryard garden the families he studied chose.

Christopher Grampp's short article *Social Meanings of Residential Gardens* (1993) is about what gardening means to Berkeley and Albany residents in California according to social class. 'For all the interest in the garden,' Grampp complains, 'one area has been ignored: the broader social meanings of gardens' (Grampp 1993, 178). Based on informal interviews, this journalistic piece develops a classification system of three garden groups: the 'California living garden', the 'well-tempered garden' and the 'expressionist garden'.

The 'California living garden' which Grampp argues, 'epitomizes the average middle-class garden in the state', is seen as a domestic extension to the house (Grampp 1990, 181). Paved surfaces and lawn give the garden an interior feel and the garden is used for domestic activities like eating outdoors, entertaining or children's play. This type of garden is constructed as an escape from city life; its emphasis is therefore on providing a space for relaxation. Plants are naturalistic, decorative and sensual and work to provide a private enclosure.

By contrast the working-class well-tempered garden is, 'formal, ordered, neat'. For these gardeners rather than the garden being a private space, the garden is conceived as 'aggressively public.' For the well-tempered gardeners, the garden is not a place of relaxation, it requires constant and laborious surveillance: 'to me its defining characteristic is that every inch has been attended to by the owner, forged into an undeniably human creation' (Grampp 1990, 182). When Grampp conducted his interviews, he found that his working-class respondents never spoke of the garden as a leisure pursuit – the task of constant garden improvement made the garden a place of work. And plant life in this garden type must bend to human will: trees and shrubs are pruned into 'contrived shapes' and grass is constantly mown to keep it in check. Garden ornaments and artefacts 'abound' and house fronts are painted in brash colours. Alongside these features, well-tempered gardeners tend to fall in with the local garden style, indeed they, 'often copy each other in great detail.' And, in line with the idea that Grampp's working-class gardeners regard their gardens as public spaces, flattery and compliments from passers-by are greatly valued.

These articles illustrate that as Douglas and Isherwood (1996) claim, gardens are sites which are used as markers of social meaning: the people in these examples use them to perform class identity and in this way, gardens are consumed in ways which tell the passer-by about social station. Kimber (1973) and Wilhelm's (1975) geographical work demonstrates that people across different historical moments and cultural contexts make aesthetic choices in putting their gardens to symbolic work. However, the problem with this type of work is that the onus is placed on the reader to interpret their geographical findings for the purposes of cultural studies. While the substance of these articles is about the cultural use of gardens as markers of social distinction, the discussion of class is confined only to economic terms.

Grampp's categories about what gardening means to a small group of Californian gardeners in the late 1980s offers the reader a focused analysis of gardening and class. Grampp's middle-class gardeners have a relaxed approach to a 'naturalistic' garden style, while his working-class gardeners labour over controlled, tidy and ordered public spaces. In this way, his work generates an interesting set of expectations about how my respondents express class in the field. However, in the context of what is a brief and journalistic chapter, Grampp tends to forego any kind of critical perspective on his findings. His descriptive account eschews any reading for example, of his working-class respondents' perspective on gardening – an approach which surely reveals considerable anxiety about the critical gaze and value judgements of passers-by. Grampp however, in the rush to celebrate gardeners whose tastes most directly fall in line with his own, tends to ignore the issues of power and identity which inhere in his aesthetic categories, falling instead to a liberal model to explain garden practices. The 'expressionist' gardeners for example, who from description are a bohemian, educated, middle-class group, are both described and celebrated by Grampp as being characterised by their 'extreme individuality' (Grampp 1990, 183).

Conclusion

This chapter has shown how gardening has been legislated in dominant national academic and literary enclaves. It argues that some of these versions of the history, places and people of British gardens resound in core British cultural institutions. Drawing on literature which charts the continued regulation of the working-class in relation to gardening and the landscape, it argues that liberal humanist, Marxist and feminist histories commit symbolic violence against women and the working-class in ways which de-legitimate ordinary male and female gardeners and their gardens. I argue that even feminist garden history has fault-lines in relation to class and gender. It either places upper-middle- and middle-class women alongside the male legislators of liberal humanism, thereby ignoring the contribution of working-class women to garden history. Or, in the absence of adequate social theory, it falls to biologistic claims about the essential superiority of female gardening without any attention to gendered aesthetics. Far more productive, I argue, is the emerging social history of the private domestic garden, which coupled with the idea that gardens perform symbolic work, show that the garden is a site drenched by class and gender. This literature, in a bid to counter the marginalisation of the ordinary cultivated plot by charting its socio-historical development since the nineteenth century, charts the aesthetic history of classed and classifiable (and to a lesser extent gendered) gardening practices. Such work also signals a history of gardening as a moral activity and of gardens as profoundly moral spaces. Indeed, according to these accounts, it was the moral imperative incited by an anxious middle-class to fix a potentially unruly working-class in place, which generated gardening as popular recreation in the first place. This book aims to add a form of contemporary garden history to this body of work: by using ethnography I give voice to ordinary gardeners, with the intention to document the contribution of working-class people and women; and secondly, drawing on the Bourdieusian framework outlined in chapter 3, I provide theoretical insight to explore the historical and social reasons why class and gendered gardening aesthetics exist in ordinary gardens.

Chapter 5 examines another institutional enclave where meaning about gardens and gardening resided at the time of the empirical study: the media. Examining the importance of gardening 'lifestyle' to the media and culture industries, I examine the themes of how the contemporary garden, gardeners and garden 'experts' were represented in television and lifestyle media. In this chapter, I argue that in dominant academic enclaves garden legislators act to marginalise the ordinary; conversely in chapter four however, I use social theory to argue that ordinariness took on an increased significance in late 1990s lifestyle media culture.

Chapter 5

Garden Interpreters: Garden Lifestyle Television and Media Culture

Introduction

Chapter 4 looked at the legislators of garden history. It argued that most dominant accounts, save for the new emerging social history of the private domestic garden, fail to provide any contextual history or location for understanding ordinary peoples' gardening practices and aesthetics *at the local level*. However, while written sources are bestowed high measures of symbolic worth in our culture, they are not the only texts which communicate values about the garden. This chapter turns its attention to a more popular and contemporary institutional site where gardens became the subject of intense focus in late 1990s: the media. It discusses how contemporary gardens, gardeners and gardening 'experts' were represented in the national and local press, magazine publishing and most especially on television.

While the 'lifestyle' media – particularly in relation to lifestyle television programming – burgeoned in Britain in the mid-1990s, 'lifestyle' generally received scant academic attention during that time (see Strange (1998) on television cookery programmes). Since then lifestyle has a new emerging scholarship (Bonner 2003; Brunsdon et al. 2001; Brunsdon 2003; Heller 2007; Hollows and Bell 2005, 2006; Moseley 2000), though *garden* lifestyle media still remains under-explored. 'They are too "ordinary"', remarks one of the few to have written about them, 'to be of interest' (Gabb 1999, 256; see also Taylor 2002). Since my concern in this study is to look at the intrigue of ordinariness, it would seem prudent to precisely focus on this compartment of the media – renowned as it is for being mundane, trivial and quintessentially ordinary (Bonner 2003; Silverstone 1994).

I argue that the continued popularity and growth of lifestyle television from the mid to late 1990s was the result of a wider cultural shift: the rise of 'lifestyle' must be understood as part of the transition from civic to consumer culture (Bauman 1987). At the local level, this shift was experienced through the fall of traditional, communal 'ways of life' to the rise in the construction of consumer lifestyles (Chaney 1996, 2001). For subjects who can no longer rely on the stability offered by the traditional way of life, lifestyle projects can act as coping mechanisms in the face of the changes delivered by modernity (Chaney 2001). The lifestyle media, I argue, offered viewers the stabilising potential to help them cope; the formal construction of lifestyle hooked into the ordinary rhythms, practices and sites of everyday life. Using Bauman and Chaney, I argue that in the context of late-capitalism, the media and culture industries had a vested interest in acting as a key site for the management of the transition Chaney describes. Hence I examine the inter-locking, mutually profitable relationship between the lifestyle media, the display of gardening lifestyle ideas and consumer culture of the time. What follows then are analyses of television and media culture that accompany the ethnographies of classed and gendered gardening in chapters 6 and 7. They chart the specific moment of how the garden figured in television and media culture and its subsequent relationship with how gardeners used mediated ideas as part of their own gardening identities in mid to late 1990s Britain.

Lifestyle television was both eminent and popular, hence its prominence in primetime scheduling in the mid to late 1990s. However, since then *garden* lifestyle programmes, as well as lifestyle media products such as gardening magazines, grew in particular. I explain this growth within the context of increased consumer spending during the period on garden merchandise and the continued popularity of the garden centre as a key British leisure site.

This chapter then divides in to two sections: the first 'Gardening People' examines how British television used strategies of 'ordinari-ization' (Brunsdon et al. 2001: 53) as a means of urging people to incorporate lifestyle practices into their daily lives. The ways in which lifestyle knowledges were presented underwent changes in the early 1970s: the authoritative tone of public service was replaced with what Ellis has called 'popular public service' (Ellis 2000, 32). Increasingly, viewers witnessed the embrace of 'ordinary' people in garden lifestyle programming and garden 'experts' became personality-interpreters (Bauman 1987), packaging lifestyle ideas from the symbolic repertoires on offer in consumer culture (Chaney 2001). I discuss how these 'ordinari-ization' strategies worked to construct a discourse of lifestyle achievability and accessibility for viewers in programmes such as *Homefront in the Garden* (BBC2, 1997-) and *Real Gardens* (Channel Four, 1998-).[1]

The second section 'Gardens', examines how the media both interpreted and showcased visual ideas about the British garden as a lifestyle space. Arguing that one needed recourse to post-modern aesthetics (Featherstone 1991; Jameson 1991) to understand the visual codes in circulation at that historical juncture, I discuss the accessibility of national aesthetics advocated in programmes such as *Gardening Neighbours* (BBC2, 1998-) and elements of the lifestyle press, for example *Observer Life*. Using Marxist perspectives on history and postmodernism (McGuigan 1999), I discuss how historical conceptions of the garden, given through the interpretative advice of garden experts, acted as a capital resource for some viewers. Lastly, arguing that especially in relation to the makeover genre, the garden 'reveal' acted to present an extension of the self, I explore whether locations of class and gender inflect the symbolic construction of the contemporary 'ordinary' garden.

In these ways, one can see that the media, a more popular and accessible enclave than academe or the literary bookshelf, was a site where ordinariness was included in a bid to extend audiences. One of the questions that struck me at the time was: might media representations provide a potential challenge to garden legislators discussed

---

1   *Homefront in the Garden* is a typical example of a popular British lifestyle makeover programme. *Real Gardens* has a magazine programme format and was screened at 9.30pm on Channel Four on Sunday nights.

in chapter 4? Could it be that ordinary people, so vilified by garden legislators, might have a stake in being part of *mediated* British garden history?

The Importance of 'Lifestyle' in Contemporary Culture

From ways of life to lifestyle

Contemporary culture is still in the process of a social and cultural transition: mass societies are moving from 'ways of life' to 'lifestyle'. In his most recent work on lifestyle, Chaney argues that traditional conceptions of culture are no longer tenable in social theory (Chaney 2001). The idea of culture as a whole way of life, based on shared traditions and communal identity has lost its capacity to define social existence as a totality. Today, social life is characterised by the severed 'umbilical link' between culture and community (Chaney 2001, 77). Whereas culture was once conceived as a set of firm beliefs and normative expectations, shared within a relatively stable community, in mass societies there are, 'a multiplicity of overlapping cultures with differing relationships with social actors' (Chaney 2001, 78). In an era of mass communication and entertainment, culture is in part about the relationship between the identities represented in media discourse and how people identify both themselves and members of other social groups. Culture, according to Chaney, has become a 'symbolic repertoire' (Chaney 2001, 78). Repertoires are adapted from images and symbols available in a mass-mediated environment which are then assembled into performances associated with particular groups. A repertoire is a set of practices through which people symbolically represent identity and difference.

According to Chaney, traditional conceptions of culture have virtually given way to new social forms. One of the most significant examples of a new social form which typifies social change is the growth of lifestyles. Lifestyles draw on the resources provided by consumer choices out of the symbolic repertoires on offer in contemporary culture. Indeed the lifestyle, in contrast to the traditional conception of a 'way of life', is utterly dependent on the leisure and culture industries and consumer patterns. Playfully and reflexively constructed by those who invest in them, lifestyles are performed improvisations in which authenticity is conceived as an entity which one can manufacture. In these ways lifestyle projects are unstable and open to re-improvisation, they converge in 'loose agglomerations'; any effort to pin down a typology of lifestyles is simply, 'chasing after a vague and constantly changing constellation of attitudes' (Chaney 2001, 86).

Lifestyle: the new coping mechanism

The cultural and social shift from ways of life to lifestyle has important consequences for subjectivity. Traditional cultural forms offer a high degree of social stability to their subjects; whereas those in the process of building lifestyles out of the freeplay of cultural symbolism lack firm social grounding and are relatively insecure. In this way, the lifestyle project as a new social form becomes a primary identity marker. People make serious investments in using cultural forms as a means to actively express their identity and differentiate themselves from others. As Chaney argues, lifestyles are also sensibilities which become imbued with ethical, moral and aesthetic significance. Even the most quotidian practices and mundane objects accrete aestheticisation in the contemporary social climate whereby tastes and aesthetic choices have become responsibilities by which one is judged by others.

More importantly, for individuals and groups who are relatively destabilised by the lack of permanence offered by more traditional ways of life, the practice of lifestyle construction can serve an important function as a means of coping with social change. For Chaney, lifestyles are reactive modes of behaviour or, 'functional responses to modernity' (Chaney 1996, 11). Changes in employment; conceptions of the family and gender relations; the development of mass society; increased secularisation; and new urban landscapes in the form of suburbia, have meant that lifestyles, 'offer a set of expectations which act as a form of ordered control' in the face of uncertainties wrought by modernity (Chaney 1996, 11). Seen in this way lifestyles serve an invaluable role for people in post-industrial societies: they act as resources of stability or coping mechanisms which help people to manage their own relationship to social change.

Lifestyles potentially act as stabilising mechanisms because they hook into the rhythms and practices of everyday life; the act of lifestyling can potentially provide ordinary comforts formed out of the habits of dailiness. Indeed Felski (2000), as I established in chapter 2, argues that dimensions of ordinariness are stabilising cognitive mechanisms which help people cope with rapid social change. Similarly, the formal construction of lifestyle television fastens onto a sense of the ordinary through its evocation of facets of everyday life, aspects identified by Felski as repetition, home and habit (Felski, 2000). The ordinariness evoked here relates not to the strand of thought which equates an authentic version of ordinary everyday life with the lives of women or working-class people (see for example, Featherstone 1995). The ordinariness of terrestrial television presenters and subjects in the late 1990s, as I argue later, was at least a lower middle-class version of ordinariness. Rather, it is possible, as Felski suggests, to consider ordinariness in a different light: the taken-for-granted continuum of the activities of daily life characterise most peoples' lives. 'Everyday life', Felski argues, 'is not simply interchangeable with the popular: it is not the exclusive property of a particular class or grouping, Bismarck had an everyday life and so does Madonna' (Felski 2000, 16). The '"ordinari-ization"' of lifestyle media describes how lifestyle programmes fasten into the sense that we are all, in so far as we connect to the backdrop of everyday life, ordinary; we are all somehow anchored to routine, to a place called home and to the mundanity of daily habit. The enactment of lifestyle ideas are rooted to the humdrum rhythms and practices of the quotidian. The garden, an inextricable part of our conception of home, is one of the key sites where the habitual and mundane, yet familiar, safe and private practices of daily life are located. Strategies of '"ordinari-ization"' work to make viewers connect the familiar, safe spaces of home with accessible and achievable lifestyle ideas.

The Popularity of Lifestyle Programming

Lifestyle and consumption have accrued increasing prominence for people in contemporary society (Bauman 1987; Chaney 1996, 2001). The credence of this argument was clearly illustrated by the eminence and popularity of lifestyle programming in the popular media in the late 1990s. By the start of the twenty first century there had been a noticeable shift in primetime British terrestrial scheduling. By the year 2000, between 8.00 and 9.00, 'factual entertainment' – an umbrella term which includes lifestyle programming – had virtually replaced the popular staples of situation comedy and high status genres such as documentaries and current affairs programmes (Brunsdon et al. 2001; Moseley 2000). Mainstay popular genres of the 1980s were being transferred to other less prestigious compartments of the terrestrial schedule in order to make way for 'the dominance of lifestyle':

> In the 1980s, variety shows, quizzes and sit-coms were a regular feature of the primetime 8-9 schedules. In 1999 they had all but disappeared. Sit-coms had moved to a later slot in the weekday schedules, variety was almost exclusively transmitted on weekend evenings and quizzes had either been incorporated into the later 'comedy' slots or relegated to the daytime schedules (Brunsdon et al. 2001, 43).

These architectural schedule changes barometered the historical rise of the popularity of lifestyle, for as Ellis argues, 'any schedule contains the distillation of the past history of a channel, of national broadcasting as a whole, and of the particular habits of national life' (Ellis 2000, 26).

These changes were the result of an elaborate interplay of factors which impacted on the British media industries. For example, the growth of cable and satellite broadcasting and the call in the 1992 Broadcasting Act that 25 per cent of programmes be produced by independents heightened the pressure for programme-makers to provide cheaper programming (Brunsdon et al. 2001, 31). This was a demand met by the economies of lifestyle genres which require no theatrical regalia or high budget stars and sets. In addition, the increase of factual entertainment from 8.00-9.00pm was a reaction to the ratings crisis endured by the BBC in the early 1990s, which spurned a will to engage more aggressively in a scheduling battle over ratings (Brunsdon et al. 2001, 40; Ellis 2000).[2] But perhaps more pertinently, primetime was re-configured because the media industries recognised the need to address wider cultural shifts – programmes in the late 1990s addressed audiences as consumers rather than citizens. The authoritarian, paternalistic voice of 'old public service discourse' was virtually dismantled in the most popular enclave of primetime television (Bondebjerg 1996, 29). In its place, as Bondebjerg argues, was a more democratised, 'new mixed public sphere where common knowledge and everyday experience play a much larger role' (Bondebjerg 1996, 29). As Brunsdon observed,

---

2   Ellis (2000) offers examples of how the BBC waged several battles during the mid-1990s with the popularity of ITV's 'early evening strengths' by successfully pitching factual entertainment programmes *999 Lifesavers* and *Animal Hospital* against the ITV 'banker' police series *The Bill*. 'Factually-based entertainments performed better,' he argues, 'than did the sitcoms which BBC1 had initially pitched against *The Bill*' (Ellis, 2000, 31).

'the BBC has differently striven to address the nation as it finds it, rather than as it thinks it should be' (Brunsdon et al. 2001, 53).

In the late 1990s, *garden* lifestyle programmes were particularly prolific. This must be seen in relation the wider popularity of gardening as a hobby at that time. Gardening has a heritage with a longer history than most leisure activities and it plays a key role as part of the lifestyle package, in fact, according to MINTEL it was, 'still the number one hobby in the UK' (2001a). The garden retail sector grew steadily during the period: garden centres multiplied and consumers were purchasing more garden goods today than they were in 1995. For example, the total garden market was worth £2.75 billion in 1996, but had risen to £3.35 billion by 2000 (MINTEL 2001b). The number of garden centre outlets rose by 17 per cent between 1998 and 2001 and total retail sales were 25 per cent higher in 2000 compared to 1995 (MINTEL 2001a). Growing consumer interest in garden goods was mirrored by an increase in popular media products about gardening during this period. Most tangibly, changes in the primetime schedule highlighted the popularity of lifestyle television and there was a concomitant rise in popularity and consumer spending on garden magazines. For example, the MINTEL *Home Interest and Gardening Magazines* report shows that the number of titles grew from seven to twelve between 1995 and 1999 and spending grew from £18.57 million in 1995 to £30.20 million in 1999 (2000). This growth is partly attributed by the garden retail sector to the change in how gardening is represented in the popular media. As MINTEL argue:

> the last five years have seen a major change in the image of gardening, thanks to the many 'makeover' programmes on television ... the trade now even refers to a 'Charlie Dimmock factor', meaning that younger presenters have made gardening of interest to a new audience (MINTEL, 2001b).

In these ways, the garden lifestyle consumer circuit was beneficial to both the media and garden retailing.

Lifestyle programmes appealed to their audiences by showcasing practical vocabularies of consumer transformation, from personal style to food and home interiors. Programmes such as *Ground Force* (Bazal for the BBC, 1997-),[3] blossomed into an extremely lucrative venture interlocking the media and culture industries in a multi-million pound business partnership. Indeed one might more usefully term the penetration of such markets 'lifestyle synergy'. In a synergy climate, such programmes become commercial 'intertexts' or launch pads from which to spawn new programme concepts and related merchandise (Meehan 1991, 48). *Ground Force*, for example, the forerunner BBC garden makeover programme was just one component in a product line that extended beyond the living room to penetrate related markets for the series book and magazine. The expert-presenters pursued equally lucrative individual projects: Charlie Dimmock magnified her multiple television, press and magazine appearances as a water-feature garden expert into

---

3   *Ground Force* was the BBC's flagship garden makeover programme. A family member secretly colludes with the makeover team, comprised of celebrities Alan Titchmarsh and Charlie Dimmock, to produce a surprise gift of a transformed garden for a nearest and dearest.

her own television makeover programme *Charlie's Garden Army* (BBC, 1999-). She went on to produce several books and sold her image for attachment to a range of humdrum, commonplace ephemera from calendars to cups. In this way, lifestyle programmes, merchandise and celebrities were able to make in-roads into the most mundane enclaves of peoples' everyday lives.

Late modernity, as Chaney argues, has provided the cultural, social and economic circumstances in which lifestyles are able to proliferate (Chaney 1996, 83). Lifestyle synergy requires the distributive global network of the media and communication industries, increased wealth and access to consumption and leisure which characterise post-industrial societies. As these examples show, British media institutions were selling lifestyle to audiences in a bid to urge people to make the transition from ways of life to lifestyles. I argue that programme makers showcased the signs and images of lifestyle through the appeal of what Brunsdon called the '"ordinari-ization" of British television' (Brunsdon et al. 2001, 53).

Gardening People

Making lifestyle achievable: the appeal of the personality-interpreter

Much of the appeal of lifestyle programming emanated from the ordinariness expert-personalities exuded. But perhaps more than that, experts came from a diversity of backgrounds. Popular gardening celebrity-experts of the time, marked a new sense of openness, legitimation and tolerance towards a set of previously marginalised voices in mainstream programming. In terms of gender and age the popular media embraced a new set of voices of expertise. There were as many female experts as there were men. There was a balance of relatively young experts alongside the more venerable. Similarly, the middle-class received pronunciation of some of the over-arching presenters became the exception among a range of regional accents. However, it would be a step too far to argue that ordinariness in class terms meant a display of working-classness; being ordinary meant being lower middle-class in the world of lifestyle programming. Interpreters with regional accents, who arguably brought aspects of working-class life to their presentation, had their claims to legitimacy bolstered using the display of their specialist knowledges. But despite this, the voices of lifestyle were *more* ordinary than they used to be and they helped to promote the accessibility and achievability of lifestyle projects.

More importantly, such experts were regularly seen to outstep traditional roles, most especially in relation to gender. In an episode of *Homefront in the Garden* for example, home interiors makeover personality Laurence Llewelyn Bowen took to the sewing machine in order to make a set of cushion covers for a tree seat; plant disease expert Pippa Greenwood offered the most scientific contribution to popular gardening debate and Charlie Dimmock was easily able to out-lift her male makeover co-workers.[4] Yet while these experts might presented the societal locations of gender, age and to a more limited extent social class, in relatively positive terms, what was the real status of their role as 'experts'? Were they afforded the capacity to set standards of horticultural or scientific expertise? Did they exist as the hallowed arbiters of historical intellectual knowledge or gardening taste? Or did they become ordinary consumer advisors, promulgating lifestyle ideas in the knowledge that the customer was 'always right'?

In *Legislators and Interpreters* (1987) Bauman argues that postmodernism has signalled a crisis of confidence for intellectuals in the West. Characterised by pluralism, openness, randomness, relativism and eclecticism, the contemporary world has replaced metanarratives with antifoundational forms of knowledge. For Bauman, these features reflect the diminishing status of the intellectual or legislator, since the modernist ideas upon which their authority was once contingent have been rendered obsolete. The massive proliferation of goods in the post-modern period has led to the further erosion of the authority of the intellectual. Legislators are no longer consulted for their opinions, rather, 'it is the market which now takes upon itself the role of the judge, the opinion maker, the verifier of values' (Bauman 1987, 124). For Bauman, authority figures have fallen in the shift from civic to consumer society. In this way, one can see that the authority of legislators, discussed in chapter 4, may be under serious challenge from the media and culture industries. The last vestige of hope for the intellectual in the context of a period in which High Culture is increasingly de-centred to such an extent that, 'the most diverse artistic products ... wait side-by-side in the "cultural supermarket" ... for their respective consumers' (Calinescu in Bauman 1987, 130), is to act as mediators or translators between cultural ideas and traditions. Intellectuals, argues Bauman, have been replaced by interpreters whose function is to adjudicate and disseminate culture in the locality of their immediate communities. Could it be that the media has become the institutional site where ordinary people, at the local level, can find a positive identification point for their own ideas and garden projects?

An examination of the specialists who present gardening in the popular media reveals the credence of Bauman's argument, none more so than in relation to the way in which gardening knowledge was presented to audiences. Despite being referred to as 'experts' by the over-arching presenters who often introduced makeovers, presenters like Anne McKevitt[5] carried no expertise in gardening – and this marked another branch of the discourse of achievability which pervaded lifestyle programming. Indeed lack of gardening knowledge was almost embraced. Certainly it provided no barrier to the garden makeover, and nor it is implied, should a lack of expertise interfere with the viewer who dreamt of renovating their garden. In an episode of *Homefront in the Garden*, for example, Anne McKevitt openly proclaimed her ignorance about grasses and bamboo: the solution was to wheel in,

---

4   It has been argued that cookery lifestyle experts were also outstepping traditional gender roles. For example, Moseley argues that there were competing strands of both hard and soft forms of masculinity in the construction of Jamie Oliver's persona in the late 1990s (Brunsdon et. al. 2001, 38).

5   Anne McKevitt is a Scottish celebrity interior designer.

'horticultural expert and gardening guru Matthew Vincent'. Anne was subsequently tutored about the ideal growing conditions for such plants. Like the novice gardener, the expert can always 'buy in' goods and expertise if specialist knowledge is not available – solutions can always be purchased in consumer culture. An important function of the expert was to out-source the ideas they provide to a host of goods that can be purchased in DIY and garden centres and related markets.[6] In these ways, some of the lifestyle 'experts' were less authoritative legislators conveying the hard facts of gardening, than friendly well-researched consumers, interpreting the latest lifestyle shopping ideas for the would-be gardener. Such 'experts' strove to establish empathy with viewers by lowering their differences in knowledge, personality and outlook between themselves and audiences. Codes of authority and expertise, as Chaney argues, have changed in public life, 'Rather than public figures presenting themselves as awesome, distant or threatening, they increasingly strive to be as one of the neighbours' (Chaney 2002, 109).

It is not that gardening expertise was entirely moribund in lifestyle television, rather, there was a shift in how knowledges were presented during the period. Within the makeover genre, gone were the didactic modes of address which once characterised early gardening programmes. The instructional close-up sequence of seed-sowing or pruning, accompanied by an authoritative voice-over was regarded as an outmoded means of engaging contemporary audiences. The more common vocabulary of address was more likely to show the personality-interpreter in mid-shot partnership with his or her clients, assessing and interpreting their needs, or re-framing their garden dreams to fit the transformative remit of a makeover design. In these ways, leisure programming has undergone a series of changes in form and tone since the late 1960s. Brunsdon (2001) charts the historic shift in the 'televisual grammar' of early 1970s 'didactic' gardening programmes to the 'generic hybridity' which characterises lifestyle gardening in the 1990s (Brunsdon et al. 2001, 55). Early programmes were distinguished by the use of close-up shots on the continuous demonstration of gardening tasks, with, 'an insistence on objects and operations, and camera, editing and commentary are governed by the logic of exposition: 'this is how it is', 'this is what it looks like', 'this is what you do' (Brunsdon et al. 2001, 55). For Brunsdon, garden lifestyle programmes of the period departed from the old through the, 'balance they offer between instruction and spectacle' (Brunsdon 2001, 54). Such lifestyle makeover programmes retained a diluted element of how to do garden tasks, but these were subordinate to the melodramatic spectacle of the programme's climax: the moment when the finished surprise made-over garden is revealed to the garden owner and the audience. It is here that the historical shift in the 'changed grammar' of the close-up is evidenced: rather than focusing on instructions the camera hones in on reactions (Brunsdon et al. 2001, 55). It is through the close-up on reaction that the climax of entertainment is achieved – has the personality-interpreter, the audience asked, successfully mediated the 'right' garden ideas to the pleasure/displeasure of the consuming client?

---

6   The advertising role played by lifestyle programmes and the expert personalities who promote goods was arguably further enhanced when broadcast by the non-commercial ethos of the BBC (Spittle, 2002, 64).

Gardening personality-interpreters were mediators who packaged garden lifestyle possibilities into styles and genres out of the symbolic repertoires on offer in consumer culture (Chaney 2001). They provided symbolic ideas for how viewers might interpret their garden aspirations and dreams. In particular, makeover personality-interpreters marked a shift away from the polarised and singular notion of purely instructional advice. They did not seek to encourage a single lifestyle, rather the focus was to expand and cater for the translation of a range of fashionable, architectural and artistic lifestyle improvisation concepts for use in the garden. Thus the job of the personality-interpreter was to make elite artistic design knowledge readable for the ordinary would-be gardener. The exclusion of ordinary people from the sanctioned enclaves of legislative accounts was becoming socially obsolete: for ordinary people as consuming clients were hailed, recognised and embraced in garden lifestyle media. In line with Bauman's (1987) argument, these texts recognised the sovereignty of the consumer, customers knew best, thus the onus was placed on the consumer to choose from a range of ideas from the symbolic repertoires offered by the culture industries.

Making lifestyle accessible: embracing ordinary subjects

The late 1990s saw ordinary people having a larger stake in primetime television, as Moseley argued, 'There are simply more ordinary people on television' (Moseley 2000, 308). But if the choice of experts and presenters of the gardening media marked a sense of openness towards those previously excluded from mainstream texts, the members of the public who were included within them extended representational possibilities even further. A whole range of people from different social groups – for example gay men, the disabled, older people and black and Asian subjects – were incorporated. As Brunsdon argued, the portrayal of ordinary England had changed on British television – the diversity of ordinary people in Britain was being recognised (Brunsdon et al. 2001, 57). The embrace of working-class subjects, however, was rare in lifestyle programming; diversity existed in terms of age, gender, race and sexuality, but it was, in the main, a lower middle-class kind of diversity.

Lifestyle largely replaced situation comedies and 'serious' high status programmes in the primetime slot, but what programme makers chose to retain from those previous genres however, were some of the main ingredients for the entertainment required from 8.00 to 9.00: drama, conflict, emotion and stereotypes. The structuring conventions of 'infotainment' took precedence over the Reithian values of information and education. Conflict was so central, that some programmes featured footage of video-diary confessionals made by the makeover subjects which charted the highs and lows of their relationships with the makeover personality-interpreters.[7] In similar vein, the need to retain the sensationalism of discord often worked at the political expense of how the previously marginalised were represented.

In an episode of *Homefront in the Garden* Anne McKevitt set out to makeover a garden owned by two men who are subtly foregrounded by the programme as being part of a gay relationship. From the outset this particular makeover is about

---

7   This was a generic feature of *Homefront: Inside Out* (BBC, 1999-).

Anne's free-reign design decisions: Anne acts as the creative, moody and largely silent authoress of the future of the garden and Martin and Trevor are subjected to her plans. The programme is oppositionally structured by Anne's strident makeover moves and the couple's increasing anxiety about how the garden is to be transformed. This strategy of creating oppositional character positions generates an opportunity to locate the ordinary subjects of the makeover into stereotypical roles. The camera frequently indulges Martin who repeatedly complains about Anne not sharing her makeover intentions, until eventually the viewer learns that he broke down and wept with frustration at the office to his co-workers. It would be unthinkable to portray a heterosexual man upset because he feels powerless – let alone out of control in the garden – a sphere positioned so closely to the home and the domestic. Martin's crying marks him out as so many conventional popular representations of gay masculinity do: as the feminine 'wife' of the couple. The makeover is prepared to include difference – perhaps even to embrace it – but the conventions of entertainment are upheld at the expense of the politics of representation. In this way, the garden makeover could be seen as a programme that was more concerned to fulfil the remit of the situation comedy it has replaced in a bid to appeal to markets, than it is about educating viewers about gardening.

In less popular enclaves, beyond the remit of the lifestyle makeover genre, gardening people were portrayed with more respect. The emphasis in Channel Four's *Real Gardens* for example was on the equal interplay between the knowledge and research embodied by the presenter and the lived experience of the 'real' gardener. *Observer* garden columnist and writer Monty Don, the over-arching presenter, introduces the viewer to programme segments which consist of expert visits to viewers' gardens. Vital to the ethos of *Real Gardens* was the manner in which the expert practically gardens alongside the visited gardener. Accompanying dialogue consists of a genuine exchange of knowledge between expert and gardener as the two assess the aspects of the garden they work upon. In one programme Monty Don gardens alongside a woman on her coastal garden in Guernsey. As they fork through her compost heap, Monty foregrounds current research on the most beneficial elements for the best results while she tempers the discussion with aspects of her composting practice. Other moments feature the experts being tutored through gardening practices that are entirely new to them. The exclusivity of the experts is continually underplayed as they strive to present themselves as real gardeners on an equal footing with the gardeners they visit. In these ways *Real Gardens* appears to genuinely value the experience, the expertise as well as the actual gardens of the gardeners they visit. Experts become lifestyle ethnographers, tempering their expertise with lived experience while showcasing and translating garden projects for audiences. In this way, even programmes which lie beyond the lifestyle makeover genre appealed to markets using the levelling strategies of 'ordinari-ization'.

The 'ordinari-ization' of lifestyle television during this moment can be read as part of the wider cultural move to help people to make the social and cultural transition from 'ways of life' to consumer lifestyles (Chaney 2001). The egalitarian embrace of a widening diversity of ordinary people, alongside the concomitant levelling down of expertise in garden lifestyle programming, undoubtedly demonstrated a move to mine new markets in the ever increasing shift towards consumer culture. But these moves are not all that the shift to lifestyle had to offer. Moseley, for example, argues that to read the primetime shift as, 'a move from hard to soft, from documentary to makeover, from address to citizen to consumer, from public to private and from "quality" to "dumbed-down" television' is to ignore the complex issues made by that shift (Brunsdon et al. 2001: 33). For her, lifestyle address straddled these dualisms: viewers were 'citizen-consumers' who could, 'on a small, local scale, learn to make changes, make a difference, improve the personal for the national good' (Brunsdon et al. 2001, 34). Analysis of lifestyle programming undoubtedly reveals that lifestyle ideas held a measure of educational value for citizens. They also offered people the opportunity, within the context of the commonplace routines of their everyday lives, to mould the strategies and sites of lifestyle in ways which helped them to navigate their own relationship to social change.

In these ways, this section demonstrates that while, as illustrated in chapter 4, garden legislators exclude ordinary people, there was an institutional place where ordinary people were included, addressed as equals and given a positive site of identification. The spaces where legislators reside, which undoubtedly remain the most culturally lauded, remain intact in academe and in traditional middle-class literary quarters and they continue to furnish educated, middle-class readers with values about the garden. Ordinary people as consuming citizens however, had the choice to turn away from legislators and towards the media as a site which allows them to see images of more ordinary people, in the context of domestic gardens, executing reasonably achievable garden projects. In these ways, as Bauman (1987) argues, the authority figures of gardening have been destabilised and consumer markets actively showcase the ordinary as a means of securing ever-widening markets. As a result, ordinariness was awarded a crucial place in garden lifestyle consumer culture in ways which potentially offered a positive location to the ordinary gardener.

Gardens

The previous section established the idea that ordinariness took on increased significance in both the contemporary media and in lifestyle consumer culture. Yet ordinariness, as I argue in previous chapters, is not defined here as belonging only to women or the working-class; rather, dimensions of the mundane – such as home, habit and repetition – are shared by people across social variables. Yet ordinariness is a sphere which is always subjectively *located* by class, race, sexuality and gender. The 'ordinary' people of terrestrial lifestyle television for example, as I argued in 'Gardening People', were usually lower middle-class, with working-class people hardly appearing as its subjects. In this section, I investigate how far the increased media significance of the 'ordinary' in relation to lifestyle was located by class and gender. Taking the garden in mid to late 1990s British lifestyle media as the central focus, I ask: was the ordinary garden, as a lifestyle site where symbolic ideas were showcased and interpreted for audiences, a classed and gendered space?

In the following section I expand beyond television to analyse a number of garden lifestyle examples. The aesthetic codes and symbolic repertoires of the contemporary garden in circulation in the media reveal that there was no one given set of lifestyle garden aesthetics: the magazine *Organic Gardening* for example, displayed a very different aesthetic vision of gardening from that which characterised the makeovers of *Ground Force*. There were multiple differences between the ways in which the ordinary garden could be made to look, differences which reveal that the British gardening public was conceived by the media industries as a socially fragmented audience. A post-modern perspective would imply that this signified the relative freedom people had to identify and access a range of different conceptions of constructing a desirable garden look. Post-modern theories, which imply playfulness, freedom of entry and fluidity of movement, tend to assume that people can traverse the social boundaries in which they are located. This book, however, uses Bourdieu's (1986) economistic metaphors to ask whether barriers to entry based on the variable distribution of cultural, social and economic capital impacted on the kind of gardening aesthetic people were able to generate. And while post-modern approaches imply that men and women are able to traverse gender boundaries, I examine the makeover genre as a means to assess if the media encouraged the fluidity of subversive gendered constructions. Acknowledging that the ordinary mediated garden was a space where more ordinary people were embraced, I ask if they were still subjectively placed by symbolic nuances of class and gender. Did the shift from civic to consumer culture (Bauman 1987) and from ways of life to lifestyle (Chaney 2001) remain underpinned by societal class and gender locations?

In the first section I examine the visual look and address of three classed modes of lifestyle garden aesthetics: the national weekend lifestyle press, the makeover and the local Sunday gardening supplement. In the second, I examine how evocations of garden history were used as a means to guide a 'new middle-class' audience in the selection of particular garden aesthetics in the makeover. And finally, arguing that garden spaces in the climate of the mid to late 1990s were used as spaces to communicate symbolic ideas about their owners, I ask how far the lifestyled garden was a classed and gendered space.

The aesthetics of the contemporary garden

Solid, traditional middle-class commentary on garden aesthetics was subtly explicated in Monty Don's Sunday gardening column in the *Life* supplement of the *Observer.* Like most contemporary lifestyle interpreters, Don avoids a directly instructional approach to gardening. Rather, he implies that the practice of effective gardening can only be understood by adopting a liberal humanist approach to the arts, from the highbrow (literature, painting and music) to the middlebrow (photography). As a result, Don's column is frequently strewn with cultural references and allusions. For example, an October piece about apples entitled, 'Cider with the roses' alludes to the writer Laurie Lee. More specifically, Don loosely adopts a quasi-Keatsian perspective both in relation to his own journalistic style and as a guide to gardening appreciation. Implied in this approach is the idea that aesthetic understanding can be acquired through the development of a sensuous appreciation of beauty. For Don, the creation of a garden is about being quintessentially alert to one's own senses. 'Last night,' begins his apples column, 'I jogged around the Herefordshire lanes and came home almost drunk with the scent of apples. Every breath was a slug of strong cider,

... not enough is made of how smell is such a feature of the countryside, from the fetid sweetness of the May blossom and the chaffy greenness of haymaking...' (Don 1997, 56). Elsewhere, sight becomes the privileged sense, '...a wigwam of purple sweet peas, the occasional iridescent petal back lit against the sky like a butterfly wing.' Similarly, the tactile quality of plants is likened to, 'a kind of delicate floral Braille' (Don 1998, 38). Thus, according to Don, the ability to distinguish beauty leads to an understanding of the visual language of gardening.

The extreme close-up photographs which accompanied Don's copy, most often supplied by acclaimed photographer Fleur Oldby, work in tandem with Don's sensuous recommendations. Instructional, literal images of plants in situ are avoided in favour of the more subtle visual strategy of allowing the reader to survey the finite, detailed minutiae of the colour, form and texture of plants. Just as Don's column has more to do with the act of writing as opposed to practical gardening, Oldby's illustrations are about enjoying the visual play that plant close-ups allow the photographer to access. Gardening aesthetics, within the pages of Don's middle-class weekend supplement begin with a cultivated state of mind which is attuned to arts appreciation. The visual organisation of the garden it is implied, is the natural addendum to a cultured approach to lifestyle. In these ways, *Observer Life* offers a traditionally educated, patrician middle-class, yet specifically English approach to the garden as a lifestyle space.

Other middle-class enclaves of the media demanded some kind of knowledge of contemporary visual codes. It is virtually impossible to discuss the visual aesthetics of the garden makeover without setting the idea against the backcloth of postmodernism. A number of central features characterise accounts of postmodernism in the arts: the obliteration of meaning as a result of the prominence of design and aesthetics; the stylistic tendency towards eclecticism and the juxtaposition of visual codes; the decomposition of the staunch distinction between high and popular culture; and parody, irony, playfulness, intertextuality and a celebration of the depthlessness of cultural forms (Featherstone 1991; Rojek 1995). A glance at the typical garden makeover of the time reveals an explicit correlation between the visual composition of these gardens and the stylistic features of postmodernism. These kinds of playful, reflexive codes appeal to the destabilised social subjects discussed by Chaney (2001). Stand-alone post-modern subjects, as Chaney (2001) describes, are more open to the new symbolic repertoires required by lifestyle projects.

The post-makeover garden was a space that above all had been subjected to the principles of design aesthetics. The decomposition of meaning through the prominence of design was a key strand of thought among post-modern writers. Jameson argues that post-modern culture was characterised by superficiality: 'depth,' he argues, 'is replaced by surface' (Jameson 1991, 12). In *The Condition of Postmodernity* (1989), Harvey discusses the shift in the conception of space from urban modern *planning* to post-modern *design*:

> Whereas the modernists see space as something to be shaped for social purposes and therefore always subservient to the construction of a social project, the postmodernists see space as something independent and autonomous, to be shaped according to aesthetic aims and principles which have nothing necessarily to do with any overarching social

objective, save, perhaps, the achievement of timeless and 'disinterested' beauty as an objective in itself (Harvey 1989, 66).

While Harvey's claim is made in relation to urban design, his comment holds credence for the consideration of the typical garden makeover – they too were most often conceived as gardens within wider urban spaces. The pursuit of a rigorous and consistent garden design concept without any recourse to a wider communal or social goal was therefore a characteristic of the makeover. In these ways, one can see how the traditional 'way of life' with its recourse to shared, communal codes, was discarded in favour of the design remit of the 'lifestyle' Chaney (2001) describes. Design was often presented as a desirable end in itself and the possibility of underlying meanings was disregarded in favour of immediate, surface impressions. For example, as part of the back garden makeovers in *Gardening Neighbours* for example, Ali Ward persuades older members of the terrace Terry and Joan to wipe every trace of their old garden away in favour of allowing the makeover team to produce a classical formal garden. By way of introduction to the feature-segment, Ali Ward's voice over sets the scene: 'The central feature of Terry and Joan's original garden at No. 4 was a raised bed full of Bizzie Lizzies'. Indeed the design of their 'undesirable' garden, is precisely the working-class design trope favoured by my grandparents in the late 1950s (see Figure 2.1). This was clearly a loaded introduction for the viewer of taste; if these are the plants and structures these gardeners choose, they need the tasteful features that a design concept provides. The saddening aspect of this act of gardening benevolence is that these gardeners clearly wanted to keep their home-made concrete raised bed of impatiens, because it contained valued personal aesthetic meanings for them. 'It was beautiful before you changed it all,' remarks Terry as the camera pans the crisp formality of the newly installed box hedges and standard bay trees. The raised bed provided colour and centrality that the new design, which Terry and Joan call 'interesting', fails to provide. This instance is typical of the values of makeover aesthetics; there is an almost clinical obsession with maintaining a coherent design (even if that theme is one of post-modern eclecticism), at the expense of plants or objects invested with value, memory or meaning. It is also an example of symbolic violence (Bourdieu 1990) *par excellence.* The programme encourages the removal of local working-class aesthetics to make way for the imposition of a middle-class coherent design concept. The message is clear: get rid of vulgar working-class aesthetic attachments which lack reconvertible capital and surrender them to the cosmopolitan eclecticism of desirable middle-class conventions. This typical instance is one of the conventions of the genre where the makeover expert and the makeover subject battle over the sentimental attachment people are accused of harbouring to garden plants or objects. Most often the casualties are working-class objects or aesthetic features. In the world of the late 1990s makeover, the depth of personal (working-class) meaning must be sacrificed to the cleansing agency of the surface aesthetics of design principles.

In order to deliver audience entertainment, each new makeover was constructed on the principle of difference; its central dynamic therefore becomes the endless pursuit of novelty. This was also manifest in the eclecticism of visual codes which typically characterised the makeover. In an episode of *Home Front in the Garden* for example, Anne McKevitt's makeover design is based on providing a series of rooms for the garden which include modern features – a heated swimming pool, a grass and bamboo garden and a lit patio area – as well as such 'updated' historical features as a perspex version of the eighteenth century ha-ha and a brightly painted khaki, aubergine and maroon representation of a walled garden. The result is a melange of stylistic trends, or what some might even regard as a miscegenation of cultural and historical codes.

This kind of playful eclecticism was also at work in the community makeover of back gardens in *Gardening Neighbours*. In all, the eight back gardens of the Sheffield terraced row are based on themes of choice – African, white city roof top, cricket, child safe, classical formal, herb and seaside, so that the experience of strolling past is almost akin to choosing lunch in a shopping mall restaurant from an array of world cuisine. For Fredric Jameson postmodernism brings a new 'structure of feeling' to contemporary culture. In *Postmodernism; or, the Cultural Logic of Late-Capitalism* (1991), Jameson argues that the 'crisis of historicity' which characterises post-modern culture is experienced subjectively and becomes manifest in a loss of temporal meaning. The past becomes nothing more than a series of unrelated signs which give no sense of the shape of material history. This leads to what Jameson describes as a 'schizophrenic experience … of isolated, disconnected, discontinuous material signifiers which fail to link up into a coherent sequence' (1990, 119). Jameson claims that the schizophrenic experience is marked by a different kind of emotional charge: it is, 'a far more intense experience of any given present of the world' (ibid.). This feeling of heightened intensity, or what Hebdige calls 'acid perspectivism' (Hebdige 1994), occurs as a result of being condemned to experience time as a 'series of perpetual presents'. As Jameson argues, 'the world comes before the schizophrenic with heightened intensity, bearing a mysterious and oppressive charge of affect, glowing with hallucinatory energy' (Jameson 1990, 120). Jameson is careful however to warn of his sense of deep pessimism, for him a loss of history is experienced as an assault against subjectivity, 'what might for us seem a desirable experience – an increase in our perceptions, a libidinal or hallucinogenic intensification of our normal humdrum and familiar surroundings – is here felt as loss, as "unreality"' (ibid.).

Not all critics have embraced Jameson's notion of a schizoid culture. Featherstone for example, suggests that 'little evidence is presented as to how men and women engaged in everyday practices actually come to formulate these experiences' (Featherstone 1991, 42). While it is difficult to assert that my analysis reveals a hallucinogenic post-makeover experience, I would argue that many makeover subjects responded with shocked emotional intensity to their new gardens. In fact the first experiential encounter with their makeover is often accompanied by tears, laughter or over-whelmed emotional astonishment. Often subjects are rendered speechless or they offer bewildered emotional statements about the garden which often speak of it as unreal or otherworldly. For example in an episode of *Homefront in the Garden* one woman, whose new communal garden included among other things an outdoor cinema, offered this perplexed statement to the programme makers: 'It's just amazing. It's really mad though, it's kind of hard for me to get used to it. I think it's just not happening …It's out of this world, it's just completely out of this world.

It's just not normal.' For other critics the power of the revealed garden is a result of the juxtaposition of intense emotion and ordinariness, 'through its close-up on the reaction of the 'ordinary' person on television' it represents a, 'moment of excess representative of *über*-ordinariness' (Moseley 2000, 303).

Jameson presents a fatalistic view of the experience of postmodernism, but one can see how post-modern codes might appeal to those interested in the playful and reflexive lifestyle practices Chaney (2001) describes. For stand-alone, educated, middle-class subjects in post-industrial societies, who have left behind the communal 'way of life', the interpretation of post-modern codes enables the re-fashioning of new forms of identity. Yet these post-modern middle-class codes resided uneasily next to the established, traditional forms of middle-class aesthetic advocated by writers such as Christopher Lloyd, Monty Don and Sir Roy Strong. Post-modern aesthetics, which rely either on high cultural artistic knowledge of both modernism and postmodernism or a familiarity with the sanction given to aestheticised objects by commodity culture, struck a jibe at the patrician 'establishment' aesthetics also being promulgated by Don in his *Observer Life* column. After all the makeover provided spectacular visual spaces which seemed exciting, youthful and hedonistic in comparison with the rather pedestrian emphasis on the colour, texture and relationships of form provided by companion planting. In these ways, garden lifestyle texts not only showcased different kinds of (middle-) class aesthetics which demonstrated the internal divisions within class groups, they also testified to the contiguous friction between different factions of a social class at that historical moment.

The garden looked entirely different in local aspects of the media. For instance, Howard Drury offers weekly gardening advice in the 'preview' supplement in the *Sunday Mercury*, a Birmingham and West Midlands local Sunday newspaper. *Howard Drury's Gardening Diary,* a cheaply produced, largely black and white 'special publication' produced annually, offers the reader a month by month breakdown of the gardening year, highlighting the seasonal requirements of the garden. Hard sell advertising for products such as orthopaedic chairs, ceramic tiles, Capo Di Monte and credit agencies reveal a working- to lower middle-class, white, 'grey' readership.

The magazine offers the reader ways of constructing a practical, sensible garden space; an aesthetic is provided, but it denies anything which might be regarded as ostentatious. In this way, the magazine alludes to the kinds of lower middle-class values which appealed to the British working-class of the 1980s: economic thrift, hard-work and an ascetic approach to leisure. These key components of the cultural aspect of Thatcher's brand of conservatism inform the few photographs provided. The magazine promotes an aesthetic ethos of plain orderliness based on conserving the respectability of traditional garden elements. Elsewhere the magazine uses close-up photographs to illustrate the copy in a utilitarian way. Where images of a garden are provided, the colour scheme is traditionally wrought: outdoor landscaping materials, such as stone paving flags, creosoted wooden fences and trellises, gravel pathways, aluminium and glass greenhouses utilise neutral, outdoor colours such as brown, beige, grey and green. The images draw upon conventional, stock garden elements such as the lawn, the flower bed containing common shrubs and space for annual bedding, trees, the shed, the greenhouse, the rockery and pots and hanging baskets. The only full colour photograph which focuses on a plant display shows a summer flower bed arranged in blocks of white and pink bedding plants consisting of begonias, pelargoniums (geraniums) and impatiens. There are no spectacular constructions, no novelty themes, no bright colours and no structural references to transnationality. Within the pages of this advice supplement, the reader is encouraged by the personal address of Howard the author to focus down on the essential information, the plants themselves. Thus, the simply conceived advice sections, 'The lawn' and 'The vegetable garden', for example – steer the reader away from what might be seen as the ostentatious excesses of consumption towards a moderate conception of how a garden should be practically constructed. In these ways, Drury's recommendations have nothing in common with the national codes of *Observer Life* or *Homefront in the Garden.* Based on plain orderliness, sincere tidiness and respectable traditional garden elements, Drury's garden is generated locally using local aesthetic visual codes.

These examples show that while ordinary people were given an identification point by aspects of the media which use the ordinary domestic garden as a setting for interpreting lifestyle ideas, the garden was a classed space at the level of representations.

Internal antagonisms within the middle-class were illustrated by the differences between the traditional, educated and somewhat staid middle-class aesthetics embodied by garden writers such as Monty Don and the new middle-class who were receptive to the post-modern cultural goods and experiences offered by the makeover. The middle-class consists of dominant and subordinate factions who, 'are engaging in endless though reasonably genteel battles to assert their own identities, social positions and worth' (Savage et al. 1992, 100). Bourdieu (1986) reminds us that the upwardly aspirant 'new petite bourgeoisie' keeps discovering that the social field it wishes to have more purchase upon is already dominated by a more patrician, long-standing middle-class generation and in a bid to mark new territory, 'previously well-established cultural traditions are thus increasingly treated in a 'pastiche' way' (Savage et al. 1992, 128). Concomitantly, in counter-response, those higher in cultural capital struggle to ensure that 'culture' remains autonomously scarce and exclusive and intellectuals attempt to find ways to maintain the value of their specialised knowledge. In this way, Bourdieu's work enables one to understand the specific class context from which different aesthetic modes of lifestyle emanate. It also shows the on-going struggle between the culturally more outgoing and the more respectable and conformist factions of the British middle-class in late 1990s British culture.

Moreover, Bourdieu's (1986) economistic metaphors show that the national media deployed techniques as a means to institutionalise particular forms of capital. As the examples from *Observer Life*, *Garden Neighbours* and *Homefront in the Garden* show, it was middle-class gardening tastes, competencies and aesthetics which were ordained as legitimate by the national media. Not everyone had the resources to enable them to access the display of middle-class taste in the media. Yet the garden lifestyle media sanctioned the symbolic power of the middle-class as the primary arbiter of symbolic capital. Monty Don for example, constructed a resoundingly middle-class presence in his *Observer Life* column; his reference to literary allusions and antiquated knowledge offered a means to display a high volume of capital. Moreover, through the use of middle-class tastes, as the example of the imposition of a post-modern design remit on working-class couple Terry and Joan in *Gardening Neighbours* illustrates, the media enacted symbolic violence (Bourdieu 1990) against working-class viewers. Yet legitimate knowledges and aesthetic codes require recognition based on the 'transferable dispositions' of one's habitus and on access to forms of capital. In this way, Bourdieu's model enables an understanding of how class inequalities were perpetuated, since those with meagre capitals simply could not exploit the pedagogic action of the garden lifestyle media, hence, they experienced problems in their attempt to accrue, exchange and capitalise on them. No wonder working-class audiences turned to aspects of the local press for affirmation of their own local garden aesthetics.

Indeed some forms of cultural and symbolic capital, in a bid to retreat from legitimate taste, were generated locally. *Howard Drury's Garden Diary* used different garden codes and conventions, which arguably functioned to contest legitimate capital. Yet these local conventions only held value within local settings. At national level, media institutions had a vested interest in conferring the symbolic power of middle-class aesthetics. In these contexts, local aesthetic codes were devalued and their tradeability is therefore limited: they simply lacked the institutional channels through which to disburse their calls for legitimacy.

In these ways, the 'ordinary garden' of the lifestyle media in the mid to late 1990s was shot through with classed aesthetics.

The evocation of history in contemporary gardens

Identified as a more culturally extrovert faction of middle-class, the 'new middle-class' emerged in Britain in the early 1980s (Savage et al. 1992). Critics have argued that this group is marked by its receptivity to post-modern cultural goods (Featherstone, 1991). Indeed Savage et al. (1992) identify a 'post-modern' faction of the British middle-class, which they argue is characterised by its indulgence in a 'wide range of disparate consumption practices' (1992, 130). Even more pertinently, Savage et al. argue that this group is also marked by its tendency to treat previously auratic forms of culture in non-auratic ways (ibid.). Hence, they give weight to the argument I mounted in the previous section: post-modern lifestyle garden aesthetics offered this new class faction a means to challenge auratic or at least highly legitimate middle-class garden aesthetics, while allowing them to indulge in the depthless, self-parodying commercialised art found in lifestyle compartments of consumer culture. In this section, I argue that the lifestyle media of the time was highly sentient of the new middle-class and its needs and, acting as guides for living, lifestyle texts promulgated the idea that the aestheticisation of components of everyday life – such as the garden – would lead to a more gratifying lifestyle.

Bourdieu (1986) argues that there is a whole swathe of cultural workers devoted to the production and dissemination of symbolic goods for the expanding new middle-class. Obsessed with the promotion of appearance, identity and presentation techniques in occupations such as the media, advertising and public relations, these workers act as 'new cultural intermediaries', ferreting out new artistic and intellectual trends, producing and crystallising particular symbolic ideas, in a bid to educate publics. A key part of their project has been to break down previous barriers to elite forms of knowledge. As cultural interfaces the new intellectuals have striven to formulate, 'an art of living which provides them with the gratifications and prestige of the intellectual at the least cost ... they adopt the most external and most easily borrowed aspects of the intellectual lifestyle ... and apply it to not-yet-legitimate culture' (Bourdieu 1986, 370). The result has amounted to a destabilisation of previously established knowledge hierarchies which in some quarters have virtually dismantled the popular versus high culture dichotomy. As Bourdieu argues, the new good which ciphers aspects of the intellectual lifestyle, 'is still able to fulfil functions of distinction by making available to *almost* everyone the distinctive poses, the distinctive games and other external signs of inner riches previously reserved for intellectuals' (Bourdieu 1986, 371).

Mindful of the new middle-class who Bauman (1987) describes as 'neither coarse nor fully refined, neither ignorant nor educated to the standards boasted by the elite' (Bauman 1987, 135), the new cultural intermediaries are concerned with the project of tutoring the new petite bourgeoisie in how to make discriminatory judgements about the positional value of symbolic goods. Taste configurations and lifestyle preferences are associated with social class and occupational status, making it possible to plot out the world of taste and its minutely graded distinctions. Within late capitalism, however, where the ever-increasing proliferation of symbolic goods can shift the value of 'marker goods', there is a potentially endless supply of work for new intellectuals (Featherstone 1991). In a context where the positional value of symbolic goods is relative, the anxiety of members of the new petite bourgeoisie to consume legitimate aspects of culture is potentially assuaged by the work of the new cultural intermediaries. Their task is to supply the self-conscious consumer with the knowledge required to both judge the cultural value of the latest goods and be attuned to the culturally befitting ways of how they should be consumed. I argue that the role of the personality-interpreter is to display and proffer the social and cultural value of post-modern modes of history to the self-conscious middle-class consumer so that they might be consumed judiciously in the 'right' ways.

For post-modern writers, the experience of the present no longer entails the possession of a coherent sense of the linear progression of history. 'Eschewing the idea of progress,' asserts Harvey, 'postmodernism abandons all sense of historical continuity and memory, while simultaneously developing an incredible ability to plunder history and absorb whatever it finds there as some aspect of the present' (Harvey 1989, 54). Similarly, for Jameson, post-modern culture is characterised by a 'weakening of historicity' (1991, 6). As a result, the past becomes a series of malleable signs without any concrete sense of the forces or narrative trajectory of material history. Other writers have identified a crisis in the representation of history. Taylor, for example, argues that the television viewer's experience of history is presented as, 'an endless reserve of equal events' (Taylor 1987, 104). Television is, he argues, 'the first medium in the whole of history to present the artistic achievements of the past as a stitched together collage of equi-important and simultaneously existing phenomena largely divorced from geography and material history' (ibid.). This kind of approach produces what has been called a, 'flattening out of history' (McGuigan 1999, 72). In this way, the relative importance of certain events is lost, since history becomes merely a surface area without volume. Instead, intertextuality dominates postmodernism to produce an endless freeplay of signs detached from their referents. The result is a 'new depthlessness' since the logic of intertextuality is that everything, including history, is reduced to textuality. Past historical moments are deliberately raided, using allusion, imitation and pastiche, to produce a simulacrum of historical reality. 'The history of aesthetic styles,' Jameson argues, 'displaces "real" history' (Jameson 1991, 20).

Indeed a consideration of the way in which the garden makeover provided reference to the historical antecedents of gardening revealed a will to ransack the surface image of historical styles in a manner which floated free of the depth of their historical significance. For example, in *Homefront in the Garden*, Matthew Vincent explains Anne McKevitt's intention to put a 'contemporary spin on a very old idea,' – they decide to construct a perspex ha-ha. The ha-ha was essentially a large ditch placed at the end of a garden boundary. When the eighteenth century gardener looked to the garden edge, the ha-ha generated a visual illusion: the garden merged with the landscape beyond to create a vista while simultaneously deterring both animal and human undesirables in surrounding fields from entering the garden. 'Capability Brown copied it from the French,' remarks Vincent, as he proceeds to illustrate their intention to produce a similar visual effect using perspex as opposed to a *cordon sanitaire*. Yet while Vincent's explanation provides a sense of spurious historicity to the makeover programme, an actual encounter with this ha-ha would almost certainly amount to a profoundly ahistorical experience. For these makeover experts the ha-ha is useful as a design concept, interesting because of its surface appearance. The wider context of its meaning as a signifier of the great age of gardening is neutralised. In the context of this garden it is no more than an allusion or an empty textual signifier, as Jameson argues, 'a "connotator" of the past' (Jameson 1991, 20). Yet while what lies beyond the historical allusion is of little consequence, the ability to be able to offer a cursory nod at historical knowledge is. The ability to drop a flattened historical vignette into the commentary on the design remit is an important signifier of cultural capital. Historical allusion is used as a means of conferring legitimation and power on those who can couch their choices in a trajectory of garden history. It was these distinctive poses that the lifestyle media was concerned to transmit to the new self-conscious middle-class consumer.

Yet as the camera moves away from Matthew Vincent's commentary on the ha-ha, Tessa Shaw's voice-over introduces the viewer to another re-fashioned signifier of the past. 'Anne,' we are told, 'had created her version of another classical design – the walled garden.' Anne's version however, has very little in common with the walled kitchen garden William Cobbett describes in *The English Gardener* (1996) in 1829. The ideal design he recommends is for a south-facing, brick walled, rectangular enclosure which is divided within and provides space for fruit and vegetable plots, a hot-bed and a tool-house. The walled garden that Cobbett advocates is a working garden, often owned by country families, which had been tended in the English countryside for 500 years. Anne McKevitt's version is more akin to an outdoor living room: its walls are angular, textured and painted in a variety of fashionable colours and it provides seating and a coffee table as opposed to offering a space to grow food. The experience of history in these gardens is based on the juxtaposition of different ephemeral, fleeting moments: from the ha-ha to the modern patio to the walled garden. Historical chronology or development was a moribund concept in the typical garden makeover: as post-modern spaces these designers felt free to quote images of history in any order they choose. Yet the ability to choose from a body of historical knowledge, no matter how superficially it is retrieved, confers power on the beholder. Such references may lack depth, but they stamp the authority of history on to the garden. As such these programmes worked to show the potential consumer how to use a sense of history as a means to legitimate taste.

One can see the same kind of strategy in the glossy monthly magazine *Gardens Illustrated* published in Spring 2001. Here a sense of garden history is pivotal to the entire magazine, from the features about historic gardens to the commodities which imitate objects from the past. A feature entitled 'Playing tag', for example, offers the reader a series of photographs of potted bulbs and herbs in order to showcase a variety of plant labels currently on the market. These labels are evocative of various moments in garden history: 'Victorian hanging alitag'; 'antique small and large glass and aluminium alitags'; 'steel "tournefort" label' are examples. Most of them, as in the case of a verdigris copper tag which can be purchased from The Conran Shop, offer a pre-designed patina. They offer the consumer the opportunity to venerate the garden with a sense of antiquity. Such features tutor the reader about the newest symbolic goods and they offer interpretations of how history can generate cultural capital in the garden.

In these ways, one can see that the lifestyle media acted as a commercial site where personality-interpreters use the garden as a space for interpreting new, yet *classed* symbolic lifestyle ideas. For the new middle-class, however, 'cultural assets need not depend on the legitimacy offered by the state. Cultural assets can be deployed and valorised in the market' (Savage et al. 1992, 129-130). In this way the media acted as a commercial guarantor for the value of new positional goods. This section has shown how garden history can be interpreted in the garden in ways which confer power on to their beholders. Lash (1990) argues that the middle-class use symbols as a substitute for things, enabling them to 'produce symbols which help realise the value of other symbols' (Lash 1990, 251). In this way, the lifestyle media shows consumers how to use distinctive historical symbols as forms of power and as a means to make the garden a legitimate middle-class space.

Gardens as an extension of the self

So far this section has shown that lifestyle ideas are always classed. This section illustrates that the ordinary lifestyle garden is also shot through with symbolic ideas about gender as well as class.

One of the conventions of the late 1990s British makeover was to extend the indoors outdoors; a typical characteristic of the 'reveal' for example, is that the patio area has been transformed into an 'outdoor lounge'. Yet makeover gardens were often more than just an extension of the home interior, they were also, in many cases, shown to become an extension of the self. A convention of the makeover involved finding out about the personality of the makeover subject, so that the garden can either be tailored to fit the individual's needs or become a means of expressing the individual. An episode of *Homefront: Inside Out* (BBC, 1999-) for example, borrows docu-soap conventions in order to construct a sense of 'Sharon' as an individual: friends and work colleagues testify to her personality traits; we see footage of Sharon interacting in the workplace; she is filmed living in the home and garden spaces that are to be made-over; she is subject to stringent cross-examination from both Laurence Llewelyn-Bowen and Diarmuid Gavin about her design preferences; and she is asked to compile a pin board presentation of favourite images and objects. All these elements construct a view of Sharon: her preferences, psychological disposition, emotional life, and her personal and professional personae are subject to scrutiny, for these are the characteristics which will govern the garden project – a project which above all is a reflection of Sharon as an individual.

Yet as Skeggs argues, 'the project of the self is a Western bourgeois project' (Skeggs 1997, 163). Seeing oneself as an individual is a liberty only those with sufficient financial and cultural resources can afford; middle-class subjects have access to the conditions which might enable them to turn their gaze inwards in order to work on the self. The idea of formulating a character portrait in order to project it onto one's personal space is a proclamation of individual self worth and value. Public exploration of one's inner traits is based on the assumption that others are innately interested (ibid.). The garden makeover tended to focus on clients whose class position allows them the prerogative of egocentric self expression – doubtless the typical makeover subject is already familiar with such practices, such as personal therapy, yoga and the art class, which also promote the idea of narcissistic self exploration. Middle-class subjects partake of individualism with the same confidence as the middle-class body moves with disinterested ease through social space – as though they are given entitlements.

To this extent, Sharon occupies a relatively privileged location as a middle-class subject in a milieu similar to the one described above: as manager of a media recruitment consultancy she enjoys a good deal of economic independence and culturally she is accustomed to the trappings of an affluent consumer lifestyle. To be sure, Sharon is afforded an opportunity to negotiate a means of expressing herself through the aesthetic codes of her made-over garden via a genre which encourages the expression of the self, but not, I would argue, without being subjected to the gendered version of Sharon's individuality that the programme makers of *Homefront: Inside Out* are anxious to construct. Sharon is entitled to bourgeois self-indulgence, but only within the prescribed parameters of a version of caring, maternal and emotionally vulnerable femininity.

Diarmuid and Laurence's assessment of the components of Sharon's personality is constructed around a fundamental set of oppositions: her private home life and her public work persona. Using Sharon's own video diary, footage of her in the workplace, the testimony of friends and Sharon's 'likes and hates', the experts conclude that Sharon is soft and vulnerable at home, but cold and hard at work. Yet the footage we see of Sharon at work, (we see her answer the telephone and later she discusses a computer question with a colleague) hardly justifies the adjectives 'icy', 'hard', and 'tough' – terms that purport to encapsulate her work persona. Rather, these words are coined because Sharon in making relatively minor day-to-day decisions and managing a small team of employees outsteps the traditional remit of domestically bound, passive femininity. Once this side of the opposition is established however, her character soon takes on a set of corresponding colours and design materials: 'there's a cold steely blue edge to her,' remarks Laurence. In stark contrast, the programme's exploration of Sharon's home life focuses on relationships and emotions. Single and childless, the viewer is shown snippets from Sharon's video diary. She confesses that she hates living alone and that her cats (her 'babies') provide her with the love she lacks. They are also, the programme implies, child substitutes. Anxious to tone down the hard edges established by Sharon's steely work persona, the viewer witnesses several moments where Sharon is shown 'caring' for her cats. The cats therefore must be taken into account when it comes to the makeover, as Dairmuid asserts, 'they reveal a softer side to her – a strong contrast to her hard-edged work persona.' But there are yet further strategies to feminise the 'bossy' aspect of Sharon's character. Building on the testimony of Sharon's best friend – 'Sharon doesn't suffer fools gladly…at home she's pink and fluffy …if she were colours she'd be pink and icy blue' – the presenters fasten onto the notion that she is 'pink and fluffy' to such an extent that it becomes the leit-motif of Sharon's essential nature. 'This is you on the inside' remarks Diarmuid as he points to a piece of fuschia pink fluff on the presentation pin board. When Sharon is asked to discuss her likes she mentions a dislike of straight lines, 'I like round' she comments, 'curvaceous,' adds Dairmuid, thereby re-positioning her statement using a term so often used to encode the female body. Finally Laurence suggests that a steel pink pen that has been attached to the pin board really encapsulates Sharon; a 'curvy, pink and cunning' pen becomes the central image for the garden and interior makeover.

While Sharon is afforded the opportunity to project herself onto her home and garden her femininity is produced, framed and ultimately constrained within *Homefront: Inside Out.* In this way the programme demonstrates the fears and assumptions that career women, who are seen as transgressing the boundaries of femininity, often provoke. The team do acknowledge the career woman in their design – the stainless steel kitchen accessories offer a nod at Sharon's work persona – but ultimately there is a drive to locate Sharon within the private, the emotional and the domestic, in short to realise Sharon 'on the inside.' She is offered a particular gendered subject position within the programme, one that offers her the ameliorative potential to recognise and experience the softer, caring side of her essential nature. In the end Dairmuid's garden design becomes in part a reflection of the process of being circumscribed and bound by a particular version of femininity. The garden becomes soft, pink and curvaceous: hard landscaping is softened by the planting scheme of mauve foliage grasses, magenta roses and pink flowering shrubs; decking is used to replace 'hard' concrete areas and structures like the decking base for the dining area are circular rather than square. Thus, historical and cultural ideas about femininity are written into the process of realising the individual through the makeover of the garden and the garden literally becomes a feminised space. The garden experts provide a particular framework whereby a softer, caring subject position is offered and taken up in the process of Sharon's own subjective construction.

In her analysis of lifestyle cookery programmes, Strange (1998) argues that in the mid-1990s cookery experts Keith Floyd and Delia Smith were characterised by conventionally gendered modes of presentation. Moseley (Brunsdon et al., 2001) however, uses Jamie Oliver's persona to argue that lifestyle experts, by the late 1990s were beginning to outstep traditional gender roles. In this chapter I argue that personality-interpreters did represent a more diverse range of voices in terms of gender, class and age. However, as the example cited in this section shows: there was still a place within the lifestyle gardening media for highly conventional gendered images of gardening people, to such an extent that the garden became the epitome of typically gendered female space. The lifestyle media was prepared to show the interpretation of lifestyle ideas in 'real' gardens and as an institution it was showing signs of egalitarian change in terms of the representation of class and gender, but there was still progress to be made in the terrain of the cultural politics of class and gender.

Conclusion

My conclusion to chapter 4 argued that the history and location of the ordinary British garden and its gardeners was almost entirely missing from legislative enclaves. This chapter has shown that the media was an institutional site that acted progressively to erode the authority of garden legislators. Ordinary people did have a real stake in the garden lifestyle media and ordinary gardens had a respectable visual location in contemporary media texts. In this sense, ordinary people became central to the on-going construction of a mediated version of garden history. These changes however, must be seen in the context of the shift from civic to consumer culture Bauman (1987) describes. The ordinary people that found an embrace in 1990s lifestyle media were, as Moseley (Brunsdon et al. 2001, 33) describes, '*citizen*-consumers'; and the increased significance of interpretative ideas centred around the ordinary garden occurred as a result of the elevated authority of the market. These shifts contain an important caveat: ordinariness, in the 1990s, became an essential component of the political economy of the media; ordinariness was only embraced within the context of the popularity of lifestyle in consumer culture.

The 'ordinari-ization' strategies of the garden lifestyle media must be seen therefore, as part of the endless search the media industries were – and still are – prepared to make for increased market possibilities. Sentient of the fact that contemporary culture remains deeply stratified in terms of gender and social class, the media was, and in the main still has, retained the social locations of ordinariness for the purposes of efficient marketing and public relations. While garden lifestyle texts like *Homefront in the Garden* and *Howard Drury's Gardening Diary* were ordinary they were, for the purpose of reaching their intended consuming client group, classed and gendered products. And as this chapter shows, as conventionally classed and gendered products they incurred costs for both working-class and female audiences. National lifestyle texts of the 1990s carried an aversion to working-class culture and women were encouraged to adopt traditional modes of gendered being.

Yet despite these caveats, the increased presence of the representation of ordinariness was an important milestone for the lifestyle viewer. This chapter has also raised a number of positive ideas about the lifestyle media and the emancipatory potential it offered the ordinary viewer. For example, it has also been suggested that viewers retained their status as '*citizen*-consumers' (Brunsdon et al 2001) and in this sense the lifestyle media retained a civic, educational address. Lifestyling, as Chaney (2001) suggests, contains stabilising strands which enable people to cope with modernity. And ordinariness, as Felski (2000) asserts, has the potential to enable people to envisage and execute innovative responses to rapid social change.

Postscript: Where is the Garden Now?

'The death of TV make-overs: what next?' (MINTEL, Gardening Review, 2007)

Television genres and their hybrid off-shoots are continually evolving. At the time of writing, it is property shows that seem to be the most fashionable lifestyle component in today's daytime and terrestrial primetime schedules.[8] If lifestyle is about 'constructing projects of the self' (Bell and Hollows 2006, 4), then property accrual would seem to be one way in which value becomes attached to the middle-class self in the contemporary. Since the late 1990s, much has changed across the televisual landscape. An encapsulation of those changes is beyond what I can provide here, but some of the shifts in television production have signalled an end to the lifestyle makeover as it was. Some of its conventions – of transformation through expertise for example – have merged with reality formats to produce generic shifts in lifestyle television: hobbyist forms of television have given way to an over whelming preoccupation with the self (Palmer 2004; Wood and Skeggs 2004); the out-link to retail consumption that lifestyle make-over programmes once showcased has become a faded convention; and there has been an extension of the use of affect and emotion that characterised the 1990s 'surprise' makeover programmes (Aslama and Pantti 2006; Gorton 2008).[9]

In this way, television genres come and go and gardening lifestyle makeover programmes belong to a specific moment in television history. For, as I browse the early January terrestrial and main digital schedules – and it may have something to with the season – I can see the weight of MINTEL's (2007) assertion about the death of the make-over: garden lifestyle programmes have disappeared. It is not that the garden is entirely moribund on television or in the lifestyle media more generally.

---

8   For example, across January's 2008 primetime terrestrial schedule, Channel 4 is showing an hour long property show between 8-9 pm from Tuesday through to Friday. That includes: *Property Ladder, Relocation, Relocation, A Million Pound Place in the Sun*, and *A Place in the Sun: Home or Away*.

9   These shifts can be seen if one compares the changes in programme content from *What Not To Wear* (BBC1, 2002-) to *Trinny and Susannah Undress* (ITV, 2006-). In the latter, there is a deeper involvement in the relationship between the look, self-image and personal relationships of the makeover subjects and as a result, far more emphasis on emotions and psychological exploration.

.

The old staples continue: *Gardener's World* has remained a perennial; as has Radio 4's *Gardener's Question Time*. The weekend press both nationally, in say *The Guardian's* supplement *Weekend* and regionally in newspapers like *The Yorkshire Post,* still carry their features which contain lifestyle projects and both new and old gardening experts. Rather, it was that production slowed down, garden lifestyle for a time was televised as repeats in daytime and some evening scheduling, and was moved to satellite and digital channels from the early to mid 2000s. Garden lifestyle makeovers are now rare – a recent exception is Channel 5's independently produced *Nice House, Shame About the Garden* (Shine, 2005-). And the move to lifestyle/ reality formats is illustrated by Monty Don's attempt to break substance abuse by involving a group of drug-users in the on-going production of a working vegetable garden in *Growing Out Of Trouble* (BBC2, 2006-). Here the transformation of a land plot is melded together with the emotional highs and lows of keeping the team on the straight and narrow. So the garden, as a trope in British hobbyist culture is still located in traditional quarters; it is just not the lifestyle flavour of the month, rather – as *Growing Out of Trouble* illustrates – it is subject to the same generic principles as other lifestyle/reality formats.

Concomitantly garden centre retailing has contracted. According to MINTEL's latest report (2007), the market in garden products has declined in value since a peak in 2003. Estimated spending on garden products in 2002 stood at 5.65 £bn compared to a 10 per cent fall to 5.14 £bn in 2007. There has been a decline in spending around manufactured garden goods such as furniture, buildings and equipment, while the market for growing stock has remained steady – 'buoyed by a trend back towards "grow your own"' (MINTEL, 2007). This change may indicate the lack of what MINTEL (2001) named the 'Charlie Dimmock effect' of retailing and its relationship to television in the mid to late 1990s.

Yet more interesting, is the question of how the garden will be represented in future television programming. My argument about mid to late 1990s lifestyle was that while ordinary people were embraced as part of a mediated contemporary form of garden history – working-class aesthetics were marginal and working-class people and women were still subject to traditional forms of representation. However, recent garden programming has acted to contest arguments I have made both in this book and elsewhere (see Taylor, 2005) about how ordinary, working-class aesthetics had no place as valued practices in national television programming in the 1990s. *Christine's Garden* (BBC2, 2006-) for example, a 30 minute programme televised before *Gardener's World* on BBC2 in 2006, is about an ordinary middle-aged Lancastrian women who is incredibly enthusiastic about her own garden. Christine Walkden, a woman who clearly has no interest in performing conventional femininity for the camera, talks the viewer through her weekly ongoing pottering and seasonal projects; she is also shown as a gardener steeped in her local community, exchanging plants, skills and favours with her gardening neighbours in her street. Even more interestingly, the programmes are made at what Brunsdon has termed the 'realist end' of lifestyle programming (2003, 18), in that they make a slight return to the instructional by showing, at some points in real time, Christine helping to cut down a clematis for a neighbour or waiting indoors for a shower to pass before she can begin gardening again. The arguments I made about late 1990s national programming are rendered obsolete in relation to *Christine's Garden*: here are ordinary, local aesthetics given time and value on prime time national television. And while it is tempting to explain such programming as yet another extension of the political economy of television, *Christine's Garden*, with its ethos of gardening as a 'way of life', would be very appealing to the people who have made the ethnography in this book possible.

Chapter 6

Class, Taste and Gardening

Maud: I couldn't bear to live in a flat and not have access to …
Rosemary: Private land.

John: … whereas some people might 'ave a shit 'ole for a garden … then there's the other end in't the, what knows all the actual names o' the plants, botanical and all this stuff and to me that's not fun, that's just overboard.

Lisa: I've had failure with clematis myself.
Margaret: Me too. And then you go past those grotty houses on Heaton Avenue (a road on the nearby council estate) and see their success and you think, they won't look at it twice.

Lisa: Have you ever been influenced by gardening programmes?
Doris: Well you've to think of the expense and you can't, can you? There's certain things that you just can't enter into.

Introduction

This chapter empirically examines how people occupy and inhabit the social and cultural positions of class. Keeping ordinary practices and aesthetics at the forefront of the analysis, it asks if the garden is a site where identities of class are played out and if gardeners make aesthetic choices according to how they are positioned by class. I address these questions by attending to the facets identified by Felski's (2000) phenomenological approach to ordinariness in everyday life: its temporality through 'repetition', its grounding at 'home' and its rhythms of 'habit'.

I argue in this book that while ordinariness has been examined in relation to consumption practices (Gronow and Warde 1999) and with regard to class identities (Savage 1999, 2000a, 2000b, 2001, 2005) in sociological work, it has a history of being somewhat maligned in cultural studies, despite the commitment to ordinary people left by the legacy of early culturalism. Accounts of the history of the formation of cultural studies argue that there seems to have been no real attempt to get in touch with the grass-roots, lived vagaries and nuances of the humdrum, mundane aspects of ordinary peoples' lives (Murdock 1997; Walkerdine 1997). While at the CCCS the initial focus was on class formations, there is no evidence that anybody really attempted to build an organic working relationship either with working-class people or with the existing labour movement. Indeed the focus on class during the 1980s and early 1990s took the form of an intense analysis of the hegemonic appeal of Thatcherite Toryism and its effective construction of 'authoritarian populism', rather than on how 'real' people occupied the social and cultural positions of class during that time (Milner 1999). Studies about class it would seem, have fought shy of the attempt to understand the truly mundane elements of the everyday life of working-class people. What cultural studies has tended to do instead, according to Walkerdine (1997), is to concentrate on resistance and subcultural ritual in a way which has tended to reproduce the idea that only the politically conscious working-class are worthy of interest. Consequently, as Murdock argues the,

> focus on refusal and non-compliance left little room for an extended analysis of caution and conservatism. In the cultural studies' hall of mirrors the centre became the margin. As a result it was unable to offer a convincing account of continuity and inertia. It was strong on disruption but weak on reproduction (Murdock 1997, 180).

In this chapter, rather than treating those who conform to the rituals of ordinariness as worthless and uninteresting, I want to explore forms of culture that are not politically subversive, spectacular or exotic. I am interested in how 'classed' subjects live, survive and get by in the complexities of common practices like gardening. Intrigued by what the ordinary people of this study have to say about ordinariness as a truly mundane entity, I ask what role the endlessly repeated humdrum rituals and habits of gardening, located in a place called home, play in the formation of classed identities? The chapter is divided in to two sections: the first asks what gardening means to people and the following section explores aesthetic dispositions. Each section takes each class group in turn.

'I Like T' Compliments at T'End at T'Day': What Gardening Means

One of the key sites where cultural capital is located is in the language of gardening. The working-class gardeners I interviewed had a limited horticultural vocabulary. They lacked access to the cultural capital of gardening knowledge which meant that they would be unlikely to trade what they knew as an asset beyond the local level. Doris referred to shrubs as 'bushes'. Keith called perennials 'per-annuals'. Doris was only able to recall some of the common names of plants, for example 'red hot pokers'. Keith kept referring to the plants he was interested in as 'eye-catching', which became a euphemism for plant varieties that he either could not or did not feel the need to reference. Most of these gardeners did not possess the capital which inheres within particular forms of gardening knowledge; and if they had scant capital they tended not to recognise that it might have legitimacy. They were therefore unable to convert what meagre capital they had into symbolic capital.

For these gardeners, there was an awareness of the impact of gardening practices on the local community and alongside that a wish to please and to some extent to serve and bend to others wherever possible. Keith removed his privet hedge and replaced it with patterned blocks, partly because the privets were pushing his walls over, but also so that local drivers could safely see on-coming traffic at the t-junction on which his house was built. The working-class people of this study 'know their place' as gardeners within a community hierarchy in which they recognise themselves as followers of rules set by others. For example, several of the working-class gardeners gardened the council verge between the pavement and the street. This was seen as part of the community service that they envisaged their gardening to be about. In this way, as Keith's verge illustrates in Figure 6.1 (see also an illustration of Doris gardening her verge in Figure 1.1), the garden was not entirely conceived as a private space. Note how Keith's verge contains a wealth of perennial plants that require labour and care to maintain.

Generosity to other gardeners was very much a part of the enjoyment of the experience of gardening. Millie missed greenhouse gardening because growing large

Figure 6.1   Merging Public and Private Space: Keith's Council Verge

quantities of plants from seed meant there was always a surplus to give away. Keith's generosity was extraordinary: he 'passes on' annuals that he has grown from seed, 'that's a service you know, for friends, neighbours'; and splits herbaceous perennials for friends or admirers:

> **Keith**: I know there's a couple of people and they often come like, and say, "Oh it's doing well", you know, and I've often said, you know, "if you wait while later I'll split it and I'll bring you some over" and I always give them a good sample of soil as well and I tell them what position it's been in ... shady or well-drained ... try and get them the same sort of setting as what I've had.

He even offers to garden for local elderly gardeners. This ethos of helping others with the physical work of gardening and sharing seeds and plants comes from a history of conceptualising gardening as a community endeavour:

Keith: Well I think that's how it was done when I was young, I don't think it was too much that everyone went out and got packets of seeds, you know what I mean, … they used to swap plants did the neighbours and I think that's where I got it from.

Many of the gardens I visited amongst the working-class respondents were maintained by labour intensive means which in many cases meant hard physical work. And the gardeners themselves nurtured the idea that gardening is hard work;

Figure 6.2   Doris's High Standards of Care for her Sieved Soil, 1999

they believe the notion that keeping a garden requires regular laborious maintenance. This was often taken to quite extraordinary extremes. Doris, for example, actually gardens the texture of her soil, 'I hoe it, I do hoe. I like hoeing, you know, if there's been heavy rain it gets a little bit solid.' The close-up in Figure 6.2 shows very high standards of care taken to dig, weed, hoe and sieve the soil in to a very fine tilth. Doris was simply not satisfied until her soil resembled a fine crumb. Only constant, almost daily repetition of hoeing and sieving could produce such large areas of exposed yet 'crumbed' soil, since airborne seeds would be constantly settling onto such perfect germination tilth. Sure enough, she gardens daily and spends a large proportion of time weeding bare earth. Similarly, David builds on the idea of 'worked earth' by actually terming it 'clean earth'. Yet the achievement of 'clean earth' is extremely labour intensive, and David told me that his soil requires regular surveillance since open soil 'gets covered in weeds.' And there are other facets of gardening which require sheer hard work. Jack and Millie for example, invest a lot of time at particular times of year potting up bedding in tubs. After Keith's industrial accident he re-designed his garden so that he could easily access his beds, but this was not a bid to make life any easier since it simply meant he would open the way to work the soil more regularly. He could, 'go in and be able to hoe and weed…I can walk in now quite easily and I'm able to weed from either side.'

Yet despite gardening regimes which required the constant repetition of the circadian rhythms of routine tasks such as weeding, gardening was described as a pleasure by all the working-class gardeners. All said that gardening was 'enjoyable', and 'rewarding' and gave a 'sense of pleasure'. Unsurprisingly only one woman said that gardening was 'relaxing'. In relation to this, comments, in particular praise from passers-by, are given a great deal of significance and indeed contribute highly to the pleasure that gardening offers them. What working-class people think of their publicly visible space is extremely important to them. Pleasure comes from knowing that when their gardens are seen by others they meet approval.

> **Doris**: And I don't let any weeds grow. One of my friends says (laughs) oh I'd better (looking at cassette recorder) he says, "I always look to see if I can find any Doris and I can never find a weed in your garden" (laughs). He uses strong language but I won't say what he says … and so I think caring for it makes a difference.

Millie and Jack have a shared garden and they recognise that as retired residents they have more time to garden than the people who work full-time in their block. The praise that they get for taking full responsibility is clearly very important to them, 'It's nice when people admire it and I mean the people that live here as well, always comment on how nice its looking … they appreciate the work that we've put into it.' Keith is embarrassed when he admits that praise is very significant for him, 'I know it might sound vain but I like t' compliments at end of t' day.' Indeed for these gardeners there was a self-conscious recognition on their part that a well-kept garden signifies something to passers-by about the up-keep of the house that accompanies it.

> **Jack**: I think, I've always thought this with houses, if the garden's nice, you're guaranteed the house is nice and tidy…You know if you go and look at a house and the garden has a kitchen sink in it, you have an idea about what it's going to look like inside.

Indeed for others a tidy garden even says something about the people who keep it.

> **Keith**: It's an extension of the house, really, and the people who live in it…I think if people can see your garden's tidy then they think your house is tidy. I mean it might seem cosmetic but really you know really at the end of the day if you reflect that you're capable of looking after plants and various bits and pieces then you're capable of doing things, you know, animals and anything, you know.

> **Lisa**: So it says something about you as a person?

> **Keith**: Oh yes, it does, you know, it shows you're caring to some degree.

These comments show that these people see and invest in their gardens as a means of signalling their capability, their worth as people. These comments also reveal an awareness of the judgement of others and alongside that a knowledge that they might be positioned as inferior or inadequate. The garden is the interface between home and the street and as such it holds a particular significance; it can act as a marker of respectability to others who might miss out on seeing that the inside of the home is tidy and by extension – clean. It therefore becomes the site by which they are able to tell others in their local community that they are that part of the working-class who know how to manage the up-keep of the home. The following exchange shows an awareness that there are particular kinds of 'scruffy' garden that should be avoided and that particular times of year prompt increased vigilance for John and Stephanie:

> **John**: I don't like right long grass. To me it looks scruffy. If my lawn were long grass, I'd cut it, just to cut it down.
>
> **Stephanie**: If I've left it I've been ashamed. I'd think oh next door's gonna think, "get out and do it."
>
> **Lisa**: Are you conscious that people look?
>
> **Stephanie**: Oh definitely! An' we 'ave, in May when we 'ave t'elections, *everybody* walks up and down for elections, don't they John?
>
> **John**: Aye and they look in t'garden.
>
> **Stephanie**: An' they stop an' look in ours, don't they? An' they say "Oh that's nice, I like that." To me, if you bother with your garden it shows, really…
>
> **John**: It shows on yer 'ouse.
>
> **Stephanie**: It shows yer house is, you bother with your house as well. If you've got a scruffy garden, if I look in what I call a scruffy garden, someone who can't be bothered, they show that they can't .. that their house is gonna be t'same. It's like *Keeping up Appearances* on tv. You look at their garden and you know t'ouse is gonna be t'same 'cos they just can't be bothered.

These gardens are regulated to ensure that those who judge from the outside cannot regard those inside as ones who do not know how to 'care' for the inside. Keith made it clear that his act of giving plants away was predicated upon knowing that the people he gave plants to would be responsible enough to care for them. In doing so he expresses doubts about other members of his class who might turn out to not care. On offering to put a plant in the garden for a neighbour,

> **Keith**: I says "well do you want some of these?" he says "alright" he says, "well yeah, just stick 'em in and I'll look after them." And that's important, if they're gonna look after them that's fair enough.

For the middle-class respondents gardening is regarded quite differently. There was a 'given' confidence about stating the value of gardens as well as an assumption that I would recognise the various types of value that were ascribed. For Rosemary gardening first and foremost is about 'having a love of plants.' There was also a different vocabulary for describing garden space. Often gardens were referred to as 'land'. Some used the acreage of their land as a descriptor of their garden, 'The garden is about one and a half acres,' Hugo told me. And Rosemary said, 'We've always had land':

Maud: I couldn't bear to live in a flat and not…

Rosemary: Have any private land (laughs).

Maud: … be able to open your door and walk into the garden. Gardening just comes naturally when you've lived in the country.

In these ways, the garden was implicitly regarded as both a cultural and a property asset and, as Savage et al. remind us, what characterises the historical formation and reproduction of the British middle-class is its ability to recognise, store and transmit such assets (Savage et al. 1992, 17).

The middle-class gardeners had access to the resources horticultural knowledge affords and this took various forms. Several of them were entirely at ease with the Latin nomenclature of plant species and genus and this was exchanged quite casually in everyday conversation. 'We're fond of viburnums,' Hugo told me 'but we also have lots of the usual: cotoneaster, pyracantha, spiraea, philadelphus …'. David, a biology teacher at the local grammar school was interested in plant reproduction and disease, so he was able to speak with confidence about plant 'stamens' and 'ovaries' and processes such as 'photosynthesis'. And Anne and Phoebe were interested in the medicinal uses of herbs and they were very knowledgeable about some of the poisonous chemical constituents of herbs and plants. In short, these gardeners were conversant with the kinds of gardening cultural capital that could be exchanged for high returns in the 'right' circles.

Interestingly, in contrast to the working-class gardeners – who clearly valued and worked hard to maintain both the friendship links, through plant exchange and the look of the street by having a tidy garden – the middle-class gardeners left the local community unmentioned. What mattered to them was the establishment of social links *beyond* the local. Indeed these gardeners by varying degree have accrued social capital: Maud and Rosemary were members of the Northern Horticultural Society, (note too that the following remark demonstrates a social link with someone in the legal profession) 'Well it was Mr Inneson, Mr. Inneson the solicitor who invited Pop to join, so we've always maintained it since.' Maud had a long-standing relationship with flower arranging societies, 'I first went on my flower course in 1957,' she told me, 'and I went to the Constance Sprye School for a five day course which they put on for teachers.' Almost all the middle-class gardeners I interviewed mentioned that they had purchased plants at Harlow Carr (based in Harrogate, with all the class connotations that Harrogate brings). And several of them mentioned purchasing plants at certain specialist garden centres. Indeed for some purchasing plants was described as a form of connoisseurship:

Thomas: What we'll try to do in the garden is something that I'm finding now with woodwork and also buying wine, is that you try to get the best of the type…for example, we don't just go to the nearest nursery and buy the cheapest plant.

Also in contrast to the working-class gardeners, who embraced the almost daily routine of garden labour as hard work, the middle-class gardeners discursively avoided ever referring to gardening as work. The middle-class gardeners I spoke to tended to gloss over the idea of labour by naming it as some other function, it was always more than just labour as a means to achieve an end: gardening was 'relaxing' or 'good exercise', digging was described as 'therapeutic' and Anne and Phoebe said that they used gardening as a means of 'procrastinating'.

And, unlike the working-class people of this study who were perpetually alerted to the idea that critical others lay in constant judgement of the order of their gardens, the middle-class gardeners made absolutely no mention of what other people, *at the local level*, might think of them. But it would be a step too far to claim that they had no care about what some people thought of them: for they demonstrated to me that they were skilled at the art of display, it was just that they were concerned to showcase their requisite capitals.

As this section of my study shows, class location made a significant difference to what everyday gardening means to people. In Bourdieusian terms, the working-class gardeners of the community had a paucity of legitimate capital assets. Lacking in formal education, they had virtually no references to cultural capital. The kinds of legitimate tastes recommended by the journalists of the time, such as Monty Don or Christopher Lloyd or personality-interpreters such as Anne McKevitt held no real interest for these gardeners. Antiquated forms of knowledge, such as Latin names had no place in their everyday lives – indeed these gardeners had no real horticultural vocabulary through which to express nationally legitimised garden capital. Their social capital was meagre or non-existent. As a result, their forms of knowledge, based as they were on local reference points became investments on which they could trade. These gardeners had built a strong sense of community garden giving; seeds were swapped and cuttings were exchanged across family, friends, neighbours and even passers-by. But while these practices had great value at the local level, they had limited value and were virtually untradeable beyond the immediate community. In these ways, these working-class people were not intent on accumulating forms of value to themselves as forms of investment – like the middle-class gardeners did. Rather, they valued themselves and honoured members of their local community through dignified forms of gardening labour, through tilling the soil with extremely high standards of care and through caring about presenting competent, decent selves through their gardens with a view to making value in the present moment.

Yet while the working-class gardeners had a dearth of nationally legitimised capitals, local community links were tremendously valuable for the working-class gardeners. Care, generosity and mutual self help that are extended through routine garden practices, are characteristics that both Hoggart (1957) and Williams (1989) sought to value in their historiographies of the working-class in the 1950s. Williams, for example, saw working-class investment in the community as a positive impetus against competitive and individualistic middle-class society. And despite Savage's

(2000b) argument that people no longer feel themselves to belong to a class in a collective sense, the collective capacity to generate shared practices – of swapping plants, or consideration of the impact of their planting schemes or hard landscaping on the wider community – is still alive in working-class enclaves of contemporary British culture. *Locally generated* practices of giving and contributing to the community using gardening was a valued competence.

But while some ordinary habits and routines were experienced positively, the habits formed in response to the upkeep of the garden, and its attendant practices of daily tidying, were indicative of more deeply felt anxieties. Given the history of how the working-class have been perceived and represented historically (see chapter 2) – as a degenerate, fecund, savage and irresponsible mass – this should not surprise us. My study reveals that these gardeners were well aware of the pejorative associations potential onlookers harboured about the capability and worth of the working-class and they fought a battle to keep such associations at bay. As my ethnographic evidence shows, for my respondents, the look – particularly of the front garden – acts as a tangible signifier of both the home interior and value and capability of the people inside. In response to the need to strive for respectability, ordinary gardening routines were devoted to the perpetual maintenance of a tidy, ordered garden. Keeping the garden tidy was repeatedly mentioned as a desirable entity by the working-class gardeners. Leaving the garden uncultivated generates powerful emotions; to be sure, the will to dis-identify with members of the working-class who 'can't be bothered' generates powerful emotions, 'if I've left it,' Stephanie told me, 'I've been ashamed.' Therefore many of the routines of ordinary gardening, for the working-class men and women of my study, were born out of a sense of anxiety and insecurity to both refuse pejorative associations about being working-class and to ensure that others recognise their respectability. Indeed as the following section demonstrates, ordinary routines of tidiness even took on an aesthetic function for the working-class gardener.

On the other hand, gardening for middle-class respondents was a pursuit into which they made high investments, especially in relation to cultural and social capital. Several of my middle-class respondents, for example, were retired teachers or they had university qualifications; they were therefore already endowed with measures of institutionalised cultural capital. More pertinently, they were often able to generically extend their knowledges out to the garden: one respondent – a retired biology teacher from the local grammar school was able to speak with authority about the reproductive features of plants; another, a fine art graduate, was able to carry her knowledge of the most consecrated compartment of the arts qualifications – art history – to her choice and consumption of decorative garden ornaments. And the ease with which they drew on Latin nomenclature showed that these respondents used their habitus to recognise the power which inheres in certain forms of knowledge and how it should be displayed. The language and advice of those with legitimate garden tastes in the media – writers such as Christopher Lloyd, whose journalism always uses the Latin before the common plant name – was accessible to these gardeners. They were in possession of social capital: they were members of horticultural societies and national floristry training schools and they took care to purchase plants and seeds through specialist outlets or botanical societies. In one interview encounter for example, I was told by Maud that a solicitor had encouraged their father to join the Northern Horticultural Society. This kind of detail, carefully hammocked around our discussion of society membership, confers and slightly increases the volume of social capital owned by the speaker. These gardeners had social capital, but they were also very keen to ensure that I should recognise it – as this search to bolster social capital illustrates. Nonetheless, the middle-class gardeners understood that their endowments in the visible outdoor space between the house and the road would be reconvertible to the most powerful species of capital – symbolic capital. This meant that their garden assets were acknowledged as socially distinctive at the local level, but also that they were recognised and valued as national assets beyond the reach of the local community.

Indeed at the local level, the middle-class gardeners were uninterested in the idea of ordinary community activities at the micro level. They never mentioned giving or swapping plants or of gardening beyond their own gardens. Indeed the only local gardening activities they invested in were institutionalised by being linked to club membership. In the case of my study this took the form of the *Spen Valley Flower Club*, a society organised and governed by middle-class gardeners and flower arrangers Rosemary and Maud. The kinds of events which were available – flower arranging events and competitions, visits to historic gardens and 'lunches' – reflected conservative middle-class tastes and pursuits; indeed, membership promoted a form of local social capital. In relation to their own gardens, however, the middle-class gardeners seemed untouched by the idea that their practices impacted on others. Several of them were more concerned with the idea that the garden was a private space and the right to privacy – linked as it is to the idea of the private ownership of assets – has always been a preserve belonging to the bourgeoisie (Savage et al. 1992). Hence Rosemary and Maud considered their land to be 'private' and the gardeners I spoke to constructed their gardens as private spaces. As Phoebe told me; 'because the garden is overlooked on two sides, it needed breaking up to become more secluded.' Already endowed with middle-class confidence, these middle-class gardeners were free from the anxiety of continually tidying the public space between the public road and their house, for they were already in comfortable possession of what the working-class gardeners strove hard to secure: respectability.

'It's Just Neat and Tidy and a Bit of Colour': Aesthetic Dispositions

When I asked the working-class gardeners if they were attempting to generate a particular garden ethos which might in some way tie in with the look of the house – I asked, for example, if they were attempting to create a 'cottage-garden feel' (see Appendix 1), it was in many cases as though I had asked a question about a possibility that had never occurred to them. They lacked the cultural capital which would have enabled them to draw on historical and architectural knowledges as a means to 'place' their houses and their gardens accordingly. As a consequence, they were denied the competencies required to design or generate a garden in keeping with planting schemes or features which displayed a knowledge of historical design antecedents.

They had no sense of aiming towards a particular garden ethos or reference point, indeed James said that he had 'no plan' the garden was 'haphazard'.

In terms of planting and plant preferences these gardeners shared a love of bedding plants; clearly prized, they were always mentioned first as the plants that were repeatedly purchased and always appreciated. Often these were used in the garden or there was a tendency to use them in hanging baskets and tubs, Figure 6.3 for example, shows a line of bedding plants in tubs in James's garden, an aesthetic feature typical of the working-class garden. One of the reasons why these plants were valued was because they provided a lot of colour as well as a range of different colours for the garden. The use of multi-colour, or placing all colours alongside each other, or as Millie described it using 'colour bunched together' was also an aesthetic tendency. Indeed while the gardeners clearly used other plants such as perennials and shrubs, as plants which contributed to planting schemes, they were rarely mentioned with the same enthusiasm as bedding plants.

Figure 6.3   A Typical Working-Class Aesthetic Feature: James's Bedding Plants in Tubs, 1999

Lacking nationally legitimated historical knowledges about garden design, the working-class gardeners tended to design their gardens in ways which 'fitted in' with the rest of the street. In this way, they used the shared aesthetic codes which had been generated locally as a reference for their own design plans. As identified by the early culturalists, the working-class gardeners still held on to locally produced shared practices and collective meanings with regard to their garden designs. When I asked these gardeners what they didn't like or what they would never consider doing in their own gardens, their answers testified to a reluctance to break the gardening patterns established by the rest of the local neighbourhood. As Keith's comments below show, there is a collective agreement on where vegetables are locally placed in his area: to break this code is to offend local sensibilities:

> **Keith**: If there was more area around the back here I think more people might be tempted to grow vegetables but I think with it being a row of terraced and everybody has a garden and you tend to sort of fit in with everybody else.

> **Lisa**: And you wouldn't want to grow veg in the front garden?

> **Keith**: Well no I don't, I mean it may be unsightly to some people. They might think, "What a strange place to put them."

But the most important aesthetic to the working-class gardeners, which became a constant feature, was that above all else a garden must be tidy. Millie repeatedly refers to the importance of keeping the garden 'just so'. For her the compliments she receives are predicated upon the garden's tidiness, 'Oh they comment yes, because it's nice and tidy. I like it to be kept looking tidy.' Keith told me, 'I like to have it neat and tidy,' and that his wife 'likes to see a nice tidy garden'. For Doris tidiness is an imperative, 'you know, you think, "Oh I'd better have it nice and tidy".' The fact that the tidiness of her garden had been noticed was a source of great pride, of a passing neighbour, she told me: 'he says, "This is the tidiest piece of Westcliffe Road", He always used to say that.' Indeed keeping the garden tidy became an endlessly repeated mantra: John: 'we like it to be tidy'; Stephanie: 'It's tidy, it's tidy'; Philip:

Figure 6.4 'Clean Earth' Between the Plants, 1999

'we look after it and keep it tidy'; Geoff: 'Oh it is tidy, we like it that way.' Indeed, the tidiness that I witnessed manifested itself in a number of ways: manicured lawns, immaculately swept paths (Millie: 'you know soil falls over, you know, I always sweep up'), totally weed-free crumbed 'clean' earth, tightly clipped hedges and shrubs shaped into spheres or squares. As you can see in Figure 6.4, some of these gardeners felt the need to see gaps between plants and shrubs so that they could be certain there were no stray leaves, no lurking weeds, no soil out of place on a paving stone, no unruly 'overgrown' plants outstretching their allotted place: in short that no area of the garden escaped their supervision. Routines of ordinariness were about these acts of surveillance: of looking, bending and relocating garden elements in to their rightful places. This made at times for a rather bleak and barren aesthetic. Lawns scorch if kept too short in summer and plants are clipped into atomised, spherical shapes between sieved tilth. Indeed there was a marked concern with the texture of the soil, 'I like to see that the soil's nice and lifted up and aerated, it doesn't want to be soggy and flat and that with all plants…I like to see a space in between them.

By contrast the middle-class gardeners were conscious of creating a particular kind of garden. Thomas and Lena claimed that their garden was deliberately designed to be 'informal' and they described their garden as a 'shrub garden'. Rosemary and Maud described their garden as 'an English garden – not a formal garden' – a categorisation which testifies to an understanding of what constitutes a formal garden within garden history. And while Hugo and Margaret said that their garden was 'hotch-potchy' they had deliberately chosen to create a herb garden.

There was also a consciousness on their part about the aesthetics of planting and of the way in which garden features could contribute to an overall aesthetic feel. Rosemary told me that her planting schemes in the garden came from her knowledge as a flower arranger, 'So if you look in the garden there's colour, form and texture… so a lot of the plants are unusual plants because they're there for foliage and for the colour and for the form.' Figure 6.5 shows the contrasting shrubbery which characterises their border; note the carefully planned complimentary differences between foliage and flowers and how knowledge of plant height and depth are planned to create a staggered border. Rosemary demonstrated a deliberate theme in terms of the kinds of plants she had chosen to plant, 'we don't grow anything rigid, we look for soft forms.' In a similar vein Anne and Phoebe, both graduates in fine art and graphic design respectively saw aesthetic beauty in the old, overgrown herbs in their garden. Anne described a lavender as 'lovely and overgrown' and spoke of the 'wonderful texture' of the woody base of the rosemary. More generally there was more of an emphasis on foliage than on flowers; two or three respondents commented that the colour of their gardens offered different shades of green.

These gardeners were not interested in using the kinds of garden sculptures or ornaments that might be purchased in local garden centres as features. But some of them did value old things – either old features of their houses or old objects and these acted as garden ornaments. In these ways, antique items lent a sense of history to the aesthetic feel of middle-class gardens. Anne told me that she had a plaster cast of the Virgin Mary that was being thrown away after the nativity play at the local church, which was now positioned in the herb garden. She also has an 'old brazier', 'rusting

Figure 6.5   Contrasting Shrubbery in Rosemary and Maud's Garden

nicely' in to a 'beautiful orange'. The antique authenticity of these objects finds a welcome place in these gardens.

For these gardeners certain plants are valued, others are not. Among the plants that are esteemed were perennials such as delphiniums, herbs, particular flowering shrubs and certain bulbs 'tulips, crocuses, aconites, snowdrops, species crocus, grandiflora crocus' (Rosemary). None of the middle-class gardens I visited showed any investment in bedding plants and such plants went unmentioned, indeed for some of them there was a continual insistence that bedding plants were undesirable. 'We don't bed out' I was told by Rosemary, 'life's too short to be bedding out.'

These gardens were not tidy, in fact tidiness was scorned by some of these gardeners. Anne commented:

> **Anne**: I don't like particular cultivated things, I like a garden to look like a garden and not be all patches and crisp.
>
> **Lisa**: So you're not bothered about tidiness?
>
> **Anne**: No, no, definitely not, I like rusty bits of metal in the garden.

Similarly Rosemary and Maud quite clearly wished to dissociate themselves from tidy gardening. Rosemary and Maud had areas of the garden where bits of garden equipment were simply left in fairly haphazard piles, in effect, niches of regulated untidiness. In line with this there was a denial or a de-emphasis on gardening labour; these gardeners were unconcerned that there were some untidy niches and plants were encouraged to have their form and in return covering the ground meant that gardeners did not have to spend hours policing the garden for weeds.

Bourdieu (1986) argues that the middle-class makes deliberate moves to distance itself from working-class practices and aesthetics, such moves are inherent in practices of social distinction. And as Savage (2000b) argues, even though people are more ambivalent about their class identity, class is still used as a measuring device to 'place' people and it affects peoples' approach to others. In line with these arguments, tidiness – recognised as an undesirable practice – was spurned by my middle-class respondents precisely because of its association with gardens in working-class districts. Indeed on one occasion, I witnessed an act of symbolic violence as Maud and Rosemary talked about their scorn for tidy gardens in the presence of Doris, who strives daily for an impeccably tidy garden:

Maud: We've some friends whose gardens are just like their houses. Nothing out of place. Too tidy.

Lisa: Right…

Maud: (laughs) You've got that. (laughs) We'll never be like that. You're not one are you? (looking at Doris who doesn't reply – laughs)

Rosemary: They dust and sweep them.

Lisa: Are you not so interested in being tidy?

Maud: Have a look around.

Rosemary: We're doers (laughs).

Maud: We've had to move all these papers (meaning newspapers).

Rosemary: Well if you plant to run into each other the weeds can't grow can they? If you've open land you've got to keep weeding. And if you have hot summers then the water evaporates from the open land.

Rosemary and Maud, confident about the legitimation of their own garden aesthetics feel quite at ease talking about the kinds of (working-class) aesthetics they never wish to be associated with – 'we'll never be like that.' Using their pedagogic authority, they recognise that anxious tidiness has no tradeable value. And at the point in the interview where Maud asks Doris, 'you're not one are you?' was a particularly painful moment, since Doris, is *precisely* 'one' of those working-class gardeners that Maud and Rosemary wish to distance themselves from. Doris surely felt embarrassment and pain in recognition that her own tastes were being devalued. She knew that to foreground her gardening style would not engender approval and in acknowledgement of her own lack of gardening knowledge she chose to keep silent. In these ways symbolic violence operates in the most mundane settings to mark the dominance and desirability of middle-class cultural values and to stamp out working-class tastes as unthinkable.

Indeed there were other aesthetic choices that middle-class gardeners made that testified to a deliberate will to reject working-class garden practices. In direct contrast to the desire for clean earth to be on show, the middle-class gardeners concurred on the need to encourage plants to cover the soil. Thomas used pseudo-scientific language to describe what he called his 'close bostitch system'[1] of allowing plants to grow until their tips were touching. Indeed, bare earth is the enemy of the middle-class gardener, as Phoebe told me, 'it wants covering with plants.'

Rather the emphasis in these gardens is on an aesthetics of 'informality' which means allowing plants to find their 'natural way'. Plants, I was told, should run into each other and spill out over lawns, shrubs should be allowed to grow into the form nature intended them to take and if leaves fall so be it. Rosemary and Maud's catmint for example, spilled over their lawn. Alongside that these gardeners wanted their garden to be 'absolutely full'. And these gardeners know what they don't want their gardens to look like. For example, Rosemary and Maud were very clear that they did not have a rockery – another undesirable working-class trope – in their garden. In the following exchange, I mistakenly identified a rockery, but I was roundly corrected:

> **Lisa**: And you've got rockery areas, haven't you? Like this for example (gesturing out through the patio doors).
>
> **Rosemary**: Not really, it's a retaining wall. It's not really a rockery.
>
> **Lisa**: Ok.
>
> **Rosemary**: If you're looking at a rockery, It's not that.

As I looked out at the garden, I was asked to re-position my thinking so as to recognise the more desirable 'retaining wall' in front of me. In fact, at Rosemary and Maud's I was invited during the garden tour, to compare their desirably chosen (middle-class) garden with their neighbours' undesirable garden which could be seen by looking carefully through the border. The difference, as Rosemary outlines and as Figure 6.6 illustrates, lies in the use of garden aesthetics:

> **Lisa**: So what you're saying is that you don't trim everything into a particular shape, you're not interested in making everything pristine
>
> **Rosemary**: Well look at next door's.
>
> **Maud**: (laughs)
>
> **Rosemary**: …and you've no form. You go out there and have a look. There's no form. Now a tree isn't rounded like a ball.
>
> **Lisa**: So you're saying that you work with natural forms and you put them together and allow them to work.

---

1   While I have never heard of the term 'bostitch system', Thomas used it to refer to the practice of close planting to keep weeds out of the garden.

Figure 6.6   'There's no Form': Looking Past Rosemary and Maud's Garden, 1999

Rosemary: and you can go and see that wonderful example by going out of there and onto our garden…you can see three illustrations of what a garden can be like …and I'll tell you why they've done it when you've had a look at them, make your own mind up. It's quite an interesting exercise out there.

As this section has demonstrated, there were profound differences in terms of the garden aesthetics the men and women of this study were able to generate. As a result of their paucity of cultural capital, the working-class gardeners had no historical or architectural reference points, and so the creation of a garden set within a known tradition, which they might have created in keeping with the ethos of the architectural moment of their homes, was beyond them. As a result, they turned to locally visible aesthetics; 'fitting in' with everybody else in the street offered a safe enough design. Moreover in the realm of plants, working-class gardeners, as Bourdieu argues in relation to aesthetics, had no recognition of form. The plants they most valued were bedding plants – but they were not interested in the form of these plants. Rather, plants such as petunias, impatiens, marigolds, plants which form the paintbox for the park gardener working on a municipal display, were required for colour. Colour – a riot of colour, multi-colours, colours 'all bunched up' – was what plants were there to provide. A plant's *function* was to provide colour for the gardener in the most valued places such as tubs and hanging baskets. Such plants served the function of ensuring the garden tantalised the observer with the pure sensation of colour as opposed to the artistic/intellectual blend of form. Moreover colour in abundance was often key to this kind of aesthetic; where an investment was made in bedding plants, they were used in quantity in order to maximise the sensation of colour. And, almost in direct opposition to the middle-class aesthetic, plants were subordinate to the whims of the gardener: the working-class aesthetic was about managing the form of shrubs and trees to ensure that there was no danger of 'take over'. Rather than allowing the natural form of plants to proliferate, some of these gardeners drew on a manner of clipping shrubs or plants into tight shapes. In the realm of aesthetics, the people of my study simply lacked the capital assets to recognise or access the resources required to accrue legitimate capital. Alongside the sensationalist abundance of colour, the working-class gardeners tended to lay emphasis on garden practices which made the best of what they had. Keeping the garden tidy by weeding, clearing leaves, hoeing the soil, sweeping paths or raking the tilth are practices which make few demands on economic resources. At the same time, they are also activities which overlaid the garden with signs of care and decency; indeed as Bourdieu argues in relation to working-class aesthetics, the garden took on a moral function for these gardeners. Their garden habitus was akin to the approach described by Bourdieu in *Distinction*; the French working-class lifestyle was based on 'a virtue made of necessity' (Bourdieu 1984, 177). Unable to make outward investments which accrue capital beyond the local, they turned to investments that the middle-class gardeners could already guarantee as a given: respectability. Neat and tidy order, having the garden, 'just so' as several of my respondents described, was a means to keep the garden respectable, for as Skeggs argues:

> Respectability is usually the concern of those who are not seen to have it…It is rarely recognised as an issue by those who are positioned with it, who are normalised by it, and who do not have to prove it. Yet for those who feel positioned by and position themselves against the discourse of respectability it informs a great deal of their responses (Skeggs 1997, 1).

For working-class people, as Skeggs asserts, respectability becomes a form of symbolic capital at the local level. Tidiness, an entity which all my working-class respondents valued, was an index of respectability. Generating order, having everything observably neat and tidy was an important element in the working-class aesthetic garden vocabulary. It was one of the (working-class) aesthetic practices which middle-class respondents both recognised and sought to distance themselves from.

In contrast to the working-class gardeners, the middle-class respondents had a sense of generating a garden with a particular ethos. Using their knowledge of garden history, they were able to at least partially set their gardens within particular traditions, for example of 'formality' or 'informality'. While my middle-class respondents could not be described as having a Kantian approach to garden aesthetics, the ethos of their planting was underpinned by a strong sense of form. While these gardeners were working with living referents as opposed to the textuality of signs, some of them were well acquainted with using plant form in a painterly manner. Companion planting – a method advocated by Christopher Lloyd – which requires a skilful understanding of how to blend the colour, tactility and lifelong architecture of plants, was pivotal to the ethos of some of the gardens I visited. In these ways, the middle-class gardeners are located within the boundaries of Bourdieu's description of legitimate taste: appreciation of the form of plants could be enjoyed just as one might appreciate Leonardo's use of chiaroscuro light effects or Seurat's use of the pointillist technique. These gardeners understood that they were generating an aesthetic visual plane using plant form as their materials, but the form of the plants took precedence over their function. In similar vein, these gardeners had a learned belief in an aesthetic of 'naturalness': plants must be given free rein to develop their forms as nature intended – the challenge therefore was to use the materials while holding respect for the form. Indeed the conservatism of their approach was reminiscent of the Darwinian aesthetics advocated by Willy Lange in late nineteenth century Germany – aesthetics subsequently adopted by the National Socialists (see chapter 4). The appreciation of form, as Bourdieu (1986, 1990) argues, was the cornerstone of the middle-class approach to aesthetics: it enabled them to spatially exhibit their legitimate tastes and cultural capital.

As my ethnographic evidence also highlights, the middle-class gardeners understood how to use strategies of social distinction in relation to ordinary gardening practices. By denigrating working-class planting aesthetics – tight clipping, bedding plants and anxious tidying – they worked to continually locate themselves in differential terms as anything but working-class. One can see the same moves to differentiate away from working-class aesthetics in middle-class garden writing. The confident judgemental tone which characterises Christopher Lloyd's writing, for example, is reminiscent of the voices of my middle-class respondents. In the garden instruction manual *The Well-Chosen Garden* (1984) Lloyd points out undesirable plants and planting practices; in short unhappy combinations which can come about as the result of insufficient knowledge or bad judgement. Monotony of form might be one error or companion planting which is ill-conceived might turn out to produce an 'indigestible bellyful' (Lloyd 1984, 40). Then there are plants themselves which embody bad taste: Lloyd tells the reader to avoid the 'crude pink' of the bedding plant ivy geranium, to steer clear of over-powering 'coarse and muscular' daffodils and to find methods to curtail certain plants prone to 'thuggery' or infiltration. These plants are like their working-class correspondents; they're out on the streets, they're tough and ill-disciplined and they're reproductively rampant. And there are modes of being in the garden, here presented as startlingly akin to the practices I found in working-class gardens, which are also undesirable. The 'ordinary' gardener (unclassed by Lloyd, but who is identifiably working-class), insufficiently knowledgeable about plants to ever 'get it right', is prone to obsessional policing practices: 'The inter-locking and weaving of plants … will rarely be met where orderliness is of the essence and every plant is allowed its place but no more. Thus the hoe is kept busy round each border clump and the next. There has to be a line of demarcating soil between one clump and the next' (Lloyd 1984, 26). And later, 'some lawn and neatness enthusiasts (they are never true plant lovers) take enormous pride in this discontinuity … lawn; cliff-edge; well-weeded border margin of clean earth; then your first border plants, neat things like annual alyssum' (Lloyd 1984, 28). The working-class gardener too uptight to sit back and think critically about their practices is prone to tidying madness, later for example, keeping a tiled roof free of mosses is described as a 'mania' (Lloyd 1984, 92). Lloyd's writing, which is devoted to castigating working-class gardening practices, is almost mirrored in the aesthetics dispositions of the middle-class gardeners I spoke to. The middle-class garden aesthetic is comprised of a set of identifiable gardening characteristics, the use of perennials, shrubs and trees in naturalistic arrangements for example, but it is also comprised of aesthetics which are formed *out of a will to reject working-class practices*. The conscious will to create untidy niches and to reject rockeries and bedding plants show that the middle-class aesthetic disposition is formed out of acts of symbolic violence; being untidy or rejecting particular plants were practices that working-class gardeners simply lacked the confidence to perform.

Conclusion

This chapter argues that while the gardeners I studied were anchored to the ordinary practices identified by Felski (2000), *class located* what gardening meant for them and it made profound differences to the aesthetic practices they were able to generate. Using the explanatory power of Bourdieu's theories, it argues that practices of social distinction still abound in mundane cultural settings. For the working-class people of this study, gardening was underpinned by the need to secure respectability and this was manifest in the aesthetic practice of tidiness that pervaded the look of their gardens. Lacking capital assets at the national level, they designed their gardens using locally generated principles and acts of community garden giving were awarded prominence. Higher modicums of capital for the middle-class gardeners, on the other hand, meant that they had nationally legitimate competencies which enabled them to design their gardens and develop an aesthetic using horticultural and historical knowledges. In recognition that their capitals had currency beyond the local, they sought to display, trade and reconvert their capitals. Already endowed with respectability, their aesthetic principles were constructed out of a will to distance themselves from undesirable working-class aesthetic practices. Savage (2000b) argues that in contemporary culture, people no longer announce an identification with class as a collective entity. In line with Savage's contention, the gardeners of this study never claimed a classed identity based on their gardening practices. However, as Savage (2000b) also argues, class is embedded in people's sense of self value, it is recognised and used as a measuring device which acts to 'position' people and it affects peoples' approach to others. In these senses this chapter argues that class pervades both the garden as a site and gardening as a set of symbolic aesthetic practices.

This book is based on a small-scale study, which can make no wide claims in terms of gardening practices and class. However, my subjects identified themselves as relating to class based groups according to collective gardening practices and aesthetics. Indeed, in this sense my findings tend to show the limitations of habitus as a conceptual tool – since in so many respects, my data shows a good deal of commonality in relation to how people use the garden as an identity marker. In an important critical essay, Longhurst and Savage (1996) argue that in *Distinction* Bourdieu is intent on seeking out variation in consumption practices, as opposed to uncovering how 'commonality and solidarities are forged between people' (1996,

275). People, they argue, have more complicated and contradictory consumer practices than is implied by habitus, in which Bourdieu conceives of consumption as a coherent set of classifiable practices. The authors quote Wynne and O'Connor's (1995) study of middle-class consumption in Manchester, where respondents' indulged in quite disconnected forms of consumption. They reason that part of the problem can be found in Bourdieu's research methods, where he concentrates on the inter-connections between variables in his use of correspondence analysis, to produce an emphasis on differences, thereby tending to miss important social processes which have little variation (for a more detailed explanation – see 1996, 285). Ultimately, in a bid to limit difference, Bourdieu falls to 'occupational identifiers' since they become, 'the sole surrogates which can stand in for this process of identity formation' (1996, 288). Longhurst and Savage suggest the need for a more complex conception of habitus which allows more room for agency, in which the internal tensions within habituses might be explored. Drawing on work in media studies, they call for the kind of work that I hope to have produced here: more ethnographically centred work which focuses on consumption practices in context, 'everyday life' and the social networks within which people live. What this study seems to underline, and this was especially pertinent in relation to the working-class people of the study where the inter-connections of community become key nodes around which some gardening practices were performed, is that habituses are not just about striking divisions between people. Indeed, through shared practices and tacit community agreements habituses are also about making similar kinds of classed identity. For contemporary ordinary gardening is undoubtedly a classed entity.

Chapter 7 uses ethnographic data to explore whether gardening practices are gendered as well as classed. Drawing on Butler's (1990) notion that gender is a masquerade, and as a means to examine how the men and women of this study inhabit gendered modes of being, I turn to investigate what tasks men and women perform in the garden. Using a case study of floristry and flower arranging, I ask whether there is a (classed) gendered gardening aesthetic.

Chapter 7

Gender and Gardening

Thomas almost entirely dominated the discussion. I have virtually no idea what kind of gardener Lena is! Do I need to interview women on their own? (extract from field notes after interview with Thomas and Lena)

John: I'm into DIY, I like to say "well I've done that garden an' our lass 'as finished it." She's dressed it, which is basically it.
Stephanie: That's what I do in t' house. He does all t' like heavy work …makes the furniture.
John: She does the trimmings.
Stephanie: And I do all t' trimmings. Even at Christmas I do all t' trimmings.

Keith: I mean me father always was a keen gardener but leaning more towards homegrown vegetables, whereas me mum always liked her plants.

Rosemary: We don't grow anything rigid. We prefer soft forms.

James: I'm a chrysanthemum man

Introduction

This chapter empirically examines if the garden is a classed and *gendered* space. I argue that the construction of gender rests on its proximity to positions of class. Working-class women, for example, have historically been denied the right to be 'ladies', because of their distance from middle-classness (Skeggs 1997). In this chapter, I interrogate what gendered proximities to class bring to gardening practices: I ask, what differences inhered in the kinds of masculine and feminine gardening working- and middle-class people did in 1990s British culture. Comprised of three sections, the first part of the chapter explores the historical antecedents of gendered gardening; the second turns to garden practices and asks if men and women do different types of gardening; and the third using case studies of floristry and flower arranging, asks if there was a specifically gendered collection of aesthetic practices among the people of the study.

In chapter 3 I set up the main theoretical framework for the empirical findings around questions of class and gender. In the previous chapter, I drew on Bourdieu's notion of 'capitals' to suggest that the gardening tastes and aesthetic dispositions of the subjects of this study were saturated by class distinctions (Bourdieu 1986).

However, Bourdieu's sociology has faced reproach from feminists for situating gender, race and sexuality as secondary to social class (McCall 1992). As Lovell argues, 'While class penetrates right through his diagrammatic representations of the social field, like the lettering in Brighton Rock, gender is largely invisible' (Lovell 2000, 20). By extension, Bourdieu has also been criticised for singling out class as the most important determinant in taste distinctions, thereby giving short shrift to factors such as gender or ethnicity as variables which impact on the meaning of consumption (Silverstone 1994). Yet as James's attachment to chrysanthemums reveals above, taste is also gendered. In this way, this study turns to post-modern feminist theory (Butler 1990) as a means to counter some of the limitations of Bourdieu's work.

Bourdieu's concept of habitus – a fairly fixed conceptual tool, faces limitations in relation to gender (Lovell 2000; McCall 1992). Theorised as a set of unconscious regulating principles, Bourdieu argues that it cannot be socially learned; rather it is acquired through social practice in ways which feel completely natural to the agent. From a gendered angle however, feminists have taken issue with the idea that women can ever feel an unconscious 'feel for the game' in patriarchal culture (McCall 1992). Rather, McCall argues that women develop self-consciousness from striving for equality in male-dominated fields. In this way the concept of habitus fails to fit the social realities of women's lived experiences. Similarly, Lovell (2000) challenges the social fixity of habitus. For her, the literal embodiment of habitus emphasises its 'corporeal sedimentation' – yet Lovell cites legion historical examples of gender passing in order to contest the unconscious element in Bourdieu's account of habitus (see also Garfinkel 1987). If women can convincingly inhabit and perform masculine attributes, then a practical and bodily 'feel for the game' can be consciously learned. it is possible for a woman to develop a masculine habitus and vice versa.

One can therefore see the problems Bourdieu's theory of habitus presents for post-modern feminists, who valorise agency and the instability of subjectivity as a means to politically transform gendered modes of being (Weedon 1987). For Butler (1990) there is no authentic self behind the masquerade of identity; rather, identity itself is a form of 'passing' since there is no 'real' identity behind the act of performance. In this way, masculinity and femininity are cultural performances which generate the effect of the natural and the inevitable. In these ways, Butler's theory offers radical potential to feminists because ironic performances or contradictory masquerades work to unhinge the social fixity of traditionally gendered modes of being.

In fact Bourdieu and Butler do share intellectual ground in that they both draw on the concept, originally developed by Austin (1962), of performativity. However, they theorise performatives differently. For Butler (1997) transgressive or insurrectionary acts can seize their own authority and change the meaning of performatives by dislodging them from their social structure. For Bourdieu on the other hand, performatives gain power firstly from the institutional authority which grants their status and through the habitus which honours that authority. For Butler, the subject has the power to transform the self; for Bourdieu the habitus is too inflexibly sedimented to allow for identity to be unfixed. I argue that both positions offer efficacy to the debate about performativity. The value of Bourdieu's argument is that he insists that indelible experiences of social learning accompany the agent throughout life; for him performativity is always freighted down by the solidity of institutions and the social. On the other hand, Butler's voluntarist position, which attempts to augment political transformation, envisages agents as relatively free to erase or re-fashion identity at will, in ways which grant freedom to the individual in relation to the new self. Left whole, Bourdieu and Butler's positions on performatives are irreconcilable, in the following section therefore, I draw on both. In the analysis of the data which follows I identify the potential for intervention by challenging the discursive construction of gender with a view to enacting social transformation while recognising the tight social and material constraints which bind men and women to their gendered roles.

The terms of the debate between Bourdieu and Butler raise questions about the relationship between institutional sites where modes of gardening were lived out or represented and the empirical modes of performed gendered gardening discussed in this chapter. If as Bourdieu insists, performatives are tethered to institutional authorisation, then one would expect a relationship to exist between the gendered gardening practices found in both the family and the media and how the men and women of my study took up modes of gendered subjectivity. On the other hand, if as Butler argues, performatives can seize their own authority without institutional tenure, it may be that the influence of institutions such as the family and the media are negligible. In the following sections therefore, I use the tenets of the debate between Bourdieu and Butler to ask if my respondents take up the gendered practices passed down to them through the family and by the media or if they flout convention by choosing *not* to perform gender in conventional ways. Can female gardeners 'make like men' despite familial influences, or can men develop a feminine 'feel for the game' and develop feminine gardening aesthetics? If so, what ordinary social circumstances produce the choice to do gendered gardening differently? Or if gender is performed conventionally, why do men and women still invest in traditional modes of gender? And finally, what impact do empirical modes of being in the garden have on the media: can the 'insurrectionary acts' Butler describes set a more politically empowering agenda for how men and women were represented in the lifestyle media?

"It's Kind of Gone Down in Generations With Us": A History of Gendered Gardening

This section explores studies which chart a history of gardening as a gendered activity. Focusing on cottage gardening, the allotment and on the lawn as a specifically masculine compartment of the garden, studies suggest that gendered gardening has an institutional base in the family. Using Bourdieu and work on masculinity which challenges familial sex-role theory as a means to explore the empirical data, I ask whether the forms of gardening the men and women of this study performed are rooted in their familial social learning.

There are several studies which cite the historical formation of gendered gardening tasks and responsibilities. In *The Cottage Garden* (1981) for example, Scott-James argues that in the Victorian family cottage garden, 'some tasks were "manly" and others "womanly"': women grew flowers and herbs and men were in charge of allotments and grew vegetables' (Scott-James 1981, 102). The historical antecedents Scott-James charts are supported in Crouch and Ward's findings in *The Allotment: Its Landscape and Culture* (1999). The authors argue that since the early 1800s allotments have been sites for the production of vegetables and as such they have been traditionally conceived as male spaces. Quoting a South Yorkshire allotment holder speaking in the 1980s, Crouch and Ward demonstrate the traditional location of the allotment as, '"an annexe to other male social sites such as the working-men's club or the betting shop"' (Crouch and Ward 1999, 89). Further evidence that allotments were kept as a male domain is provided by the Thorpe Committee Report (1969) – it noted that only 3.2 per cent of women were allotment holders and only 1.8 per cent were housewives. The committee saw no evidence that gardening was less popular with women than with men, so they were forced to conclude that it was allotment gardening specifically which women found less appealing, '"women generally prefer the cultivation of flowers to vegetables and often reach a tacit agreement that they will take charge of the home garden while their husbands look after the allotment"' (Crouch and Ward 1999, 91). But while the Thorpe Report implies that it was women's own preferences that led them to avoid vegetable growing, evidence suggests that women were not encouraged to grow vegetables either. Crouch and Ward for example, cite a 1986 Lancashire local newspaper report where it was regarded as newsworthy that a woman should even have an allotment, '"Up North – where men and women are expected to know their places – Mary Ellis came as a bit of a shock. For the petite Ms Ellis … has been invading the traditionally male stronghold of the allotment"' (Crouch and Ward 1999, 90). These studies reveal a historical legacy of gendered activities: in horticultural terms vegetable production has been a male preserve, while women have tended decorative plants such as herbs and flowers.

The masculine aesthetic preference for lawns and attachment to garden technology is historicised, albeit in a more populist vein, in Fort's book *The Grass is Greener* (2001). Fort charts the English lawn from the early seventeenth century as a specifically male history; lawns, as far as Fort is concerned, are 'man's business.' The book's prelude takes the reader through every suburban Englishman's first seasonal Saturday morning ritual of re-discovering the lawnmower. It is an act which in itself evokes a history of great mowermen: 'He may put his nostrils close to the damp mass of cuttings, inhale that fresh, innocent smell which speaks to him of his history as a mower and the lawns he has mown' (Fort 2001, 10). Fort juxtaposes his own celebratory autobiographical moments with his lawnmower against a history of lawn developers from the seventeenth to the twentieth century citing advocates and writers from Francis Bacon to Walter Godfrey. Theorising men as essentially competitive, Fort argues that men's interest in lawns is driven partly by the need to retain the national superiority of the English lawn – an asset that has historically been the envy of world gardeners. But for Fort, it is not just the aesthetic quality of the lawn that moves men, the whole paraphernalia of caring for lawns – the mower as technological apparatus, the familiar ritual of mowing, the mower's shed and the act of escaping both 'the wife and children' – are essentially male pleasures. Further,

Fort adds, men are interested in lawns and greens because the act of caring for them literally prepares the ground for male sports such as cricket and golf.

My study of lived gendered gardening practices gives credence to these historical studies. Present day gardening is not organised around food production in the ways that Scott-James, Crouch and Ward and other writers who have concentrated on civilian wartime vegetable production demonstrate (see for example, Davis 1993). Nonetheless, as section two shows, contemporary female gardeners still perform decorative gardening tasks using flowers and herbs; and while men do still produce vegetables, men's gardening has shifted to doing structural projects using construction tools and garden technology. One of the first sites where these historical modes of gendered gardening become embedded and are perpetuated is in the family. Significantly, when my respondents mentioned their parents it was the case that without exception, the parents of my respondents had all performed the gendered tasks highlighted by the authors cited above; most of the gardeners over 50 for example, told me that their fathers had grown vegetables on an allotment. And when I asked my respondents where they had acquired their gardening skills, several of them cited their parents as formative influences on their interests and competencies. In this way, Bourdieu's argument that performatives are institutionally sanctioned is offered empirical credence; the following responses demonstrate the power of familial social learning in relation to gardening. While Maud told me that gardening, 'just comes naturally when you've lived in the country,' her mother and father's skills were clear influences:

Lisa T: Did you learn from your parents? Or is it something that you acquired yourself?

Rosemary: Grandma had a cottage garden. Your mother had a cottage garden, didn't she?

Maud: Yeah.

Rosemary: Yeah.

Lisa T: And are these skills that you've passed down to each other then? (Maud laughs, turning to Rosemary)You learnt from your mother? (Maud laughs)

Rosemary: Well, my father taught rural studies – they've always been there.

In their concern to demonstrate natural skills that have 'always been there' Rosemary and Maud show a reluctance to foreground the acquisition of skills through an actual learning process. Yet the blend of educational and experiential influences from Maud's parents had a crucial influence on her and they have clearly been passed down to her daughter Rosemary. But even if we assume that Maud learned from both her parents, both herself and her daughter express a preference for flowers, herbs and soft fruit as opposed to vegetables, this marks their garden out as a more typically feminine space.

As children, in some cases, sons tended to identify with their father's activities and daughters identified with their mothers; and later in life, as I show in section two, cohabiting men and women in particular tended to adhere to activities designated masculine or feminine. Stephanie quite consciously felt that a love of flowers had been passed down a female family line, beginning with her grandmother, 'Grandma always 'ad flowers in t' house and me mum 'as tended to go that way a bit, and then I've always liked things like that, so it's kind of gone down in generations with us.' Living with husband John, Stephanie lives out her preferences by being in charge of the flowers in her own garden. David's garden consisted of both flowers and vegetables; he told me that he had learned all his gardening skills from his parents. David's father had had an allotment for growing vegetables and like other working-class men in this study, his father had grown chrysanthemums. Like his father, David grew both vegetables and chrysanthemums. But while he had benefited from the knowledge of both parents, he only talked about the particular appreciation he had for his father's knowledge, despite the fact that unlike Stephanie, David was responsible for both the feminine and the masculine tasks in his garden:

Lisa T: She was more flowers than vegetables?

David: Yeah. I'm glad he was vegetables as well, because a lot of people would have all flowers and trees and stuff wouldn't they? But I'm glad he was more vegetables…

These discursive strategies reveal that David felt more comfortable identifying with his father's gardening role, even though he clearly also spent much of his gardening life performing tasks that his mother had taught him.

It is certainly the case therefore that some gardeners did live out the historical legacy of gendered gardening practices through the lineage provided by their parents' activities. Indeed these instances seem to shore up the efficacy of Bourdieu's view that performatives are tied to the institutional bodies which sanction them. Yet while gender studies has long acknowledged the role of the family in perpetuating gendered identities, more recent work has attempted to provide a more complex way of theorising how people become particular kinds of men and women. Heward's (1996) work on masculinity for example, argues that Parsonian sex-role theory, where daughters identify with mothers and sons with fathers as an essential component in the division of labour within the nuclear family, is simplistic and tends to remove the construction of masculinity from its social and historical context. Using personal biographies of a small sample of men who studied at the same minor public school, Heward shows that a host of factors, encounters with feminism within higher education, enhanced employment opportunities for mothers and girlfriends and men's recognition that 'macho' masculinity is often problematic, mitigates against straightforward same-sex parental identification. These new social trends have meant that, 'patriarchal control is being weakened by decades of bargaining and negotiation' (Heward 1996, 46). Men, she argues are taking a more fluid and experimental approach to the construction of their masculinity in terms of their families, intimate relationships, their leisure interests and within the world of work. Turning to my sample, while it was the case that my respondents' parents took on quite rigid gendered identities, the generation I interviewed alongside their children, presented a more complex set of practices. The changing face of masculinity and femininity perhaps explains why it was not always the case that men and women aligned their gardening apprenticeship with the same-sex parent. Keith who does all the gardening and whose garden is singularly devoted to flowers also came from a family where tasks had been gendered, 'I mean me father always wa' a keen gardener but leaning more towards home-grown vegetables and what have you, whereas me mum always liked her plants.' But in what follows he foregrounds learning from his mother as a source of knowledge:

Lisa T: And did you learn about flower plants from your mum at all?

Keith: Well I often wondered, you know, I mean when she used to take cuttings and what have you, she used to show us at certain times of year and I suppose some of it stayed with me.

Similarly Millie told me that her parents had divided their activities, 'dad was veg, mum was flowers', but Millie, like her brother, had acquired pea, onion and sprout-growing success from her father:

Lisa T: And that's things passed down from your father?

Millie: (very definitely) Yes it is, yes. And my brother's the same.

The examples cited here show that there is a history of gendered gardening tasks and responsibilities which, despite class, is still being lived out. It was the case, especially among respondents over 50, that women associated themselves with flower gardening and men with growing vegetables. Moreover gendered gardening carries, once again in relation to older respondents, the legacy of being sited in the family; the men and women of the study tended to identify with same-sex parents in relation to the activities they performed. In these ways, Bourdieu's argument that performatives adhere to institutional authority is offered credence, since the family as an institution sanctioned and wielded a powerful influence in relation to the allocation and performance of specifically gendered tasks. However, work on masculinity (Heward 1996) suggests that social trends have conspired to weaken traditional institutional bases which have sanctioned traditionally gendered roles. The advent of feminism, changes both to employment structures and to the family have led to a more fluid and experimental construction of gender in contemporary culture. These factors might explain why the younger contingent of my sample were prepared to cite both parents as gardening influences and to announce that they eschewed staunchly traditional modes of gendered gardening. In this way, while Bourdieu's argument in relation to performatives might still carry credence among an older generation, younger ordinary gardeners were beginning to challenge their gendered practices in the face of weakening institutions. The tasks and responsibilities associated with masculine and feminine forms of gardening were showing signs of change.

"I Build it and She Plants it": Doing Gender and Garden Practices

Jack: I'm the grassmower.

Thomas: Lena has always grown chives, mint and parsley.

Lisa T: So you live on your own? Do you do all your gardening on your own?

Doris: Yes, the lot.

Lisa T: Absolutely everything?

Doris: Mmm mumm.

Using Butler's (1990) notion that there is no authentic gendered self beneath the performance of identity, this section turns to how contemporary gardening is done by the men and women of this study. For Butler gender is a 'corporeal style', a copy of a copy, an act, a repetition, a set of strategies with cultural survival as their ultimate aim. The parody of gender Butler describes does not presuppose an original, since it is the idea of an original that is being parodied. For her gender is a 'regulated process of repetition', a series of recurrent acts that congeal to look like something that has been there all along. But if, as Butler argues:

> the inner truth of gender is a fabrication and if a true gender is a fantasy instituted and inscribed on the surface of bodies, then it seems that genders can be neither true nor false, but are only produced as the truth effects of a discourse of primary and stable identity (Butler 1990, 136).

it must also be possible to 'act' gender in ways which highlight the constructedness of gendered identities in ways which reveal they have a vested interest in passing themselves off as 'natural'. In this section, I investigate the circumstances which contribute to the construction and performance of heterosexual gender identities in relation to gardening. I ask: do the ordinary people of this study act gender in conventional ways and if they do, why do they invest in traditional modes of being; or, do some people live in ways which allow them to flout traditional gendered modes in ways which disrupt and unfix the foundational construction of gender? Finally, I examine the relationship between media representations of gendered gardening and my empirical examples of what and how men and women, somewhere in the North in the late 1990s, 'did' gardening.

The interviews I conducted with my Yorkshire gardeners took various forms: I spoke with both men women on their own and with women in pairs, but most of my sample consisted of interviews with married heterosexual couples. The practice of interviewing couples can raise specific issues and difficulties for the researcher, particularly in relation to asking about how a division of labour is established in relation to the garden. Other academics have faced similar problems: when Kirkham (1995) interviewed Ray Eames, wife of the internationally renowned husband and wife modernist design collaboration, she mentions how difficult it was, even though her husband Charles Eames had died several years before the time of the interview, 'to get beyond generalizations about all the work being a joint effort' (Kirkham 1995, 217); in similar vein Cockburn, in her study of gender and domestic technology, *Machinery of Dominance* (1985) claims that the couples she interviewed typically answered with a set response when asked to talk about how domestic work was divided up: 'Before I had got beyond the introductory phrase, "I'm interested to know how responsibilities are divided in the home", it often happened that whoever I was talking with, woman or man, would break in with "Oh we share everything." It seemed something that confirmed a loving relationship, to believe all work is shared' (1985, 216); and Gray in her study of the domestic uses of the VCR found that couples tended to insist that labour in the home is shared (Gray 1992). In fact, when I asked one of my interviewees Keith how labour was divided, he fell to the same discursive strategy, immediately following it with a contradictory statement, 'Well, it's shared. I would say I do the majority of it.' Yet what unifies Cockburn and Gray's research and my own, is that when men and women co-habit, labour is divided – men and women perform different tasks. Cockburn, for example, found that once the interview moved to the individual tasks in question she unearthed a different version of events and a starkly conventional delineation in terms of the chores done by men and women began to emerge. Similarly, Gray found that, 'for the majority of women the home is first and foremost a work place' (1992, 54) but she found that in some cases if men did become involved in 'sharing' the housework they betrayed through their use of language who they really considered housework to belong to; one man for example called it helping with, '*her* vacuuming and dusting' (Gray, 1992: 50).

One of the findings in Cockburn's interviews has particular resonance for one of the structuring principles of gendered labour in my study. Writing of an interview with one couple she expresses surprise, 'we arrived finally at a hobby they shared: upholstery. Ah, I thought. Something that *both* of them do? "I repair the wooden frames, she puts on the fabric"' (Cockburn 1985, 218). In fact this kind of divide between men and women's gardening tasks is a common feature of the textual images of gardening in the contemporary media. The advertisement for the Mantis garden maintenance system featured in a 1998 edition of *Gardens Illustrated* for example, shows a conscious will on the part of the company to include women in an advert for garden technology. However, there are still only three women alongside five men in the illustrations where the models wield the tool. More significantly, the man in the advertisement is shown using the system for structural maintenance and heavy ground work, whereas the woman is relegated to the more decorative, 'finishing off' tasks such as edging and planting. In terms of the co-habiting men and women I interviewed, from both middle- and working-class households, it was predominantly the case that men provided structure using tools and technological machinery and women created decorative effects.

Thomas conceded he had discussed the garden design with his wife Lena but, he told me, 'I would do the manual work.' He then proceeded with a comprehensive list of the hard landscaping he had done in the garden, he had: erected trellis, constructed the paths, built a retaining wall and had done any necessary tree felling. While maintenance was 'shared' Thomas was responsible for trimming the high hedges which bordered the garden. Lena took responsibility for pruning and growing herbs. Similarly in the case of Millie and Jack, Jack was 'grass-mower' and did 'any heavy work that needs doing' while Millie 'does all the planting.' Anne told me that when her ex-husband Richard had lived with her, she had relegated heavy tasks, such as digging out old roses from the garden, to him. Yet it is interesting to note that after

Richard left, Anne very capably continued the heavy tasks Richard was no longer available to carry out. Indeed as I show later, her aspirations to build and construct became even more ambitious when her husband left.

John continually stressed his dislike of gardening, which he defined as being about plants and planting, 'I like a nice garden. I like to look at one, but I 'ate gardening and she likes a tidy one.' His way of circumventing any involvement with plants was to filter out the masculine aspects of creating a garden – the feminine aspects of plants and planting were quite clearly delegated to Stephanie. Interestingly, when he spoke about his contribution to the garden, he continually referred to it as being about preparing the space *for* Stephanie:

> **John**: I will dig a garden, plant turf, do owt *she* wants…I'll do the basics, build them, any walls, owt *she* wants that way, but other than that I don't do owt.
>
> **Lisa T**: What was it like when you first arrived?
>
> **John**: Bomb site (laughs). New house.
>
> **Stephanie**: But it was open plan with next door …we built a wall at the front and up in the middle.
>
> **Lisa T**: (to both) And did you do that work?
>
> **John**: That was me. And I framed it up, and put *her* soil in and laid *her* grass. Laid *her* some flags 'round

As John later said about a future garden they envisaged they would inherit with a new bigger house, 'It'd be just basically what *she* wants. I'd build it and she plants it.' By continually stressing that his role is to prepare a space for her decoration, John manages to place a discursive, as well as a material distance, between himself and feminine gardening tasks. He lays the structure and then completely withdraws his contribution so that she can make the decorative decisions of which he wants no part. The language of doing becomes increasingly gendered in the following exchange; John's tasks are 'heavy' and associated with DIY and they prepare the way for Stephanie to trim and titivate:

> **John**: I'm into DIY, I like to say "well I've done that garden an' our lass 'as finished it." She's dressed it, which is basically it.
>
> **Stephanie**: That's what I do in t' house. He does all t' like heavy work…makes the furniture.
>
> **John**: She does the trimmings.
>
> **Stephanie**: And I do all t' trimmings. Even at Christmas I do all t' trimmings.
>
> **John**: I like to look at it. I like to think, "that's nice. Looks good."

Lisa T: So you've worked in partnership, but you've done different things towards the finished effect?

John and **Stephanie**: Mmmmm.

Stephanie: I'm the labourer.

John: She does the labour and I do the work and she finishes off, don't yer?

Stephanie: Yeah (laughs) ...I do...

John: She does the main bit ...carried to and fro.

Stephanie: (laughs) Titivating (laughs).

Here the garden becomes an extension of the way in which 'extra' household tasks, for example constructing furniture or putting up Christmas decorations are divided. Interestingly, Stephanie describes herself as doing 'labour' and John uses the synonymous term 'work' to describe his tasks – but Stephanie provides a final decorative layer through her act of finishing off. For John, decorating the garden is an extension of how women construct a feminine appearance using the face and body:

John: Well that's what women are for, that's why you get dressed up innit and put make-up on.

Stephanie: Yeah.

John: Yeah, it's like your garden is an extension of you, to me.

John and Stephanie revealed that their garden is an important public space through their discussion of people walking past the house and looking at the garden on their way to the local polling station during elections. For them, an unkempt garden reflects on those within, 'If you've got a scruffy garden ...their house is gonna be t' same', Stephanie told me, to which John added, 'if you bother with your garden it shows on yer house.' As a result of being conscious of the critical gaze of others they strive to keep the garden tidy, 'If I've left it I've been ashamed,' Stephanie told me. Significantly Stephanie then likened her care for the garden through an identification with Hyacinth Bucket, the aspirational lower middle-class character from the popular situation comedy *Keeping Up Appearances* (BBC, 1990-1995). Hyacinth Bucket is obsessed with attempting to acquire the mores and etiquette of a cultured, middle-class lifestyle. Her fear and anxiety about 'getting it right', as well as instances she actually fails to 'get it right' offer the programme makers a set of endless comic possibilities:

Stephanie: 'Cept I'm not Daisy. I'm more like Hyacinth these days because I think you feel proud that you've done something. It's like washing your windows an' getting your whites, getting your whites right. People used to be so concerned about not hanging anything on t' washing line that weren't pure white. So if your garden's not exactly right now you do feel that somebody's saying, "so and so 'an 't' done their garden – look at that in there, oh so and so.."'"

Stephanie recognises the comedy inherent in identifying with Hyacinth's position, but more importantly, Hyacinth's character offers her a means to express her own doubts and fears about not getting the garden 'exactly right' for the scrutinising gaze of local passers-by.

It was not always the case that I managed to interview couples together. Several of the interviews include only one half of the partnership, or where partners had separated or died the remaining partner was able to speak about gardening both with and without their partner. In these cases, the gendered locations of absent partners were represented by those who were available to speak. James a retired ex-professional head gardener, worked for 25 years in private service for two wealthy industrialists before running a floristry business in partnership with his wife Joyce. Since Joyce had considerable experience as a florist, it seemed somewhat unusual that she played no part in the large domestic garden the couple owned. James did offer an explanation as to Joyce's lack of involvement in the garden: she 'hated gardening', hated what he called, 'finger work', had arthritis and he told me, 'she's not a strong person'. For James, more than for any of my other respondents, physical strength was an important credential for being able to garden.

As a teenager James decided he didn't want to follow his father and work in the local mill. But his medical condition, epilepsy, prevented him from realising his aspirations to become a joiner. But epilepsy had also closed off another possibility – it meant that James was prevented from joining the army:

James: I had to have a soft option which was gardening. That was the only thing they could put me to. It's been one of the hardest jobs, probably, is gardening.

James's illness had effectively foreclosed the possibility that he might pursue a truly masculine career path, interestingly here he follows his description of gardening as a 'soft option' with the assertion that it is, 'one of the hardest jobs.' Throughout the two interviews I conducted with James the idea that gardening is hard physical labour was central to his sense of what gardening means, indeed I got the distinct impression that James thought that gardening was unsuitable for women. He had experienced working alongside women who were employed on a casual basis at one of the nurseries he had contracted out to while running the floristry. Their work had been 'pricking out' (a term which probably relates back to his use of the term 'finger work' above), they, 'didn't fill barrels'. Interestingly while talking about these 'ladies' he turned the conversation immediately back to his wife, 'and neither', he said 'could Joyce. I wouldn't expect her to, she hasn't got the strength for it.' It was as though the idea that gardening might be a 'soft option' could be held at bay as long as it was conceived as hard, physical labour. Keeping women out of the physical aspects of gardening acted as a means to re-enforce its meaning as a tough and specifically masculine profession. Indeed this might explain why it had been decided that Joyce stay out of gardening altogether, particularly through her choice to reject the 'finger work' that might have been available for her to contribute. Joyce's involvement might well have led to a de-valuation of James's lifelong construction of gardening as a means through which masculinity can, contrary to those who define it as somehow feminised, be performed. As a consequence of Joyce's lack of involvement, however, James is responsible for all garden activities, the decorative as well as the structural. I come to how James dealt discursively with the decorative aspects of his gardening later.

James's view that women are too frail to garden has its contradictions. For one thing, Joyce clearly could garden. James told me that while he was in hospital having his heart by-pass operation, Joyce 'looked after the garden'. Also gardening presenter Charlie Dimmock had not escaped James's notice – but not as the national press at the time had constructed her – as a sex symbol. James was far more taken by her absolutely extra-ordinary physical ability:

> **James**: But I mean, to me I mean, I've never seen a woman work like that girl works. She can show fellas up nearly. She's as strong as an ox. She's tremendous strength. ...(talking about *Ground Force*) They were fetching breeze blocks or concrete blocks and they were carrying one to start with, then they carried two and Alan Titchmarsh was ...and she came through with three and Titchmarsh didn't you know...Oh I think she's as good as a fella anytime in the garden that lady. I mean gardening's physical and she could match any man.

Talking of Charlie led him directly on to a memory James had of a similarly physically able woman who made quite an impression on him, a woman he can still recall almost forty years later:

> **James**: I've only ever seen a lady perform like her when I was at Toothill. We bordered on a potting shed ... and the middle-aged farmer's wife there, youngish woman, about thirty-odd, there when it came to hitching the hay and things on to the top of the step she could match a fella anytime. But you don't find that generally with ladies, I mean they usually aren't built like that, I mean they aren't supposed to be built like that.

Making these women extraordinary serves an important purpose for James, particularly in relation to his bid to keep gardening a masculine preserve. For James, these robust gardeners can only be explained away as aberrant women who outstep the physical remit of femininity. To see them as representative as opposed to exceptional would be to acknowledge that women too have the capacity to perform 'masculine' work. They come too close to shattering the fragility of his belief that only men can cope with the physical challenge that gardening presents.

Keith told me that he has undertaken all the structural work in his garden and that heavy work, such as moving plants, is his responsibility. The statue they have in the garden was chosen by his wife Joy, who works part-time as a bank clerk, at the local garden centre. Joy chose the site for the statue and Keith was called in to carry it to where Joy wanted it. Nonetheless, while Joy made the decision to purchase their decorative sculpture, she has a limited input into the decorative decisions within the garden. It is Keith who researches plants and designs the planting scheme, so like James, Keith is responsible for the decorative aspects of his garden.

In relation to James and Keith's interview transcripts, however, one could be forgiven for thinking that these men had no relationship with decoration. Yet the gardens these men produced were adorned with plants which clearly served an ornamental function for their owners. Unlike John, who was in possession of a specific vocabulary through which to describe his wife's ornamental contribution, James and Keith used discursive strategies which allowed them to write the idea of decoration out of their versions of what gardening means. My interview with James, for example, consisted of a number of topics: his working conditions as a gardener in private service, his forte for propagation, the correct way to use and clean gardening tools, his opinion about gardening lifestyle programmes, his memories of which plants his bosses preferred, his production of chrysanthemums and his experience of floristry – but none of these topics touched on the idea of garden embellishment or beautification.

In these ways, my study demonstrates that many of the gardeners I interviewed chose to act out staunchly traditional heterosexual gendered gardening roles. Most of the couples I interviewed divided and executed their tasks into heavy/structural masculine duties and light/decorative feminine tasks. Elsewhere, the people of my study used discursive strategies to gender their tasks in appropriately traditional ways. For example, where gardening had been a form of masculine employment it was defined as a physically tough and demanding profession and when men strayed into decorative gardening domains, they found ways to discursively avoid any reference to feminine forms of beautification.

Turning to the media, such findings should not really surprise us. While I argue in chapter 5 that the lifestyle garden media embraced a shift in gendered identities using personality-interpreters such as Laurence Llwelyn-Bowen and Charlie Dimmock, the media was also replete with images of traditionally gendered gardening. For example, the features in a *News of the World* Sunday supplement entitled *Gardening from Scratch* typically demonstrates the different tasks men and women were traditionally assigned in the garden. One feature *Tough Turf But We Managed It!* shows a photo-strip lawn make-over where two men are shown heavy digging and turf laying in a North London garden. Several pages later, *Emmerdale Farm* actress Lisa Riley is shown planting containers and hanging baskets using a variety of bedding plants. Unfortunately, these examples are illustrative of how gardening was, and still is, predominantly represented in the media: men do heavy structural work and women do decorative gardening tasks.

These kinds of images had some bearing on lived garden practices. Peoples' gardens are leisure sites – yet they are spaces which are fastened to the institutional backdrop of the media. The process of how men and women come to recognise themselves as gendered subjects depends to some extent on the process by which they synthesise textually constructed versions of masculinity and femininity. Textual mediations of how and by whom garden labour is performed had an important bearing on the ways in which some men and women of this study chose to become particular kinds of gendered subjects in the garden. Conventional images of gender in publishing and advertising, like the ones mentioned above, act to give institutional social sanction to the polarised differences in what kinds of gardening some of the men and women take up. As my sample demonstrates, this kind of institutional legitimation may have acted as a powerful impetus for men and women to offer agency to traditional modes of performed subjectivity. In several cases and regardless of class, the men and women of my sample gardened in ways which affirmed conventional gender roles. Social circumstance – in particular male/female co-habitation – was a major factor in the take up of traditional garden practices. When men and women lived together, they made a tacit agreement to perform normative gendered garden practices: men used tools and technology to produce structure and women planted to make the garden decorative. For example, men tended to build trellises, lay lawn turf and mow lawns while the women planted flower beds and herbs. Taking these examples, the relationship between the media and gardening viewers would seem to be straightforward: men and women perform the sanctioned images offered to them by the media.

Bourdieu's position in relation to performativity has particular pertinence here, indeed it gives further weight to the idea that traditionally gendered media images are straightforwardly adopted by viewers. For Bourdieu, performatives are saturated by the structural conventions of institutional social norms. From his perspective, images of gendered performance in magazines or on lifestyle television are powerful precisely because they carry the weight of institutional sanction. As a further consequence, the take up of traditional modes of subjectivity by the media is in line with Bourdieu's thinking, for contained in his account is the idea that the unconscious attributes of habitus tend to accept the authority of institutionally sanctioned performatives. For Bourdieu, people are unable to simply unfetter their social boundaries since the gendered attributes of habitus and doxa work to resist the easy slippage in to politically radical performed modes of being. What Bourdieu's perspective offers, with its emphasis on the powerful social bind of habitus, is a means to recognise why traditional gendered performances are so powerfully persuasive: men and women simply find they can easily fit in to the predestined positions that are marked out for them.

On closer inspection however, my empirical evidence would suggest a more complex view of why men and women garden in traditional ways. Though undoubtedly mediated images have a bearing on audiences, I would argue that the men and women of this study did not simply take up roles assigned to them because the media ordained them; rather, they recognised that traditional modes of being offered social rewards. For example, like several of the working-class couples I interviewed, John and Stephanie gardened in classically traditional ways: John worked on structuring the garden and Stephanie was left to 'titivate' it. Like many of the men in this study, John strove to preserve the means through which his wife could fulfil middle-class conceptions of femininity – by performing decorative tasks and by steering clear of hard manual labour. To make way for one's wife to 'titivate' is to offer the space for her to imitate the genteel elegance of middle-class femininity. For Stephanie, the investment in normative femininity is also about being able to appear middle-class. In this way, some of the men and women of this study made the choice to perform traditionally gendered gardening because it offered high social returns.

However, when women live without men, women do decorative work, but they also take on heavy gardening work themselves and they use tools and garden technology with confidence. In some cases, they designed new structural plans for hard landscaping in their gardens and were sufficiently confident to execute some of the building work themselves. Anne and her daughter Phoebe, an unemployed textiles graduate, have plans to convert the old wash house at the bottom of their garden into an art studio:

Lisa T: You two, yourselves, you'd undertake to design it yourselves and build it yourselves?

Phoebe: Oh yeah, yeah (laughs) …and we know enough people to give us a hand.

Anne: I know I can do it …it's only that you're brought up to think "well you can play with the doll and the chaps can play with the Lego" or the…

Both university educated, Anne and Phoebe bring their encounter with the feminist idea that gender is socially acquired to bear on their sense of what they can achieve in their garden. As a result of building room sets at Ikea, Anne had developed a measure of assured competence, as the following exchange indicates, with tools and technology:

Anne: To be perfectly honest Ikea's quite good for that, because, you know, like today I had to climb up to the third layer at work to lift out some boxes, you know, so we get used to doing things, you know, and I build all the wardrobes.

Phoebe: You've got used to using power tools and since you've started work on the house, you see, as an extension of that…

Anne: You're starting to put floor boards down in the…

Phoebe: Yeah, I've learned how to use an electric jigsaw (laughs).

Anne: Oh yes and I cut out the bit in the kitchen.

Phoebe: Shelves up and…

Other feminist researchers have found that even women who use technology in the workplace tend to relinquish technological questions and tasks to the men they live with (Cockburn 1985; Gray 1992). In these contexts there are no men to whom those tasks need be surrendered – the women simply get on with finding the confidence and skills to execute DIY in the home and they extend those skills to the garden. And these women thought nothing of taking on heavy digging – they had plans to dig up the lawn and replace it with decorative bricks, and 'at the same time,' Anne added, 'I can start digging foundations for this business, 'cos it will need er, proper foundations.'

In other instances even much older women took on a wide range of maintenance tasks. With Maud and her daughter Rosemary, labour had to be divided according to age:

Lisa T: And who gardens? Is it both of you?

Rosemary: We don't have any help.

Maud: Rosemary cuts the lawns and looks after the roses. I do the herbaceous borders. My hobby is growing sweet peas, chrysanthemums and runner beans. Rosemary looks after the raspberries.

Rosemary: Raspberries and blackcurrants.

Lisa T: OK so you've got set tasks between you?

Rosemary: Well, mother does obviously she can't do the lawn, can she? (laughs)

Lisa T: No I realise that. I'm just interested in the way you divide that up between you… and so it's according to your interests and expertise?

Maud: Yes, that's right.

Rosemary: And (laughs) physical ability.

Indicative of their middle-class status, when Maud and Rosemary refer to 'help', they mean staff. And interestingly, Maud defines her tasks as 'hobbies', thereby providing a distance from the idea that gardening might be conceived as labour. Elsewhere they were careful to dissociate themselves from domestic labour, 'I don't like it and it doesn't like me,' Maud told me, and they were anxious to generate the impression that they had no time for tidiness, order and labour-making gardening tasks. Aware of the lack of value that these kinds of activities yielded within middle-class circles, they sought to distinguish themselves from them.

There were other cases where older women took on the entire gamut of gardening tasks, including manual work. Doris an 80-year-old woman who had been a housewife before being widowed, even built her own garden paths.

Lisa T: And so, who did all the …? Because, you've got like rocks … and your pathway?

Doris: Oh yes, I did it all.

Lisa T: You did all of that?

Doris: Oh yes.

Lisa T: Because that's heavy work!

Doris: Mmmmm, I've done it all. In fact I think some people are surprised, because they think 'cos I've three sons they do it, but they haven't done a thing.

In these ways Doris's differences from Maud and Rosemary are starkly drawn. Like Stephanie and John, Doris considers her garden to be very public. She is anxiously tidy and devoted to a highly routinised daily rhythm of gardening labour in the hope that others will notice and value her work. In this way, her willingness to perform manual labour is an extension of a set of tasks – the endless leaf sweeping, the daily hoeing – that she already performs in order to maintain an impeccably tidy garden.

While these instances are cross-cut by the proximity of gender to class, what is most significant is the preparedness these women have to perform masculine gardening tasks. These instances expose the limits of Bourdieu's conception of performativity. In particular, in cases where women found themselves living alone, either from the death or divorce of a spouse, they performed all the gardening activities – including those normatively assigned to men. For example, one female respondent told me that while she had lived with her ex-husband she had tacitly agreed to 'leave him to do things'. When he left however, she made the conscious decision to continue the 'masculine' tasks he had done for herself, using her own skills and aptitudes for structural and technological DIY. Similarly, widowed grandmother Doris simply did all her own gardening, including heavy digging and pavement slab laying, without the help of any of her male relatives. In these ways, one can see that female gardeners can 'make like men', they are, given the social conditions, able to develop a masculine 'feel for the game'. These gardeners were not out to gender-pass, but they were able to make the *conscious* choice to leave behind traditional gardening practices. Old forms of subjective recognition were discarded and new practices were taken up. As such, Bourdieu's conception of institutionally sanctioned performativity, with its insistence on the rule-bound unconscious normativity of habitus, simply cannot account for these instances of performative subversion. Moreover, the female gardeners who 'made like men' did so bodily, they took on heavy gardening labour, hence challenging Bourdieu's view of habitus as a literally embodied concept. In order to understand these instances, one needs Butler's insights on the possibilities offered by discursive agency. The men and women who broke gendered gardening conventions used their bodies as tools through which to re-enact gender. These men and women were not content to simply fit into pre-destined roles; rather, they re-constructed their identities with a degree of consciousness. From Butler's vantage point, this is a consequence of the flexibility whioh she argues can be accommodated within the theory of habitus, which she argues Bourdieu leaves out of his account:

> What Bourdieu fails to understand, however, is how what is bodily in speech resists and confounds the very norms by which it is regulated. Moreover he offers an account of the performativity of political discourse that neglects the tacit performativity of bodily "speech", the performativity of the *habitus* (Butler 1997, 142).

Moreover, for Butler, 'speaking the unspeakable' can destabilise social institutions and offer performatives an unpredictably radical future (Butler 1997, 142). For the men and women who gardened in unpredictable ways did manage to unhinge traditional modes of gender; as Butler argues, these gardeners seized their own authority and in doing so they carried out transgressive gender acts in the ordinary spaces of their everyday lives.

Indeed the wider implications of Butler's argument directs the discussion back to the institutional backdrop of gardening as a leisure activity: the media. According to Butler, 'insurrectionary acts' can shake the foundations upon which the power of institutions are based. My data would suggest that some people are gardening in ways which transgress gender norms. This would go some way towards offering an explanation of why conceptions of gender in the gardening media underwent change in the 1990s. While traditional images of gendered gardening still pervade television and magazines, lifestyle experts, as I argue in chapter 5, were represented in ways which were challenging staunchly traditional ideas about how men and women should garden. Charlie Dimmock, whose presence was arguably the most important in terms of gardening lifestyle since the mid-1990s, could indeed 'make like a man' in ways which astonished television audiences. It may be that ordinary insurrectionary acts of gardening were working to set the agenda for more politically empowered images of how men and women were represented in lifestyle gardening media.

"The Young Girls' Bouquets They Were Frothy and Frilly": A Case Study of Gendered Aesthetics

In the previous chapter, I argued that the aesthetic disposition of the gardens I visited expressed the habitus of their owners and that social class determined particular gardening tastes. In the previous section of this chapter, I argued that gardens are gendered as well as classed through *doing*. But it was through my respondents' interests in floristry, showing and flower arranging that I found a means to explore gendered tastes expressed through horticultural aesthetics. In this section I show how writers have modified Bourdieu's (1986) economistic metaphors to show that gender can also be traded as a form of capital (Skeggs 1997). I argue that gendered gardening aesthetics – located by differential class locations – carry power for their beholders. In what follows I examine the relationship between working-class masculinity and floristry and middle-class femininity and flower-arranging as a means to examine how the men and women of my study invested in both masculinity and femininity as forms of aesthetic capital.

Bourdieu excludes gender as a form of capital in *Distinction* (1986). Indeed feminists have pointed to of the lack of 'fit' between his theory of capitals and the position of women in contemporary culture. Lovell (2000) for example, argues that while women appear in Bourdieu's conception of the social field in *Distinction* (1986), they feature, 'primarily as social objects, repositories of value and capital', whose role is to circulate between men in the capital accumulation systems of families and kinship groups (Lovell 2000, 20). The problem with Bourdieu's schema, is that women have only a secondary form of status, 'as capital-bearing objects whose value accrues to the primary groups to which they belong, rather than as capital-accumulating subjects in social space' (ibid.). Even the advent of industrial capitalism and women's involvement as workers in the labour market has had little impact on Bourdieu's dogged insistence that women be counted as objects which accumulate value as opposed to subjects capable of accruing value in their own right. One of the means by which some feminists have circumvented the gaps and silences in Bourdieu's work however, is by modifying his metaphors in order to fully include femaleness and femininity in the circuits of capital exchange in which they are located. Skeggs (1997) for example, uses Bourdieu's economistic metaphors for understanding the lives of white working-class women, but she modifies Bourdieu's account of capitals by theorising femininity as a form of cultural capital.

Significantly, and presumably because feminist critics have found habitus a relatively inflexible concept, Skeggs uses Bourdieu's theory of 'capitals' as a framework for her study. Indeed she errs towards Butler's theory of gendered performativity for her analysis of the investments her respondents made in femininity. But in the context of British culture where whiteness and masculinity are valued forms of cultural capital, the young women she investigates had only a paucity of capital endowments with which to trade. They made investments in female identity as nursery carers, but their feminine capital could only be converted into limited economic gains through a declining labour market. Heterosexual marriage was one of the only other avenues for trading their scant amounts of capital. Providing a feminine appearance was a means towards securing a higher exchange rate on the marriage market – but perhaps more significantly, performing femininity offered a means through which to access what Skeggs argues has historically been denied working-class women: respectability.

Skeggs argues that by the nineteenth century ideal femininity had become established as white and middle-class. Femininity was regarded as, 'the *property* of middle-class women who could *prove* themselves to be respectable through their appearance and conduct' (Skeggs 1997, 99). Essentially passive, femininity came to be equated with characteristics 'of ease, restraint, calm and luxurious decoration' (ibid.). Working-class women, on the other hand, were defined negatively as physically robust against the genteel fragility of middle-class women. For Skeggs contemporary constructions of working-class femininity are framed by these historical antecedents: working-class women continue to be systematically denied access to respectability. For Skeggs's subjects therefore, investments in femininity offer a means to provide a distance from the pejorative associations of working-class femininity as devalued and sexually promiscuous. The anxious desire to obtain female respectability frames many of their life decisions, particularly in relation to appearance, demeanour and the interior decoration of their homes.

Bourdieu himself acknowledges that women play the chief role in their families by transforming economic capital into symbolic capital through their consumption of cultural taste – yet women's choices only 'count' in class terms in relation to their families. Hence the blindness in *Distinction* (1986) to the gendered inflections of taste that women might exercise as subjects in their own right. Skeggs's formulation of feminine cultural capital counters the omissions in Bourdieu's schema. Firstly her work has a vested feminist interest in singularly theorising women's movements through the social field; and secondly, her work offers a historical means of understanding why both middle- and working-class women make investments in femininity as a form of capital – and by extension, why the cultivation of feminine taste acts as a capital investment. Using the idea that gendered taste generates forms of cultural capital, the following section turns to the particular investments the men and women of my study made in flowers and floristry. Proximity to class, I argue, had a direct bearing on how gendered investments were manifest.

Floristry is defined by Scott-James as 'the intensive cultivation of flowers to achieve a perfect bloom' (Scott-James 1981, 80). Imported originally from French and Flemish artisan refugees – in particular weavers, flower breeding began to appeal to cottage gardeners as early as the seventeenth century in Britain. Floristry was the ideal hobby for the cottage gardener whose garden would typically have been small, for it required time as opposed to space. The cottage weaver, who worked at home at his loom, had access to his prized plants and could therefore afford them the special attention they required: in this way, contrary to popular assumptions that floristry is a female pursuit, floristry started life as a recreation for working-class men. The centre of the movement was located in the cottages near to mill towns in the north of Britain – in Scotland, Staffordshire, Derbyshire, Lancashire and importantly in Yorkshire. Later, flower breeding offered a release from the oppression of industrial working conditions, as Scott-James argues, 'when the industrial revolution made the artisan's life increasingly grim and mechanical, floristry was more precious to him than ever, perhaps the only lifeline connecting him with the natural world' (Scott-James 1981, 81).

As cottage gardeners began to produce exceptional flowers and new varieties, florists' clubs and flower shows were founded so that choice plants could be exhibited. At the start florists applied themselves to a wide range of garden flowers, but even as early as 1638 writers had begun to distinguish which kinds of plants were regarded as worthy of selective breeding. Note the gendered distinction the Rev. Samuel Gilbert makes here about the worthless, ordinary flowers grown by country housewives – plants that the florist, here by implication male, should avoid:

> There is your garden mallows, double hollyhocks, snapdragons, toadflax, foxgloves, thistles, scabious….trifles adored by countrywomen in their gardens, but of no esteem to a florist, who is taken up with things of most value (Scott-James, 1981, 82).

Since the seventeenth century the canon of valued floristry flowers tended to both contract and expand at specific historical moments, so that certain plants came in and out of floristry vogue. Post-1800 however, the list of eight accepted plants was enlarged to include the dahlia, pansy, iris – and among others, the chrysanthemum. In these ways the development of floristry and flower shows and the specific kinds of plants which were valued in floristry circles have a specifically northern, male history. It therefore comes as no surprise that several of the working-class men of my study can be seen to continue aspects of the historical legacy of floristry; it acted as a form of masculine cultural capital which could be traded for economic capital at the local level.

Philip told me that his father had grown chrysanthemums for show. Philip also grew chrysanthemums and he had successfully sold them, along with eggs, at work for many years. Chrysanthemums had also played a significant role in James's life: he had grown them by the thousand to sell on local markets as an income for the private gardens he tended; they were a significant staple flower in his floristry business and he was a proclaimed chrysanthemum enthusiast: 'I'm a chrysanthemum man,' he told me. These men felt entirely comfortable announcing their enthusiasm for the chrysanthemum; significantly, these were the only instances where men freely announced their admiration for a particular flower. Yet while the chrysanthemum was aesthetically valued it was also a flower that held significant economic capital for men located in working-class economies: it won cash prizes in flower shows and as a commodity with mass appeal it could be sold on both large and small scale markets. It was safe to like the chrysanthemum; because it was linked to work and earnings, it carried masculine capital for working-class men. Other men in their families and local communities found it pleasing aesthetically, but it could also be traded for economic capital and that imported masculine economic value – with its links to employment and bread-winning – onto the appreciation of the flower, one that made it acceptable in masculine taste circles.

James's early apprenticeship in floristry had begun at Lassett Hall in the sixty foot baronial-type hall where the gardeners had been required, on a regular basis, to fill the huge urn there with a large floral arrangement using, among a range of flowers, gladioli and a select number of chrysanthemums. But the chrysanthemum was not a plant the owners of Lassett Hall were especially interested in:

James: I think it's personal taste. I like chrysanthemums. I'm a chrysanthemum man.

Lisa T: And were chrysanthemums equally prized by these owners?

James: No. No. It was purely a money machine. They all went to the market, all these things. They all went to the wholesale market in Halifax. It was to help cushion the cost of the rising estate.

Lisa T: Didn't they want any of them themselves?

James: Well, they took what they wanted, but that was a fleabite.

Chrysanthemums were to James's employers a mass-produced good, useful as a 'filler', but more serviceable as a plant that could satisfy working-class tastes in exchange for a useful profit. The owners of Lassett Hall had tastes which were not just confined to local produce, their travels around the world had meant that they would come home from far flung destinations with requests that James and his team grow exotic fruit or plants that were unsuitable for the British climate. James's wealthy owners, mindful that chrysanthemums were prized by the working-class moved on to plants that signified their ability to travel and appreciate exotic plant varieties.

One of the gardeners who had shown James how to arrange flowers in the urn at Lassett Hall was to have an important influence on him. Mr Burton had nurseries at Elland, was a florist himself and he had shown flowers at Southport – he was, James told me, 'a pretty good fellow and he had a pretty good feel.' He also began to show James how to make wreaths – a skill on which James would come to depend when he moved into his 'florist's horticultural shop'. James's account of his work as a flower arranger at his shop in Brighouse throws up interesting contradictions about gender, floristry skills and aesthetics. On the one hand, he told me that while floristry could be learned, one needed 'flair', 'feel' or 'touch'. James had, 'the flair for making-up', the kind of innate skill that his wife Joy and her sister, who also worked in the shop, lacked – they didn't have, 'the touch.' But despite James's essentialist conception of himself as someone with the skills to use his hands sensitively to combine flowers in aesthetically imaginative ways, he relegated wedding bouquets to his wife, her sister and casual female employees while he took on wreath work:

James: I remember I got 'flu (laughs) and Joyce was having to bring flowers into the bedroom and onto the bed for me to make wreaths.

Lisa T: Is it unusual for men to be doing that kind of work or not?

James: No it's not unusual. There are one or two excellent men makers-up, particularly in this area. But it's more a feminine, majority it's female without a doubt. I think generally women have more flair.

Lisa T: Do you?

James: I think they've more feel than men, well for that kind of thing, for weddings and bouquets. I mean although mine were quite acceptable, when I got help in …florists from Huddersfield, young girls learning in a more modern way, I thought their work was a lot more sensitive than mine, it had more touch and feel about it. From my point of view I was heavier with my make-up but the girls were flimsier, but to me that's more feminine. It was light and fair. I mean my wreath, my bouquets…she did it with less wires than I did, she finished up with a much more sensitive piece, lighter…

Having already admitted his own flair for 'making-up' his step away from light, sensitive, flimsy floristry, demonstrates his comfort and pleasure with aesthetics which he defines as manly; he felt free to use his skills on the serious, public floral signifiers required for funeral wreaths, but his masculinity acted as a barrier when it came to arrangements for women. Masculine cultural capital was located in flower arranging, in ways which could be traded at the local level both economically and culturally; but it involved the careful selective culling of the manly attributes and skills which for these working-class men inhere in flower-arranging.

When I first met Rosemary one of the first things she told me was, 'I'm a flower arranger.' Both Rosemary and Maud were key organisers of the *Spen Valley Flower Club* – an organisation that ran flower arranging competitions and set a calendar of monthly demonstrations of florist demonstrations. Rosemary's involvement in floristry was intimately connected to her choice of garden aesthetics. Their beds and borders were organised around the key aesthetic tenets of flower arranging:

Rosemary: Well, I'm a flower arranger.

Lisa T: Right.

Rosemary: So if you look at the garden there's colour, form and texture.

Lisa T: Right.

Rosemary: But not necessarily flowers (pause).

Lisa T: OK …What about how flower arranging works in terms of the beds then?

Rosemary: Well I belong to a flower club and have done for a long time. So a lot of the plants are unusual plants because they're there for foliage and for the colour and for the form.

Colour, texture and form were principles that were very deliberately fed back into the garden and this made for effective companion planting and gave a painterly contrast of colours and textures to the borders. Mostly, the plants that were grown specifically for flower arranging were foliage plants, the flowers used in arrangements would be purchased from a shop such as the one owned by James. But when I asked Rosemary and Maud what kinds of flowers they grew and admired, Rosemary told me, 'we don't grow anything rigid, we prefer soft forms.' Indeed, (see Figure 6.5) demonstrates the kind of soft forms they valued; note the bells of the white campanula, the lacey delphiniums and the soft flowering shrub at the centre of the image. Their preferences for their summer borders were for blues, pinks and whites to be found in roses, sweet peas, penstemons, and their most prized plants – the delphiniums. See Figure 7.1 for a close-up of the blue delphiniums, 'people come in taxis to come and see our delphiniums,' Maud said to me. And Rosemary told me that summer flowers were mostly pale blues, yet it would be entirely possible to create 'hot' areas using the sharp yellows, oranges and scarlets found in the exotic forms of summer perennials such as red hot pokers, lynchis, or achillea. Their

Figure 7.1 Rosemary and Maud's Delphiniums

tastes were organised around feminised forms and shapes: the lacey spires of the delphiniums and the deep-throated, bell-shape of their cerise penstemons. While these women have the cultural capital to companion plant effectively, their choices of colour, form and texture help to display a feminised planting aesthetic. Indeed the logic of Skeggs's argument can be seen in relation to the different investments my respondents made in feminine cultural capital in relation to gardening tastes according to class. Rosemary and Maud for example, had a love of 'soft forms' in the garden and this was expressed through a *penchant* for feminised forms and shapes, for example the lacey spires of delphiniums. They made a conscious will to display feminine capital through their planting aesthetic. Already placed at close proximity to middle-class femininity, these women made an investment in feminised aesthetics as a means of holding their grip on the performance of ease, frailty and luxury associated with middle-class 'ladies'. In connection with this they recognised that being ladylike involved a passive and restrained approach to activity and as a result they were careful to indicate their dissociation from gardening labour or tidying. By contrast, the working-class women of the sample had less time for feminised garden aesthetics. More taken with the concern to produce respectability, my study revealed that on the whole order, cleanliness and bare earth took precedence in the working-class women's gardens I visited. The desire to keep order was such a burdensome and laborious activity that they lacked the resources for thinking about a gendered aesthetic. In working-class women's lives, the need to dis-identify with what they knew were the pejorative associations people made in terms of their class took precedence. Femininity was a luxury reserved for my middle-class respondents.

Conclusion

Using ethnographic evidence, the previous chapter argued that the ordinary garden is a site where identities of class are performed and lived out. This chapter continues to present new local knowledge 'from below' about ordinary garden practices, however, building on the conclusions presented in chapter 6, it argues that the ordinary garden is both classed and *gendered* and that gender is constructed in relation to its proximity to class. Using Butler's (1990, 1997) idea that gender is performed and the debate waged between Bourdieu and Butler with regard to the institutional anchorage of performatives, it explores three key sites of gendered gardening. Firstly, it argues that there is a history of gendered tasks and responsibilities which are rooted and socially learned within the family. Bourdieu's argument that performatives require institutional sanction is affirmed by older respondents who still followed same-sex parents in their gendered tasks. However it also faced challenge since some younger respondents drew from both parents in ways which upturned traditional gender conventions. Secondly, it revealed that when men and women occupy the same living space, they tended to make a tacit agreement to perform heterosexual gender by adopting traditionally gendered gardening practices. It argued that conventional modes of gendered being are given institutional sanction by the media. However, the performance of gendered gardening and its potential for radical change was shored up by examples of women who lived outside heterosexual relationships and who lived alone. In those cases women unfettered by institutional sanction, 'made like men' and performed extraordinary physical gardening feats. In this way, these ordinary, yet radical examples of gardening 'gender trouble' (Butler 1990) may well be responsible for the more politically empowering images of gender found among garden lifestyle personality-interpreters of the late 1990s. Thirdly, using feminist work (Skeggs 1997) which has modified Bourdieu's (1986) metaphors of capital, I argue that forms of gendered capital which inhere in garden aesthetics confer value on to their beholders. For example, already assured of their proximity to respectability, some of the middle-class women of the study invested in feminised aesthetics as a means to maintain their middle-class location. This chapter therefore concludes that ordinary gardening of the 1990s was undoubtedly a classed and gendered entity.

Chapter eight uses ethnographic data to explore the relationship between the media and its gardening audience. It investigates how class, gender and age impact on garden lifestyle media consumption and it examines whether ordinary gardeners felt incited to use or interpret lifestyle ideas. Did the ordinary people of my study use gardening as a way of life or did they 'lifestyle' and do such practices help people to cope in the wider social context of rapid change?

Chapter 8

Questions of Consumption: What Ordinary Gardeners Do With Garden 'Lifestyle' Media

Margaret: We don't watch them for instructions.
Hugo: No!
Margaret: We're critical.

Phoebe: (about Diarmund Gavin, *Homefront in the Garden*) I like his ideas very much. I wouldn't steal them, but some of the … like painting the walls that marrakesh blue, that was lovely. That was a nice idea but we wouldn't necessarily do it in paint. It might be in plants instead.

Introduction

This chapter turns to the relationship between my respondents and the garden lifestyle media texts they were consuming in the late 1990s. In earlier chapters I argued that lifestyle texts might be conceived as agents which enable subjects to make the transition from 'ways of life' to 'lifestyle' (Chaney 2001). Central to processes of 'ordinari-ization' adopted by such texts, however, was their address and formal ability to hook into the ordinary rhythms, practices and sites of everyday life. Such 'ordinari-ization' strategies included the more popular tone of contemporary public service broadcasting (Bondebjerg 1996; Ellis 2000); the accessibility and achievability of the presentation of lifestyle projects; and the increase in more ordinary 'experts' and lifestyle subjects. This chapter examines the lived consequences for ordinary subjects of the shifts in the ethos of public service broadcasting, programme changes and promotional lifestyle culture at the time the data was gathered. It investigates how those changes concretely interacted with the sites that ordinary gardening viewers both experienced and imbued with meaning. In these ways, it aims to contribute to an historical understanding of how such macro changes are experienced at the micro level by people at the point of media consumption.

This chapter is divided in to three sections. Firstly, I investigate how and what viewers consumed. In chapter 5, I argued that ordinary people had a larger representational stake in mediated garden lifestyle texts, however, I argued that media representations of ordinary people were still located by class and gender. In this first section, therefore, I ask if the consumption of lifestyle media was also subject to locations of class and gender. Section two looks at how ordinary viewers read garden lifestyle texts. Lifestyles are seen as the new social form, replacing 'ways of life' (Chaney 2001). According to Chaney, people destabilised by modernity use lifestyling as a coping mechanism. Analysing the responses of my respondents I asked: how did ordinary viewers respond to the garden makeover and to 'personality-interpreters'?; and how did people conceive of the notion of garden media 'lifestyle' as both citizens and consumers? Using Chaney's ideas that lifestyling acts to enable people to cope with social change, I consider whether my respondents used garden lifestyling in the ways he suggests: did the people I studied in a semi-industrial town in the North of England need to draw on the resources offered by lifestyle or did they garden in ways which drew on more traditional, local garden competencies? As a means to address Chaney's argument, the final section examines the relationship between lifestyle ideas and garden practice. I ask: did gardeners actually execute the ideas that personality-interpreters promulgate in lifestyle media texts?

Modes of Consumption: inflections of class, gender and age

How they consumed

Part of the formal construction of lifestyle texts is the manner in which they fasten into a sense of the ordinary through their evocation of facets of everyday life; aspects identified by Felski (2000) as repetition, home and habit. I argue that the "ordinari-ization" (Brunsdon et al. 2001, 53) of lifestyle media was linked to the sense that we are all, in so far as we connect to the backdrop of everyday life, ordinary. Lifestyle texts were rooted, from production through to consumption, to the humdrum rhythms and practices of the quotidian. Garden lifestyle texts fit around the habitual, hap-hazard rhythms of domestic, family life, therefore, written into the textual organisation of the garden lifestyle media product is the anticipated sense that their consumption will be random, partial, fragmentary and casual.

There is an extensive media literature, perhaps most especially in relation to television, which emphasises the capricious manner in which media texts are consumed within the context of everyday life. Ellis (1992), for example, theorises the television viewer as inherently casual and inattentive in the context of the domestic family home. Similarly, Grossberg argues that television is moulded, 'into the mundanities of everyday life', and as a result faces, 'constant interruption by and continuity with our other daily routines' (Grossberg 1987, 34-5). Indeed switching on the television may have an entirely different purpose than the one anticipated by the media producer. Bausinger, for example, argues that switching on television may, for some, have quite another domestic purpose, it might for example mean, "I would rather see or hear nothing" (Bausinger 1984, 344). And television is not the only medium to be 'read' randomly and inattentively. Hermes, in her study of women's general interest magazines, argues that readers do not always consciously register or fully ingest textual messages: 'everyday media use is identified with attentive and meaningful reading of specific texts, and that is precisely what it is not' (Hermes 1995, 15).

These studies usefully contextualise my own findings on how gardening lifestyle programmes and journalistic features were consumed. My respondents, regardless of gender or age, consumed lifestyle texts across a range of media – from television, magazines and radio to the local and national press – *casually*. Lifestyle media texts certainly failed to command total attention, or cover-to-cover modes of reading. Keith for example, described his own way of using the local press for features on new plant varieties as 'browsing'. In fact, the argument that Hermes mounts, that magazines are read with 'less concentration and … detachment', could be extended to the way in which my respondents consumed lifestyle across the media (Hermes 1995, 14). There was a lack of attention to the detail of gardening lifestyle that tended to pervade the atmosphere of several of my interviews. The following exchange typically demonstrates what I came to think of as 'garden lifestyle amnesia':

Lisa T: Do you watch gardening programmes?

Catherine: Yes, watched one last night but I don't know what it was.

Lisa T: Was it *Carol Vorderman's Better Homes?*

Catherine and **Philip**: Yes.

Philip: I think I fell asleep.

Respondents forgot programme titles, the names of personality-interpreters and generally had a medium to low lifestyle information absorption level. One makeover programme became 'that building gardens thingie', Diarmund Gavin was called 'the Irish chap' or 'the Irish gardener' and another presenter, 'the young woman with curly hair.' Casual media consumption, for most of my respondents, became intertwined with everyday inattentiveness: being an audience for such texts was a humdrum activity and the meanings my respondents took away were half-remembered, partial or even fuzzy.

There were references to casual consumption of lifestyle texts throughout the sample. However, class made a difference to the ways in which respondents talked about their agency in relation to the selection of lifestyle texts: some respondents made quite careful statements about how they came to be either watching a lifestyle programme or reading a gardening magazine. For example, in relation to television, the lower middle-class respondents were concerned to distance themselves from the act of *consciously selecting* lifestyle gardening texts. I was told by Millie and Jack, for example, that they would only watch makeover programmes, 'if they are on', thereby signifying a complete lack of interest in seeking such programmes out. Rosemary tried to suggest that lifestyle television entirely dominated broadcast television, thereby suggesting that she and her mother only watched them because they had no choice – 'we watch them because they are always on' she told me. Similarly David denied his own agency in turning lifestyle programmes on with the following comment, 'I do watch them if I happen to just be sitting down … just toddling.' In these ways, these viewers generated the sense that they watched lifestyle texts almost under sufferance, when clearly they watch enough gardening lifestyle programmes on which to base a number of evidenced opinions as to their value. These kinds of distancing strategies may indicate, as both Brunsdon (1997) and Leal (1990) remind us, that middle-class people in both Britain and South America consider television to be a 'bad cultural object' (Brunsdon 1997, 114). Similarly, Seiter's (1992) ethnographic work shows that people she interviewed about soaps felt ashamed to admit, in the presence of an academic, their appreciation of what they felt to be unworthy television.

But while it might be argued that television as a medium is denigrated by middle-class consumers, lifestyle magazines were also held at arms' length. This suggests that both the medium and the notion of lifestyle were regarded as unworthy. For example, several of my respondents demonstrated the need to show that they were only 'secondary' magazine readers; that is, they would only ever read them if they were passed on by a relative, or if they 'happened' to come across magazines while doing something else. 'I've looked at them because my mum buys them' Millie told me and Rosemary said, 'we used to have one passed on by a relative, now we only read them at the dentist (laughter)'. The pervasive view of lifestyle as somehow 'trivial' (Brunsdon et. al., 2001) is likely to contribute to the need for these middle-class gardeners to efface their actual enjoyment of lifestyle. Indeed these distancing strategies are reminiscent of middle-class approaches to garden taste and aesthetics explored in chapter 6. Using Bourdieu (1986), I argue that middle-class people are skilled at differentiating themselves from the vulgarity of working-class aesthetics; indeed, I argue that middle-class garden aesthetics are forged out of a will to reject working-classness. Here I extend the Bourdieusian argument: such differentiation strategies are also at work in how middle-class people discursively positioned themselves in relation to lifestyle consumption.

What they consumed

When I asked my respondents what aspects of the gardening media they consumed, their choices were starkly demarcated, most especially in terms of class. I argue in chapter 5 that there were differences between national and local garden media aesthetics. Legitimated compartments of the media, which are always national, assumed the possession of measures of institutionalised cultural capital on the part of their audiences. This was certainly the case with regard to particular elements of terrestrial television and some elements of national magazine and newspaper publishing. One need only consider, for example, journalist/presenter Monty Don – with his patrician persona, waxed Barber coat and corduroys and resoundingly middle-class English received pronunciation – to know that his weekend column in *The Observer* and the gardening programme he presented *Real Gardens* (C4, 1998-) was to be consumed by middle-class audiences who were either rich in, or at least moderately equipped, with cultural capital. Local capitals, often found in aspects of the local evening or weekend press were constructed to appeal to working-class consumers. And so it was: when I asked my small sample of gardeners which aspects of the media they used, the middle-class respondents predictably recounted their use of middle-class publications and the working-class gardeners quoted more down-market, local aspects of the gardening media.

Radio Four's *Gardeners' Question Time* was popular with my middle-class respondents, as was Christopher Lloyd's gardening column in *The Guardian* weekend supplement. And, since as I argue in chapter 6 that my middle-class respondents were in possession of social capital, that is, they were members of horticultural societies, several of them read the Royal Horticultural Society monthly journal *The Garden.* While most of my middle-class respondents made definite claims that they never purchased gardening magazines though they read ones passed on by relatives, Anne and Phoebe told me that they had bought and enjoyed *New Eden.*

By contrast the working-class gardeners had come into contact with more cheaply produced garden lifestyle television programmes on cable and satellite channels and they drew on the local press for inspiration. Keith told me that he used gardening features from the tabloid press. Almost all these gardeners insisted that they too never bought gardening magazines: 'Never,' Philip told me, 'I have never bought a gardening magazine ever'. However, Millie said that while she had bought *Gardeners' World* magazine, she had bought what she described as a 'gardening book' called *Gardening Made Easy* which she bought every week, which was collected into plastic folders to make four volumes. Exceptionally, Stephanie told me that she did read magazine features on gardening, but in her monthly women's general interest magazine as opposed to a gardening magazine.

However, while there were stark classed differences between both the mediums and the texts my respondents selected, all the gardeners I spoke to were fully conversant with the makeover garden lifestyle genre. All the gardeners I spoke to had a reasonably extensive knowledge of the genre: they were conversant with its conventions, they were familiar with a number of personality interpreters and they had seen the execution of a range of garden lifestyle projects. The makeover programme they were most familiar with was the BBC's flagship garden makeover programme *Ground Force.* Each of the gardeners I interviewed, regardless of class, age or gender, had been hailed by the popularity of the terrestrial 8-9 p.m. lifestyle slot.

Questions of Access and Consumption: Class, Age and Gender

Class

Using Bourdieu (1986) I argue in chapter 5 that access to media images and lifestyle ideas which display legitimate garden aesthetics is incumbent on the habitus of the reader/viewer and on their access to forms of economic, cultural and social capital. Access or blocks on entry to forms of capital has real effects on people's ability to organise the visual language of gardening, as chapter 6 empirically evidences. The competencies and knowledges specific to my respondents' class location had a direct bearing on both what they consumed and how they were able to synthesise lifestyle images.

Several of my middle-class respondents, for example, had been teachers or they had higher education qualifications; they were therefore endowed with measures of institutionalised cultural capital and this had a bearing on their access to lifestyle image consumption. Anne, for example, a fine art graduate, was able to carry her knowledge of surely the most lauded arena of the arts qualifications – art history – to bear on her reception of lifestyle ideas. In my discussion with Anne about the garden media, she was able to identify the historical and cultural artistic allusions which inhered in some media lifestyle ideas. Describing a roof garden makeover that had utilised desert plants, grasses and mirrors, Anne drew on her knowledge of Spanish art as a means to describe it as, 'having a Gaudi feel to it.' Similarly, Anne and her daughter Phoebe, a textiles graduate, showed their ability to display what Bourdieu would describe as 'elite taste' (Bourdieu 1990b) in relation to magazine photography. In an exchange about the magazine *New Eden*, for example, Anne and Phoebe demonstrate that their appreciation of photography goes beyond merely looking through representational form at utilitarian images of plants:

Anne: There was this really expensive one, wasn't there?

Phoebe: I was gonna buy it the other day.

Lisa T: Which one, can you remember?

Anne: It's a new one, what's it called? It's square …

Lisa T. *New Eden*.

Phoebe: Lovely!

Anne: Beautiful photographs. Now that does attract me to them. I like to take close-ups of flowers, or close-ups of anything.

Phoebe: Yeah, mum's a really good photographer.

Here the appreciation of the form of close-up photography, a medium described by Bourdieu as a 'middle-brow medium' (1990), takes precedence over the use of photographs for their function of portraying plant varieties. Aesthetic appreciation of lifestyle form is privileged over its function. It was the possession of cultural capital amongst my middle-class respondents which enabled this particular mode of lifestyle media consumption. The cultural references encased in magazines such as *New Eden* was only available to those with sufficient capitals to unlock them: class determined access to particular aesthetic codes and allusions.

Age

Class, however, is not the only determinant which might either provide access or block entry to media lifestyle consumption. Age, a variable – especially in relation to older viewers – that has been given relatively short shrift in media reception studies (see as an exception Tulloch, 1989), was also a factor which hampered gardening possibilities provided by the garden media. One of the questions I posed during the interviews was: 'Do you have any dreams or aspirations for the future?' The pattern that emerged from this line of enquiry was that if respondents had few dreams and diminishing aspirations, they were unlikely to be hailed by media lifestyle ideas. It was by no means always the case that older respondents had a more static conception of their garden, however, when being older co-incided with being working-class, there were virtually no new garden plans. Class and age provided a double block on entry to new garden projects; for them, mere maintenance became an aspiration in itself. This had a direct bearing on their reception of garden lifestyle ideas.

When I asked Philip and Catherine if they had ever been influenced by the garden media, they responded by immediately discounting themselves as an appropriate garden lifestyle audience:

> **Lisa T**: Can you ever think of a time when you've been influenced by a gardening personality?

> **Catherine**: I might be I think if we were younger and didn't have things how we want. You know my son has just bought a brand new house. It's just a mass of weeds. They just don't know what to do with it, you know.

> **Philip**: I think they'll be influenced by watching those sorts of programmes.

> **Catherine**: They would, because they've got a bare garden there with nothing and they want ideas as to what to do with it.

Here Catherine immediately falls to thinking of her son, as opposed to herself, at the consideration of new ideas for the garden. Catherine and Philip have the garden 'how [they] want it'; here they shift the idea of new projects and aspirations to young, relatively mobile people like their son and his new wife. In these ways, Catherine and Philip have a means of watching makeover programmes while writing themselves out of the lifestyle possibilities the programmes offer.

Doris also had watching strategies which precluded her sense of herself as an active consumer of media lifestyle ideas. She watched *Ground Force* without ever being hailed by its ideas. Always mindful of her own constraints of space and economic resources, such as money and lack of transport, she placed a barrier between herself as gardener and the programme's incitement for her to take up its ideas. One of the strategies she used as a means of curbing her involvement in programme content was to 'outsize' gardens shown on television, in this way she was able to strike a vast difference between gardens on television and her own garden. As a result, any comparison between her garden and television images of gardens became entirely unrealistic and unachievable:

> **Doris**: I mean you watch programmes on the television and they show you these marvellous gardens, well they're massive aren't they so they can take big plants, and that, like pampas grass, well it's far too big for a garden like mine. It isn't that I don't like plants, you know, it's I can't have them, if you understand me, rather than don't like them, I just can't have them for my size of border.

Even though, as I argue in chapter 5, using Bauman (1987) and Chaney (2002) contemporary 'experts' strived to lower their differences in knowledge, personality and outlook between themselves and audiences, Doris could only see a chasm of difference between herself, Alan Titchmarsh and his access to garden resources:

Doris: This, erm, Titchmarsh. What do you call him?

Lisa T: Alan Titchmarsh.

Doris: Well he shows yer, and he's lots of garden and he's doing this and doing the other and putting, you know, making them in arches, and I think, "It's all very well (laughs) but you've a lot more space than I have." And, like I say, you like these things but you just haven't the space to do it.

Indeed, for Doris the mention of *Ground Force* only served as a reminder of a list of resources she simply could not access:

Lisa T: Do you watch *Ground Force*?

Doris: I've watched that, yes. They've to do it in a certain time.

Lisa T: What do you think about that?

Doris: Well as I say it's alright, they're all experts. Erm and they can do it and they have all their plants, everything, all at the ready.

Lisa T: Yeah.

Doris: Well I 'aven't a car so I've to depend on someone taking me to the garden centre and that …

Lisa T: Sure.

Doris:…if you're wanting to do things like that. I mean you can 'ave people in, but they're quite expensive you see and you've to think of the expense as well, haven't you?

Lisa T: Yes … so that's something you'd watch but you wouldn't be influenced by?

Doris: No …no because you can't can you, there's certain things that you can't enter into.

For Doris maintenance of a tidy garden was all she could hope for:

Lisa T: Dreams or aspirations?

Doris: Not really. Well, I mean it's tidy and I keep it tidy. Probably if I was younger I might, but when you're older, you don't 'ave dreams like.

Gender

Throughout this book I argue that gardening is both classed and gendered. In chapters 5 and 7, I explore the traditionally gendered images of gardeners from the late 1990s, where men mow, clip and construct and women decorate and plant. I argue that even the madeover garden, with its use of 'curvy' hard-landscaping and pink planting schemes, was used, as I demonstrate using *Homefront: Inside Out,* as a means to express the 'latent' femininity of the makeover subject. In chapter 7, I empirically evidence that traditional, gendered ways of gardening continued to be practiced in ordinary gardens – though some gardeners represented a challenge to traditional modes of being in the garden.

In terms of lifestyle media consumption however, I found only scant empirical evidence to suggest that gender impacted on the consumption practices of the men and women of this study. Only one instance of gendered lifestyle consumption was offered during the time I spent with my respondents: interestingly it was an example culled from a compartment outside the garden lifestyle media.

In chapter 7, I argue that when men and women lived together, regardless of class, age or gender, it was almost as though they had made a tacit agreement to perform staunchly demarcated, gendered modes of gardening. For example, working-class couple John and Stephanie had a starkly drawn model of gendered garden tasks: John's role was to provide a structural, DIY garden canvas for Stephanie to 'titivate' using her essentially female decorative skills. Interestingly, Stephanie was the only respondent who made any claims to gendered lifestyle consumption, but the gardening lifestyle media was not where Stephanie went for inspiration:

> **Lisa T**: Have you got any gardening magazines?
>
> **Stephanie**: Well. I 'aven't any actual gardening magazines, but women's magazines do 'ave garden sections in them.
>
> **Lisa T**: Do you pay attention to those?
>
> **Stephanie**: Oh yeah, yeah, 'cos they 'ave like, what you should be doing in your garden this month an' each month as it goes along. They'll say, "Right, prune this or so and sos in season." An' they'll usually have some nice colour photo. pages that I suppose if you wanted you could frame yourself and make a little picture (laughs).
>
> **John**: We 'ave done that 'aven't we?
>
> **Stephanie**: We 'ave done that in the past.

For Stephanie, the monthly advice offered by general interest magazines seemed to suit the rhythm of her own instructional requirements. And the images, here valued not for their form, but for their ability to realistically and functionally portray beautiful gardens, also held a cut-out-and-keep appeal which was good enough to adorn the walls of her home. Indeed, reading about gardening in a women's general interest magazine – an aspect of popular culture devoted to the construction of femininity – suggests that gardening is seen as both an extension and compartment of femininity. The exchange went on:

> **Stephanie**: I think its mainly women that's noticing 'cos they're the ones that have time to do it an' we've got better ideas anyway. Obviously … we've got better ideas about co-ordinating.
>
> **John**: Well that's what women are for, that's why you get dressed up innit and put make-up on.
>
> **Stephanie**: Yeah.
>
> **John**: Yeah, it's like your garden is an extension of you, to me.

For couples who perform traditional modes of gendered gardening, lifestyle garden media texts may not be sufficiently conventionally gendered. If the decorative aspects of gardening are a logical extension of how women adorn themselves through clothes and cosmetics, then the general interest magazine is a more convenient place to search for ideas.

This book argues that people live out classed and gendered identities in the context of their ordinary gardens. In chapter 5, I argue that while the media was an institutional site where more ordinary people were embraced, representations of the ordinary were still located by class and gender. This section shows that class was the most significant variable in determining how people navigate their consumption of media texts. Bourdieu's (1986) theoretical approach to class was also salient from the production to the point of the consumption of lifestyle texts because access to being able to consume the knowledges which inhere within lifestyle ideas was largely determined by the distribution of (classed) capitals. Age was also significant to the consumption of lifestyle texts, especially when being older was combined with being working-class. For respondents over fifty-five there was a sense that they lacked sufficient future to fundamentally change the garden. And older working-class people simply lacked the economic capital to consume new lifestyle ideas. In these cases, people suspended their own subjectivity from the address of garden lifestyle texts in the acceptance that garden maintenance, with its emphasis on making the best of the resources they had was 'for the likes of them'. I found only scant evidence to suggest that gender had a real bearing on modes of garden lifestyle consumption.[1] It would seem from my data that women's general interest magazines, through which the construction of femininity was more pervasively given emphasis, served to feminise aspects of lifestyle, including gardening, perhaps more obviously for my respondents than garden lifestyle texts. Subjective locations had a bearing on how ordinary people consumed media lifestyle texts.

---

1   This may well have more to do with the types of questions I asked during my interviews than with whether gender mattered to my respondents' consumption of lifestyle texts. I never directly asked whether gender affected their consumption. See appendix one.

Reading Garden Lifestyle Texts

In chapter 5 I drew on social theory as a means of understanding the impact of rapid social change on the media and culture industries. In this section I examine how ordinary people consumed the 1990s shifts in media policy and programming in the context of wider cultural change.

According to recent social theory, contemporary culture is still in the process of social and cultural transition: mass societies are moving from 'ways of life' to 'lifestyle'. Traditional cultural forms offer a high degree of social stability to their subjects; whereas those in the process of building lifestyles out of the freeplay of cultural symbolism lack firm social grounding and are relatively insecure. In this way, the lifestyle project as a new social form becomes a primary identity marker. People, according to critics like Chaney (2001), make serious investments in using cultural forms as a means to actively express their identity and differentiate themselves from others. For Chaney, lifestyles, 'offer a set of expectations which act as a form of ordered control' in the face of changes wrought by modernity (Chaney 1996, 11). Seen in this way lifestyles can act as resources of stability or coping mechanisms which help people to manage their own relationship to social change.

Chaney is careful to point out, however, that the move from 'ways of life' to 'lifestyle' is *currently in transition*; in this way his work offers an interpretation of, 'social change as it is happening – a form of contemporary history' (Chaney 2001, 86). It is not simply the case that ways of life have been wholly replaced by lifestyles, as he argues: 'Ways of life and lifestyles are not mutually exclusive, as they clearly to some extent co-exist in contemporary experience' (Chaney 2001, 83). In what follows, I asked whether ways of life are currently in the process of being replaced by lifestyle in the small semi-industrial town of this study, in the manner Chaney describes. As a means to do this I asked: what do ordinary people think about the makeover, the personality-interpreter and the social uses of garden lifestyle practices?

Approaches to the makeover

As Chaney (2001) argues, a central feature of the changes wrought by modernity is the breakdown of old established communities. Lifestyle media programmes of the late 1990s recognised the inherent instability of contemporary social life – indeed lifestyle producers understood that the wane of civil society was producing stand-alone subjects capable of inventing their own present and future identities. Yet my empirical data revealed that there were enclaves in British culture, beyond the urban anonymity of the city or the suburb, where subjects still retained strong community ties and roots. All my respondents had been born, brought up and had lived to middle- or old-age in the small town where they were interviewed. Even in cases where respondents had studied for qualifications at Universities located outside the region, they had returned 'home'. As a consequence, the majority of my interviewees lacked the need to utilise lifestyle as a coping mechanism and tended to reject the idea of gardening as a consumer activity. Indeed, several of them interpreted lifestyle garden ideas as undesirable and symbolic of a wider, lamentable decline in traditional, authentic garden practices.

John told me, for example, 'I've seen two or three programmes and I think "garbage"'. But beyond decrying the makeover, respondents had a critical approach to the garden media. There is by now a long-standing tradition in media and cultural studies which credits the powers of the discriminating, critical and 'active' media audience (Gillespie 1995; Jenkins 1992; Nava and Nava 1992; Seiter et al. 1989; Willis 1990). In line with this work, the people of this study had a thought-out rationale on which to base their criticisms of garden lifestyle. For many of them, gardening was an authentic hobby which had to be performed in real time. The 'instant' makeover had no real relationship with gardening in the true sense. Authentic gardening was conceived as a skill-set which requires perseverance across years of practice. Instant gardeners had no business calling themselves 'gardeners'. As David told me:

> **David**: I don't like instant gardening. It's taken sixty years to do that and for these people to say they're gardeners and then you can get a lorry to take all the muck away and get another lorry with £100.00's worth of plants all at one go. So you've got so much new stuff to look at in one go…
>
> **Lisa T**: It goes against …
>
> **David**: Anybody who's done that can't call themselves gardeners really.
>
> **Lisa**: No.
>
> **David**: It shows that they want a nice garden and they want to spend a week at the seaside don't it?

Similarly, Rosemary told me that makeover programmes were a 'good idea for people who are not gardeners,' adding, 'a garden grows over years.' For others, 'real' gardening was about carrying out garden labour methodically and appropriately.

While Chaney (2001) argues that those who embrace lifestyles accept the production of authenticity using resources from the consumer and leisure industries, the gardeners I spoke to excoriated manufactured gardening consumption and bemoaned the fall of traditional methods of garden-making. Take for example, the following points made by David about his soil and compost making:

> **David**: I have a feeling that a lot of these blokes on gardening programmes have some lovely soil there. They've made it look so easy for people to garden. But you see I don't go off into a – say garden centre – and see all these lovely green and yellow coloured bags. I never buy any. I have things out there that have been there years and years. The soil's improved. Dug over and composted, year after year.

For these gardeners, media makeover gardening was aligned to the unnecessary expense of the garden centre. Rosemary described makeover programmes as, 'expensive', remarking that her retaining wall, would be far too expensive for such programmes to create using 'original' materials. These gardeners turned a blind eye to lifestyling from symbolic consumer resources. Gardening for them was about working with the authentic and sometimes inclement, raw materials offered by the garden itself. And there was an acceptance that that meant bending to seasonal conditions, traditional garden knowledge and hard labour.

For Chaney (1996, 2001), the lifestyle is a new social form, redolent of the wider social shift away from traditional, civic ways of life. I would argue that the gardeners I interviewed were at least partially sentient of that shift. Experientially, they regarded the move to lifestyle as a decline in traditional local methods and aesthetics. For Rosemary the outdoor spaces subject to makeover on programmes such as *Ground Force* were 'shapes' which even when finished lacked any sense of three-dimensional garden space. 'Well,' she told me, they're usually very flat aren't they, an absolute flat square. There's plenty of spare earth, but no garden.'

Approaches to personality-interpreters

In chapter 4 I argue that media garden legislators, who addressed audiences up until the late 1960s using an instructional mode of address, had by the later 1990s largely been replaced by personality-interpreters. As part of the discourse of achievability which pervaded the lifestyle media, presenters such as Anne McKevitt and Diarmund Gavin carried only scant measures of gardening expertise. In line with the argument that society is undergoing a transitional shift from civic to consumer culture, personality-interpreters have became friendly well-researched consumers, interpreting the latest shopping ideas for the would-be lifestyle gardener. However, those who interpreted lifestyle as an erosion of traditional garden aesthetics and knowledges, tended to be unreceptive to the friendly advice of media garden presenters My group of gardeners, with their roots in a relatively stable semi-industrial community had investments in the continuation of traditional gardening as a way of life. As a result, most of them tended to bemoan the demise of the instructional, public service gardener.

Several of the gardeners I spoke to had a wistful nostalgia for late 1960s gardeners such as Percy Thrower and Peter Smith. When I asked Geoff, for example, if he had ever been influenced by the contemporary gardening media, he told me that he still refers back to his 'Percy Thrower books upstairs' for help with how to garden. As Keith told me, 'Percy Thrower and Peter Smith …they showed actual gardening techniques and they were showing people as we were taught when we were kids.' And many of my respondents were deeply sentimental about the late Geoff Hamilton. Many of them spoke of their 'admiration' for a what Millie called, 'a marvellous man'. Interestingly, as Geoff reveals below, Geoff Hamilton straddled instructional gardening advice and lifestyle ideas:

> **Geoff**: I tell you who we used to like, we used to watch that one, that Geoff Hamilton, that died. He was sort of in-between, sort of serious and games really.

But perhaps the most vociferous critic of the gardening personality-interpreter was James. James, who, at the end of his lifelong career as a professional gardener and florist, had a great personal investment in arguing for the preservation of traditional methods of gardening that had been his stock-in-trade. For James, contemporary television programmes such as *Gardener's World* and *Ground Force* only serve to remind him of the severed link between the gardener and traditional gardening tools. Neglect for how garden tools work with the soil has led to a decline in techniques for the care and preservation of tools:

> **James**: Today, I mean these people paddle about, you never see them come out with a clean spade. It's always a dirty, grubby spade and its ten times harder to use. Titchmarsh is as bad as them all. It's ten times harder because it doesn't slide in the soil and it's like a drag, it's like a parachute, it's simply slowing you up as you're going in.

The problem with these kinds of programmes for James is that they simply lacked instruction. From his point of view, audiences need to be shown what he termed 'the basics':

> **James**: They don't teach it now and they're going more gimmicky than they were. I say they're not showing enough of the basic potting and growing. And it's time they taught people how to garden and how to use the tools. I mean for newcomers and people new to it, it's what they want to see.

Lifestyle gardening for the social good

To malign lifestyle as a signifier of consumer culture alone, is to choose to ignore the attributes in factual entertainment which might promote citizenship. Moseley (2001), for example, argues that to read the primetime shift as, 'a move from hard to soft, from documentary to makeover, from address to citizen to consumer, from public to private and from 'quality' to 'dumbed-down' television is to ignore the complex issues made by that shift' (Brunsdon et al. 2001, 33). For her, lifestyle address straddles these dualisms: viewers are 'citizen-consumers' who can, 'on a small scale, learn to make changes, make a difference, improve the personal for the national good' (Brunsdon et al. 2001, 34). Analysis of lifestyle programming in the late 1990s undoubtedly revealed that lifestyle ideas hold a measure of educational value for citizens, and while most of my respondents were too firmly bound to their stable communities to be motivated to activate the possibilities of consumer gardening lifestyle, many of them recognised the benevolent role of lifestyle gardening in promoting the social good.

Of all my respondents, university-educated mother and daughter Anne and Phoebe had the most positive response to the makeover genre, personality-interpreters and the idea of lifestyle garden transformation. Marked out as the only respondents to have studied higher qualifications outside of their hometown, they were people who had experienced a sense of temporary uprootedness. In this way, they serve to support the efficacy of Chaney's argument, that subjects open to lifestyle improvisation are relatively destabilised. Garden lifestyle programming was positive for these women because they could act as catalysts of creativity:

> **Lisa T**: And what do you think of them when they're finished after a couple of days? They've used things like stapling and decking?
>
> **Anne**: I'm all for it. I think a garden helps people. I know I used to go out if I'd had a row with Richard. I'd go outside and I'd dig. That's creating something and a lot of people

have difficulty being creative, whereas if you stick a plant in and it goes there's a great deal of satisfaction in it.

Anne and Phoebe recognised that while creativity held therapeutic value and could be used as a coping mechanism for the travails of everyday life, ordinary people need some kind of reassurance for its release. Lifestyle programming could help to get people started:

Anne: Most people, if they had a completely blank canvas it would be like a clean sheet of paper, they wouldn't know where to start, they'd be frightened. So in a way them talking about, you know, just draw your garden and measure around it, just outlining ways of doing, it is sort of increasing their confidence.

Phoebe: I think that they help people to see what's possible as far as their gardens go.

And even those who bemoaned the 'gimmicky' feel of the lifestyle makeover programme tended to concede that the aims of the lifestyle garden media were positively laudable. Despite James' reservations, for example, he told me that garden lifestyle programmes were serving to democratise gardening as an activity: 'I like some of the developments they're making,' he said, 'They're opening up avenues for anybody.'

Moreover, the wider 'social good' of garden lifestyle was linked, for some of my respondents, to the idea of urging people to keep their gardens from falling into dilapidation. In chapter 2 and 6, I argue that working-class gardeners have historically been urged, either by the council estate regulatory handbook or through an invidious self-regulation, to monitor their gardens in a bid to maintain respectability. For some of the working-class gardeners I spoke to, the garden lifestyle media served a function in continuing the project of local councils by urging other working-class people to take 'responsibility' for the space outside their homes.

Keith: These programmes help get people interested in gardening again basically. Because I think people will ignore gardening for as long as they can, but if they have a responsibility to look after something then they tend to go and look after it ... and then they start looking at garden centres. I suppose at end at t'day, I just want 'em to realise what they've got.

For others, the media was already playing a central role in promoting gardening as citizenship into the working-class societal enclaves that need it most. Stephanie and John believed that garden lifestyle television made some gardeners sufficiently self-conscious to keep their gardens tidy. 'If it wasn't for telly,' Stephanie told me, 'people wouldn't do owt with their gardens.' Her husband John backed her up – demonstrating even less trust in his working-class counterparts:

John: Yeah telly's doing some folk good 'cos whereas some might 'ave a shit 'ole for a garden, they've actually got some flowers and they're taking a bit more pride in it.

In these ways, my data demonstrates that some of my respondents recognised that lifestyle programming was socially beneficial for the nation, for generating creativity amongst ordinary people and for democratising gardening knowledge. But for some of those located as working-class, the importance of lifestyle programming lay in its efficacy to address *others* as 'citizen-consumers' in a bid to help the working-class to 'improve.' In this way, the 'national good' was effected by communicating values of respectability to those likely to neglect their untidy (front) gardens in ways which 'let the side down' in areas where working-class people live.

The experience of my respondents testified to the continued existence of 'ways of life' in relation to gardening as opposed to the import of garden lifestyle practices. No doubt in other sections of contemporary British social life, garden lifestyling is replacing traditional ways of life in relation to gardening in the ways Chaney describes. However, in the small semi-industrial town where my data was gathered, my respondents enjoyed the security offered by shared communal garden practices where authentic, local gardening traditions were still valued. Indeed it was through my respondents' approach to garden lifestyle media consumption that I discovered gardening was still regarded as a traditional 'way of life'.

From Lifestyle Ideas to Garden Practice

The uses of media lifestyle ideas

Thus far, this chapter argues that my group of ordinary gardeners were too firmly rooted to their traditional 'way of life' to be interested in the pursuit of new, consumer-driven lifestyle garden projects. But the garden lifestyle media were by no means superfluous for these gardeners; indeed, while they were more traditional in their approach to the garden, they still used garden media products in specific ways.

For several respondents, television lifestyle gardening, in particular the makeover, offered an important source of 'entertainment'. As Philip told me, 'they're for entertainment now as much as teaching.' Similarly, Kate told me that it is, 'the entertainment rather than anything' that motivated her to watch *Ground Force*. Another use for the garden makeover, and this was especially the case among female respondents, was that it allowed one to be a voyeur of other peoples' gardens. 'I think I'm quite nosey about other peoples' gardens,' Phoebe told me. And Catherine said, 'it's entertainment, it's peeking into somebody's private life.'

Others approached the garden media as 'consumer-citizens'; for them it served an educational role by providing information, tips and advice. As Millie told me, 'You get ideas, but you also get good advice. I mean I've learnt quite a lot from them. How to take cuttings, what to do and what not to do and what to put them in.' One of the most popular educational television features amongst my sample of gardeners, however, is the *Gardeners' World* slot where, as Thomas describes, 'they take you to an established garden and show you around it.' What was of primary interest to several of my gardeners was the fact that these features provided valuable information, as Alan continued, about, 'what grows in those conditions, the colour combinations, the height.' Millie and Jack also use these features for their information about plants:

Lisa T: What features interest you most?

Millie: I like to see the country ones, the bigger ones, where they go 'round and they're all … and they're saying well you could grow this, but we've tried now and you know.

Jack: And they give you various plants that you grow in a certain situation, you know, like shade, or they like dry … this will grow in acid soil and this will grow in a clay soil …

These responses give weight to Moseley's (2001) argument: that the 'citizen-consumer' address of lifestyle was designed, at the micro level, to help people make a small personal difference and thereby contribute to the national good.

Others recognised that the role of these programmes was to address audiences as consumers and some respondents were grateful to the media for showcasing new products and for proffering product advice. Anne and Phoebe, for example, used the media to find out about products for pest control and mulching. But perhaps even more significantly, some of them recognised the part presenters played as adjudicators whose role is to *interpret* new ideas for the would-be gardener. As Kate describes:

Kate: They show you what you can do. They show you what is available and, you know, whereas you just have these set ideas and they come up with different variations of it. Like flagging, you know, we don't just want square flags everywhere, we want it nice.

Preparation, plans and ideas: gardening and modern imaginative hedonism

What is perhaps most interesting about Kate's response above, was that her remarks testified to a willingness to *apply* media interpreters' ideas to her own garden. While most of my respondents were too 'rooted' to traditional garden ideas as a way of life to be hooked in to what the lifestyle media had to offer, I found that not all of them were immune to lifestyle ideas. For some, lifestyle captured the gardening imagination; the new ideas of lifestyle tapped into their dreams and aspirations. For Kate and Geoff, for example, the lifestyle media had captured their fantasies of making a Mediterranean garden. Notice the imaginative possibilities sparked by the lifestyle media in the following exchange:

Geoff: I was going to create our own bit of the Mediterranean, aren't we?

Kate: Yeah. Terracotta, definitely, I love the terracotta. We love Greece. You see things out there and these television things show you …blue … to tell the truth and the brilliant colours. It's just lovely.

And Anne and Phoebe showed enthused engagement with lifestyle images, particularly in relation to the ways in which personality-interpreters used design in the garden. As fine art and textile graduates, they were able to use their cultural capital as a means to both understand and imaginatively appropriate the post-modern eclecticism of how design is used in the makeover genre:

Phoebe: (about Diarmund Gavin) … some of the ideas he's come up with are really nice. I like his way of thinking. To me he's a designer and it wouldn't matter what he was designing … He has a vision of what is good design and he could be designing cars and he'd still be a good designer. And it's that imagination that he's taken into the garden and it's appreciated.

Anne: We appreciate that …

Phoebe: 'Cos he's asking people to make a leap of faith in essence.

What is important about these comments is that Anne and Phoebe were prepared to use 'experts' as interpreters. According to Chaney (2001), as a new social form lifestyles are fashioned out of two distinctive components: sites and strategies. Sites are the physical spaces where people can appropriate their own agency; they are places which become meaningful because they afford people a measure of control. Strategies are the projects in which people invest; they become manifest as implanted metaphors which articulate identity (Chaney 2001, 86). The 'leap of faith' Anne describes was a recognition that lifestyle interpreters suggest lifestyle strategies for audiences to appropriate and order in the context of their own garden sites. In what follows, Phoebe and Anne discuss how they have selected interpreters' ideas which they plan to go on to translate through their own creativity:

Phoebe: (about Diarmund Gavin) I like his ideas very much. I wouldn't steal them, but some of the … like painting walls that marrakesh colour blue, that was lovely. That was a nice idea but we wouldn't necessarily use it in paint. It might be in plants instead.

Lisa T: So you wouldn't, alright, so you'd actually be quite uncomfortable with just nicking an idea?

Anne: Oh no!

Phoebe: Oh no!

Anne: You'd never … I mean our space is our space and therefore it's quite unique to us. So no matter what idea you've chosen, it wouldn't be exactly the same because it would have to fit.

Making it 'fit', using plants rather than paint showed their own aesthetic use of lifestyle programming in order to adapt their own strategies into the physical environment of the garden site. Yet even though, as these comments show, lifestyle ideas were powerfully attractive to some respondents, I saw no evidence of practised engagement with transformative gardening as action. Rather, I found that lifestyle ideas captured the head rather than the hand or arm; the idea of transformation tended to exist in the imagination and at the level of conversation rather than in practice. Why, I wondered, was it the case that even those imaginatively fired up by the notion of lifestyle gardening showed no evidence of putting those ideas in to action?

In his book *The Romantic Ethic and the Spirit of Modern Consumerism* (1995), Campbell argues that consumption must be understood in relation to the modern self's unique ability to generate pleasurable thoughts through fantasy. Modern consumerism, which Campbell dates from the eighteenth century English consumer revolution, is characterised by, 'an outgrowth of modern, autonomous, imaginative hedonism ... the widespread adoption of the covert habit of daydreaming' (Campbell 1995, 88-89). Modern hedonism, for Campbell, is distinguished by the distinctive faculty of being able to generate illusions and fantasies which are 'known to be false but felt to be true' (Campbell 1995, 78). In this way, fantasising and day-dreaming become so pleasurable that it is wanting, as opposed to having, which becomes the key element in the pursuit of pleasure. Indeed, consummating the desire to have things by actual acts of consumption can be relatively 'disillusioning' for people. Campbell goes on:

> Individuals do not so much seek satisfaction from products, as pleasure from the self-illusory experiences which they construct from their associated meanings. The essential activity of consumption is thus not the actual selection, purchase or use of products, but the imaginative pleasure to which the actual product lends itself, 'real' consumption being largely a resultant of this 'mentalistic hedonism' (Campbell 1995, 89).

The credence of Campbell's concept of 'modern, autonomous, imaginative hedonism' is directly relevant to the responses some of my ordinary gardeners had to the actual consumption of garden lifestyle ideas. Kate and Geoff testified to their dream of a Mediterranean garden, but I know through my continued contact with this community of gardeners that their plans remain plans. Stimulated by the Mediterranean 'looks' they have gleaned from viewing the garden makeover genre and from their holidays in Greece, they continue to defer the gratification of fantasy rather than to actually execute the work. Similarly, Anne and Phoebe were full of new ideas to transform their back garden using the inspiration of garden designers such as Diarmund Gavin, but they have never moved beyond excited sketches and animated talk. Acts of mixing cement or laying bricks are not yet in evidence.

Integral to Campbell's argument about the nature of modern consumption is the idea that a whole swathe of cultural artefacts which represent goods, for example, calendars, posters, works of art – and texts which advertise goods in the media and communications industries – work to *facilitate* imaginative hedonism. Indeed 'window-shopping' which is performed without purchasing goods, is itself a pleasurable experience. In this way, Campbell provides a useful way of conceptualising why my respondents used lifestyle ideas to dream and fantasise about how their gardens might have been, without ever feeling the need to actually purchase or actively garden. Pleasure, he argues, 'comes from the imaginative use of the objects seen; that is from mentally 'trying on' the clothes examined, or 'seeing' the furniture arranged within one's room' (Campbell 1995, 92). Lifestyle interpreters captured the imagination of some ordinary gardeners, but rather than inciting people to manufacture garden lifestyles, they often provided material for garden day-dreams. Wanting, longing, fantasising and day-dreaming were more desirous activities than the messy, flawed, imperfect realities of actually executing the plans.

Conclusion

My analysis of the consumption of garden lifestyle texts, using ethnographic evidence 'from below' reveals that media public relations, advertising and marketing strategies work effectively to secure the audiences they target, especially in relation to class. In this way, this chapter argues that Bourdieu's (1986) model of capitals offers explanatory power both to the textual production of how lifestyle texts represent class and to how audiences receive and consume them. The uneven distribution of different types of capital determines access to lifestyle ideas; in this way, those without the requisite capitals lack the competencies to be able to consume legitimate middle-class aesthetics. These patterns of consumption illustrate the chain, from production to consumption, of how class inequalities are concretised, perpetuated and experienced as power relations. It argues that while class determined what and how people consumed lifestyle texts, age was also a barrier to the reception of lifestyle ideas: working-class older people simply lacked the economic resources to even allow themselves to be subjectively addressed by lifestyle ideas.

Class was also significant for how people regarded the social value of the garden lifestyle programme. I argue that working-class viewers regarded their uses as both educational and productive. Historically denied respectability (Skeggs 1997), I argue in chapter 6 that the drive to both acquire and secure respectability through garden aesthetics was especially salient for my working-class respondents. Aware that there were members of their class who refused to 'improve' in ways which fuelled representations of the working-class as lazy and worthless, this chapter shows that these gardeners saw the lifestyle programme as an educational aid which might urge the lazy working-class contingent to get motivated about gardening. In this way, these gardeners recognised and valued the civic aims of lifestyle because of their class location.

However, this chapter also argues that the macro changes identified by contemporary social theory – such as for example, the transition from 'ways of life' to lifestyle – are not yet in evidence in the micro context of the small British semi-industrial town. For the bulk of my respondents, gardening remains a traditional enthusiasm, fastened to a relatively stable sense of a 'way of life'. While the lifestyle programme was lauded by working-class respondents because of its potential to improve *other* working-class people, its 'lifestyle' ethos courted criticism. The trappings of lifestyle which find their expression in the garden makeover and the personality-interpreter were largely rejected as superficial and expensive products of popular entertainment. For the people of this study lifestyle, regardless of their locations of class and gender, remains a media construction rather than a lived experience. This does not mean that they were entirely untouched by lifestyle ideas, indeed in some cases, people made innovative interpretations of the ideas they encountered. However in these exceptional cases where imaginations were captured by fresh lifestyle ideas, people tended to allow their interpretations to remain at dream or fantasy level (Campbell 1995). Gratifying their dreams through actual consumption held small priority for these ordinary gardeners.

Chapter 9

Using Sentimental Capital: Class, Emotion and Value

Introduction

In this final chapter, I want to encapsulate the book's historical findings on classed and gendered taste cultures in the ordinary garden and its relationship to lifestyle media culture, recording as I do my concluding remarks about a particular moment in British media and cultural history in the late 1990s. I also want to end the book by tentatively sketching out an attempt to theorise how the working-class people of the study use and make their own forms of value through gardening. In doing so, I revisit Bourdieu by extending his concept of capital as a means of exploring the emotional resources, produced out of affective familial ties, which become fastened to the skills, knowledge and assets that are drawn upon to make gardens. Arguing that such a resource is held, circulated, exchanged and traded in local contexts I draw on both Nowotny (1981) and Reay's (2000) concept of 'emotional capital' to argue that the valuing located in this small-scale study might act as a form of 'sentimental capital.' I chart how gardening with sentimental attachments became manifest in the empirical data: through what gardening means, familial passed down practices and in relation to sentimental feelings provoked by condemnation of lifestyle garden television. For it was here, where opposing aesthetic value systems (national vs. local and lifestyle vs. ways of life) met, that I got a clear sense of how the working-class gardeners in particular, had developed a way of conceptualising their hobby using emotional resources of self-valuing. In this final chapter I argue that these affective resources are expressive of a local alternative value system that insists on reproducing community valued aesthetics in an emotional politics of resistance to lifestyle culture, aesthetics and consumerism.

Gardening with Sentimental Attachments

One of the findings that emanated through the study was the specific set of emotions experienced by the respondents. What comes through aspects of the data, was that in talking about their gardening as an everyday enthusiasm, the people of the study felt at certain points, 'tender, comforting emotions and gentle feelings' (Knight 1999, 411). They felt caring, affection, sympathy and sharing but also wistfulness, nostalgia, maudlin: emotions that are commonly associated with sentimentality. Some of them were powerful – particularly in relation to the deeply sentimental feelings about their conception of traditional gardening that came through some of their pejorative and at times quite angry views about garden lifestyle make-over television. But many of them were routine, embedded into the diurnal rhythms of gardening practice and were felt most especially by my working-class gardeners who gardened in resource constrained contexts. To give you a flavour of gardening with sentimental attachments, there were three key areas of emotion. Firstly, there were *sentimental practices of what the garden meant for the working-class gardeners of the study.* To my working-class gardeners there was a desire to keep gardening a community endeavour within the context of relatively few economic resources. Particular aesthetic codes of how gardens, especially at the front, should look, were adhered to:

> **Keith:** With it being a row of terraced …everybody has a garden and you tend to fit in with everybody else
>
> **Lisa :**And you wouldn't want to grow veg in the front garden?
>
> **Keith**: Well no I don't, I mean it might be unsightly to some people. They might think, 'What a strange place to put them.'

Seeds, cuttings and perennial plants were exchanged and freely given in a context where high ethical ideals of caring and sharing in the community were both held and acted upon.

> **Keith:** I don't think it was too much that everyone went out and got packets of seeds … they used to swap plants did't neighbours and that's where I got it from.

And there were dignified, ideal standards of tidiness and respectability that meant enormous investments in how peoples' gardens looked (see chapter 6). Then there were *sentimental practices formed out of passed down familial gardening practices.* Respondents' parents had transmitted tastes for plants, and had expended time and effort in passing their own skills about how to sow seeds or grow vegetables – to the people of the study. Several respondents expressed wistful and nostalgic feelings when they related how their mother and fathers had taught them how to garden (see chapter 7). 'I'm glad he was vegetables' David said of his father. And Stephanie talked about a female line of flower appreciation:

> **Stephanie:** Grandma always 'ad flowers in 't house and me mum as tended to go that way a bit, and then I've always liked things like that, so it's kind of gone down in generations with us.

And finally, there were *sentimental feelings that arose out of condemnation of the make-over and its conventions* which were channelled back to deeply sentimental ideas about old-fashioned gardening practices in the past. It was here where my respondents held me in dialogue about what they thought gardening should be about. It is in these exchanges where mutual valuing and 'talking back' to lifestyle is located. I return to a more detailed analysis of this data in relation to lifestyle consumption later.

I want to draw on Sara Ahmed's (2004) 'sociality of emotions' model for thinking about how feelings were shared and exchanged amongst the people of the study. She argues that objects or practices of emotion circulate and become saturated with affect within a community. And since this is a 'grey' study, her argument that emotions accumulate over time in ways that accrue affective value is especially germane. This chapter is an attempt to cautiously outline the tensions coming out of my empirical data around the question of emotional value. If the people of the study make emotional investments in gardening as hobby – what do such sentimental investments motor? Are they transmitted to other people or do they reside in practices, skills or in aesthetics? This focus on the question of emotional value takes me to Nowotny (1981) and Reay's (2000) work – scholars who extend Bourdieu's concept of capital to develop what Nowotny first termed 'emotional capital'. Could the emotional resources I identify in my data exist as a type of emotional – or perhaps even sentimental capital? But if sentimentality is given, as Knight argues, 'near universal condemnation ... taken as a fault that it is taken as a mark of moral decline (or worse) in moral or aesthetic sensibility' (Knight 1999: 411), can 'sentimental capital', which I later show is a resource which has shared value for the people of the study, have any exchange or conversion potential beyond its local contexts?

Emotional Capital

The newcomer to the concept of 'emotional capital' could be forgiven for making the economistic assumption that emotional capital is generated out of positive attributes that might confer further forms of capital accumulation. In fact, it is a complex type of capital, which also carries potential for halts and barriers to further investment and tradeability because it circulates in classed and gendered contexts. For Nowotny, emotional capital is a species of social capital that belongs specifically to women and is located firmly in the private sphere. It consists of 'knowledge, contacts and relations as well as access to emotionally valued skills and assets which hold within any social network characterised at least partly by affective ties' (ibid.) Its forms consist of the resources generated within the affective circle of family and friends, which are transmitted as investments from mothers to children and husbands; in this sense it is a self-less form of capital: devoured by others, for the benefit of others. Moreover, in Nowotny's thinking, emotional capital cannot be converted to economic capital: 'limited to the private sphere ...it is of little value in the outside world' (ibid.). What Nowotny's model shows, is that emotional capital is generative of positive attributes – support, skills, valuing and encouragement – but it is a form of capital that nourishes the tradeability of other capitals. I want to argue that in relation to my study, where there were scant cultural resources, emotional capital fuelled forms of self-valuing within local contexts with meagre currency beyond it. In this way, the link between capitals shows how local affective investments in particular aesthetic practices continue to reproduce themselves in local alternative circuits.

Reay (2000) also theorises emotional capital as gendered capital in her empirical work on mother's involvement in children's schooling, and she builds on Nowotny's model by looking at how class impacts on its efficacy. However, no straightforward model emerges from her data on the relationship between emotional involvement and educational achievement. She found for example, that some of her working-class mothers found it significantly harder than their middle-class counterparts to supply their children with the resources of emotional capital. Often constrained by economic struggle, lack of educational competencies and confidence – some of the mothers she spoke to were using their emotional energies to survive the everyday with limited resources. Conversely, she also found that middle-class mothers' anxieties about their children's academic success meant that while their cultural capital increased as a result of being forced to do homework – there were costs for their freedom and their emotional capital was reduced. In these ways emotional capital, 'is context and resource constrained' (Reay 2000, 581); as a form of capital, its complexity lies in the fact that it eschews clear links between class, value accrual and success. But perhaps most significantly, Reay found that even in the face of the knowledge that their children were failing at school, in contexts where emotional capital had little cultural capital to nourish, working-class mothers insisted on supporting the emotional well-being of their children. This idea is central to my own findings of how emotional resources continue, even when those concerned are sentient that their practices are not valued beyond local contexts, in ways which turn a blind eye to the values of the dominant system. My working-class gardeners were not interested in accruing value beyond the local. In the following section, I explore sentimentality – a term which represents a family of emotions which reinforced positive feelings within the gardening community I studied, but which place further blocks on particular gardening aesthetics beyond the local.

In Defence of Sentimentality

'I think we must face,' argues Knight, 'that sentimentality cannot be defended' (1999, 411). She goes on :'One cannot coherently praise the irrational, the shallow, the simple, the passive, the fantasized, the confabulated' (1999, 418) Indeed, in Knight's thoroughgoing review of the standard philosophical and aesthetic literature sentimentality is associated with a fault, a spiralling down of standards in moral or aesthetic sensibility. And despite the fact that sentimentality acts as an umbrella term for a host of humane and appropriate emotional attributes, 'it is taken as a mark of psychological decline … in ourselves as cognitive and moral agents' (ibid.) The critical language condemning sentimentality is also undoubtedly gendered, think excessive, passive, self-indulgent, shallow: 'sentimentality is a *femme fatale,* only she wields a contagion rather than a gun. Masquerading as an innocent, and working on the inside, it is the undoing of the rational self' (Knight 1999, 418). Other critics note the ways in which sentimentality has been excoriated: Gorton (2005) argues that television studies has marginalised critical engagement with sentimental or emotional programmes, categorising them as 'easy, constructed and simplistic, and watched by lazy audiences' (Gorton 2005, 72). And Warhol (2003) argues that one of the legacies of modernism was its aesthetic and philosophical recoil from feminine forms of popular culture and its need to distinguish 'authentic' emotions from the false and sentimental. But these feminist critics also argue for the re-appraisal of the sentimental. Gorton's work on emotional television uses Kay Mellor's tv writing as an example of how the 'emotional journey' of comedy drama weaves intellectual and emotional engagement together to make 'good' television. Such programmes, she argues, require formal aesthetic qualities in order to 'move' their audiences. Such devices are part of the pedagogical politics of connecting audiences to societal issues and to a 'sense that relationships, whether in the family, community, workplace, matter and that they will enable us to cope with everyday struggles and pressures of life' (2005,78). The idea that sentimental texts connect viewers and readers to the good things in life is echoed in Warhol's writing: 'To those who ask, "what's 'good' about 'the good cry'?" I respond that the ideals of sentimental culture – the affirmation of community, the persistence of hopefulness and of willingness, the belief that everyone matters, the sense that life has a purpose that can be traced to the link of affection between and among persons – are good ideals' (Warhol 2003, 56).

The dual-edged properties of the 'sentimental' enable an understanding of why this type of capital is not valued outside its community of users: it is condemned in the wider culture for the reasons Knight outlines, while also carrying a host of valuable good life ideals for the community in which it circulates.

Sentimental Capital

Sentimental capital is an emotional resource, which is produced out of affective familial ties and becomes fastened to a repertoire of shared ideas about the skills, knowledge and assets that might be drawn upon to aesthetically make gardens. Interestingly, while sentimental capital was in abundance among the middle-aged, it was held in equal measure by both the men and women of the study. In the context of this study it was not so much transmitted or used up, rather, in line with the sentimental feelings that were being experienced it was continually re-visited and re-experienced. 'Sentimentalism,' as Warhol argues, 'is pointedly not cathartic … it rather encourages readers to rehearse and reinforce the feelings it evokes' (2003, 18). When it is was drawn upon amongst the working-class gardeners of my study, it was shared and circulated through practices of sharing plants and seeds and by adhering to communally sanctioned practices about garden aesthetics. It was used in relation to the acquisition of traditional skills, such as caring properly for tools or growing vegetables. And sentimental capital had a temporal dimension – part of its wistful nostalgia came out of conceiving the act of gardening as an old practice. The passing down and then passing on of plants and practices were part of the emotional investment in gardens. Moreover, the working-class respondents were attuned to owning their sentimental feelings through what seemed to me to be an oral tradition of narrating stories about gardening practices. I am by no means the first to note the how sentimentality operates specifically within British working-class culture. In Lusted's (1998) discussion of the affective appeal of light entertainment for audiences, he makes a particular case for sentimentality and the working-class:

> It is the *display* of emotion which characterises working-class social interaction. Working-class cultures celebrate sentiment and the display of sentiment (sentimentality?). It is part

of popular memory, the cultural equivalent of the museums…and other monuments of middle-class history (Lusted 1995, 186).

He goes on to argue that telling stories about cultural practices is often infused by sentimentality as a means of holding together a historical sense of community:

> For working-class communities without resources and organisation to build monuments to their own class histories, oral history becomes crucial in popular memory which must bear witness through stories of communal traditions and practices … sentiment is the affective agency which works to bind listeners into a common community and class memory (Lusted 1995, 187).

In these ways, gardening practices and traditions, as told through the sentiments of oral testimony, become historical monuments to working-class history and culture.

I turn now to discussions of lifestyle television culture where sentimental capital was drawn upon as a means of both decrying lifestyle culture and allowing my respondents to rehearse sentimental emotions about how gardens and gardening should be. In these informal semi-structured interviews I asked my respondents what they thought of the aesthetics promulgated by lifestyle programmes and if they drew on the resources offered by lifestyle in their gardening.

The Uses of Sentimental Capital

Most of them interpreted lifestyle garden ideas as undesirable and symbolic of a wider, lamentable decline in traditional, authentic garden practices. Some respondents reacted quite violently to the mention of the garden make-over genre. As David remarked:

> **David**: It's since this blooming *Force* came on.
>
> **Lisa T**: *Ground Force*?
>
> **David**: I think it's blooming awful.

And John told me, 'I've seen two or three programmes and I think "garbage"'. For many of them 'real' gardening was a pursuit that required the investment of time. The make-over was therefore seen as 'instant' and had very little to do with gardening in the true sense. Authentic gardening was a pursuit that took many years of perseverance, and those who gardened 'instantly' simply had not earned the right to be called 'gardeners'. For David, who still lived in the house where he was born and which his parents had occupied, the garden had been a lifelong project:

> **David**: I don't like instant gardening. It's taken sixty years to do that and for these people to say they're gardeners and then you can get a lorry to take all the muck away and get another lorry with £100.00's worth of plants all at one go. So you've got so much new stuff to look at in one go…
>
> **Lisa T**: It goes against …

David: Anybody who's done that can't call themselves gardeners really.

Lisa: No.

David: It shows that they want a nice garden and they want to spend a week at the seaside don't it?

Similarly, Rosemary told me that make-over programmes were a 'good idea for people who are not gardeners,' adding, 'a garden grows over years.' For others, 'real' gardening was about executing garden labour properly and methodically. For John and Stephanie, instant gardening was the antithesis of authentic garden construction; it meant superficial, slip-shod work that simply did not warrant the title 'gardening'. Hear Stephanie's conception of communally generated garden-giving in this exchange:

Stephanie: Cuttings and things like that, that's how gardens are built up I think over't years. Cuttings from each others things.

John: All these programmes seem to do is change stuff that look different. They don't actually do any gardening. They just dig an 'ole, put a water feature in, stick some trellis in.

Stephanie: Yeah, but they've only two days 'aven't they? Takes time.

John: They just throw a bit o' bark over rough ground instead o' diggin' it out or riddling it and putting plants in how yer should. It's just quickness, it's just hype.

While Chaney (2001) argues that those who embrace lifestyles accept the production of authenticity using resources from the consumer and leisure industries, the gardeners I spoke to decried manufactured gardening consumption and bemoaned the fall of authentic methods of garden-making. Take for example, the following points made by David about his soil and compost making:

David: I have a feeling that a lot of these blokes on gardening programmes have some lovely soil there. They've made it look so easy for people to garden. But you see I don't go off into a – say garden centre – and see all these lovely green and yellow coloured bags. I never buy any. I have things out there that have been there years and years. The soil's improved. Dug over and composted, year after year.

For these gardeners, manufactured, media make-over gardening was linked to what they saw as the unnecessary expense of the garden centre. Hear too the commitment to the old practice of turning the soil and adding compost oneself as a means of caring for and respecting the garden without manufactured products. Others noted that the problems with make-over recommendations were that they were based, as Keith remarked, on 'spending all that money in one go'. Going to the garden centre, for John, quite simply, 'wastes brass'. These gardeners were not interested in improvising new lifestyle ideas from the symbolic repertoires on offer in consumer culture. Gardening for them was about working with the authentic, and sometimes challenging, natural materials offered by the garden itself – and if that required time, respect for the seasons, authentic garden knowledge and methodical labour – then so be it. Experientially, they regarded the move to lifestyle as a decline in traditional local methods and aesthetics. David, for example, suggested that lifestyle media ideas, with their preference for convenience gardening, were serving to render traditional garden features obsolete: 'they're doing away with lawns 'cos they're too difficult.' For him this has had an impact on the aesthetic look of gardens – he added, 'but you're loosing the green, aren't you?'

Sentimental capital is a type of emotional capital which acts as resource of self-valuing. It was a specifically working-class resource because of its sociality, its emphasis on traditional passed-down practices which were shared, sympathetically within a community and because it was embedded within a tradition of sentimental oral testimony. Gardening with sentimental capital, with its emphasis on nostalgia and gardening in the past also meant that working-class aesthetics, like the sentimental feelings they evoke, are also rehearsed repeatedly, with very little change. In these ways, it continues to produce gardening as a 'way of life' – continually repeated through practice to honour previous historical traditions of clean earth, of colour through bedding plants and through high ethical approaches to caring for the soil. In these ways, the tight grip on traditional working-class tastes and skills enabled my respondents to build an alternative value system that fostered an emotional politics of resistance to consumerism and national lifestyle aesthetics.

Conclusion to the Book

This book began autobiographically by considering my classed and gendered position in relation to the ordinary enthusiasm of gardening in the mid 1990s. It explores the gaps that appeared between my (once) working-class gardening competencies and the taste cultures promulgated by television and media culture of the late 1990s. It demonstrates what I had long suspected: that the private domestic garden, a mundane consumption site attached to most peoples' homes, is a space where class and gender are continually made and re-made.

Using empirical detail, the book has traced some of the lived processes through which class and gender pervade gardening as a mundane hobby. Using an inter-disciplinary theoretical framework, it charts the historical antecedents of gendered practices and working-class regulation through autobiography of my own family's classed and gendered gardening on a Yorkshire council estate since the mid 1950s, and a larger socio-historical backcloth of popular gardening since the nineteenth century.

The book has examined how the garden has been legislated in official histories as a means of geographically and historically locating the empirical data. Arguing that most official histories have ignored the ordinary and the working-class, the book turns to recent social history of the private domestic garden as a means of framing its findings. As such, my hope is that this book has made a contribution to that growing literature, recording as it does, the voices and experiences of ordinary gardeners – a group often marginalised from official accounts. In this way, it has documented a finite moment in British 1990s cultural history. It offers a small-scale, yet detailed account of how gardening has been practiced in the North of England; it offers an analysis of how the garden and gardeners were represented in media and television culture of the time; and it explores how such mediations were consumed and synthesised by the people of the study in relation to their own gardens.

By tracing these threads, the book has pursued a number of key arguments. First, that gardens are classed spaces, shaped by knowledge differentials and unequal resource access. The middle-class people of the study were able to use their gardens as an exchangeable form of culture; while the working-class were unable to deploy their gardening resources beyond the local. Second, this was why nationally 'legitimate' 1990s garden lifestyle media failed to appeal to most of the people of the study: such texts lauded middle-class practices and where working-class gardening aesthetics appeared (and this was rare) they were bulldozed through practices of symbolic violence. Third, that gardening is often performed in conventionally gendered ways, though some were choosing to navigate gender roles in ways which make gardening 'gender trouble'. Though to be sure, gender is inflected by its proximity to class and the investment in gendered aesthetics depended on the class location of the respondent. Fourth, the study uncovered ways in which, by declining the move to do 'lifestyling' working-class gardeners developed their own 'way of life' meaning-making practices and aesthetic dispositions based on local codes and knowledges. By adding to the oral tradition of infusing their accounts of cultural practices with sentimentality, they continued their own sense of historical community – rejecting lifestyle consumerism in the process.

The working-class subjects of this book were not interested in trying to secure value through acquiring middle-class gardening tastes; nor did they seek out ways of making their 'land' into an enterprising form of culture, exchangeable beyond local contexts, in the ways in which their middle-class counter-parts did. But while sentimental capital has value for those who use and make it, according to the Bourdieusian conception of capital exchange-value, it holds none beyond local circuits. Skeggs's (2004b) work on exchange, value and affect in Boudieu's work is germane here. In her reading of the habitus as obsessively out to generate value as part of a, 'future-projected ...exchange-value self', she asks how we represent subjects who are uninterested in playing, 'the dominant symbolic game' as a means of accruing value to the self (2004b, 89). For if we hold with Bourdieu's model, ultimately working-class practices are rendered value-less, a bad set of cultural choices. 'How,' she implores, 'do we represent them with value?' (Skeggs 2004b, 87).

One way, according to Skeggs, is to think beyond exchange-value, by being attentive to alternative working-class value systems. We need, she argues, ethnographies which investigate elements of working-class culture which lie outside the dominant symbolic: elements valued not just by the working-class, 'the anti-pretentious humour, the dignity, the high ethical standards of honour, loyalty and caring'; different ethical value systems, such as working-class re-evaluations of respectability; and forms of culture which simply de-authorise the dominant exchange-value system, 'the habit of recalcitrance, of non-belonging ... the f*** off and 'so what' of utterances' (2004b, 88). Calling for a shift to investigate how use-value works through emotion in working-class culture as a means to understand, 'those who cannot or who do not want to make property out of their relations to others' (2004b, 91) enables the exploration, 'of how something has different values in different relations, different contexts, enabling us to break through the dominant symbolic understandings premised on exchange' (2004b, 89). In this way, we can begin to move beyond simply seeing working-class culture as lack or bad choice.

By making the shift to thinking about the use-value of sentimental capital and its attachment to gardening, one can appreciate the forms of valuing which inhere in how it is continually re-made by the working-class people of this book. Focusing on how sentimental capital is used shores up its good things: caring for the garden as part of the home and for the people past and present who have been part of those processes. In these ways, gardening practices become bound by sentiment as an affective means by which those who told and listened became part of the on-going history of a shared community.

Appendix 1

The Research Process: A Methodological Account

Between December 1998 and July 1999 I took a period of leave from my role as full-time Lecturer at the University of Wolverhampton and I took up residence with my parents in West Yorkshire. It was there that I began to involve myself in a small community of gardeners. However, despite my familiarity with the area, the garden community I was to study was just three miles away from the council house my grandparents had lived in back in the 1950s, I had left as a teenager in 1984 to study a degree at University and I had come back to an area I was familiar with, rather than to a community I still knew. And as many academics who have conducted qualitative research readily admit, gaining access to ethnographic respondents, especially for the purposes of studying domestic consumption, is fraught with difficulties (Hermes 1995; Moores 1996). When I began the research, the unappealing idea of knocking on doors or of hailing passers-by in the local town centre seemed like an awkward and intrusive method of finding respondents. I had also tried to enquire about outreaching interviewees by asking a garden centre worker about the possibility of somehow advertising for informants through her. In her ethnographic study of romance novels Radway (1987) finds 'Dot', a bookshop worker who put her in touch with a whole community of readers buying novels from her shop. I was trying to find someone like Radway's 'Dot', but my conversation with the garden centre worker was stilted and awkward. I found it difficult to explain my needs to a stranger and I decided to find another method to access respondents. I mentioned my problems and feelings of discomfort to my parents and it was then that my father offered to ask neighbours, members of his local painting group and workers – at the carpet factory where my father had worked until retirement – if they would be willing to be interviewed. Nobody refused and there was therefore no need to use the local press or magazines as a means to advertise for informants, as other researchers document in their methodological accounts (Stacey 1994). I had managed to gain access to a community through a relatively informal channel, and moreover, this group of gardeners were willing to talk to me as a favour for my father. Acting as an invaluable mediator between myself – the already embarrassed researcher – and my interviewee/s, my father set the interview time and dates and always accompanied me to the first meeting as a means of providing an introduction. However, not all of the interviews were garnered by my father, in particular, several of my middle-class respondents were contacted through what is described as 'snowballing' (Hammersley and Atkinson 1995) or 'friendship pyramiding' (Hermes 1995). In these ways Maud became a key informant. As a principal organiser of the *Spen Valley Flower Club,* she set up interviews for me with other educated middle-class gardeners.

While interviews were not the only resource I drew on for gathering data about my respondents, they offered the bulk of information on which the findings of this project are based. All of the interviews took place in and around the home setting of my respondents, but they were never entirely statically located in the living room. I was always taken into the garden and through conservatories and greenhouses if they were in existence, so that I got a sense of the particular specificity of garden sites and how they were fastened to the domestic space of the house. While the interview would begin with a set of questions (detailed in appendix 3), it invariably became informal and meandering and the 'tour' across the garden and its related sites generated further informal talk. In these ways, what began as a semi-structured interview became an unstructured informal conversational encounter in a natural setting. All interviews were tape-recorded, photographs were taken and notes about the 'tour' were committed to fieldnotes and diaries. Interviews took between two to three hours.

The subjects of the research

I interviewed, observed and gardened with 21 gardeners: 12 were women and nine were men. All the respondents were white and heterosexual. Their ages ranged from 27 to 96. I locate my respondents broadly into two class groups: working-class and middle-class gardeners. However, classifying in class terms is always fraught with difficulties. For some, to attempt to fix or abstractly define class is to ignore the historical construction of class as a site of struggle: 'Analysis of class should therefore aim to capture the ambiguity produced through struggle and fuzzy boundaries, rather than to fix it in place in order to measure and know it' (Skeggs 2004, 5). Nonetheless, I drew on Bourdieu's theory of capitals (for a detailed discussion of capitals see chapter 2) to 'place' and understand my respondents' class location. In this way, I used the research encounters to assess, in ways that cannot be easily measured, how far economic, social, cultural and symbolic capitals were held, deployed and exchanged by the people of the study. In this sense, the empirical snapshot offered by the data bears the marks of the internal power structure constructed by the differential access to the (capital) resources at stake in gardening as a field. I also took a range of other factors in to consideration in order to 'measure' class: I accounted for my respondents' housing, car ownership, educational qualifications, occupation and their own and their parents' class position (see tables 1 and 2). It must, however, be noted that measuring class using tables in these ways is problematic for women. The personal biographies of my respondents are to be found in appendix 2. I use pseudonyms to protect the identity of my subjects.

Table 1: Class, Parents' Class, Educational Qualifications and Age

Name	Class	Parent's Class	Ed. Qualifications	Age
Maud	middle	middle	Prof. qualification	96
Rosemary	middle	middle	Post graduate	55
David	middle	middle	Post graduate	68
Hugo	middle	working	Prof. qualification	78
Margaret	middle	middle	'O'Levels	68
Anne	middle	working	Degree	54
Phoebe	middle	middle	Degree	26
Thomas	middle	working	Prof. qualification	68
Lena	middle	working	None	72
Jack	middle	working	Prof. qualification	57
Millie	middle	working	Prof. qualification	56
Keith	working	working	CSEs	46
Geoff	working	working	'O'Levels	48
Kate	working	working	CSE	46
Philip	working	working	CSEs	55
Catherine	working	working	None	56
James	lower middle	working	'O'Levels	72
John	working	working	CSEs	41
Stephanie	working	working	None	38
Doris	working	working	None	86
Nancie	working	working	None	66

Table 2: Housing, Car Ownership and Employment

Name	Housing	Car ownership	Occupation
Maud	owner-occupied	Yes	Retired school teacher
Rosemary	owner-occupied	No	Retired university lecturer
David	owner-occupied	Yes	Retired grammar school teacher
Hugo	owner-occupied	Yes	Retired chemical dye-house technician
Margaret	owner-occupied	No	Housewife
Anne	owner-occupied	Yes	Set builder/sales worker Ikea
Phoebe	owner-occupied	No	Unemployed
Thomas	owner-occupied	Yes	Retired sales executive

Lena	owner-occupied	No	Housewife
Jack	owner-occupied	Yes	Retired bank manager
Millie	owner-occupied	Yes	Retired deputy bank manager
Keith	owner-occupied	Yes	Production foreman
Geoff	rented	No	Carpet factory plant operator
Kate	rented	No	Part-time super-market worker
Philip	rented	Yes	Carpet factory production planner
Catherine	rented	No	Carpet factory winder
James	owner-occupied	Yes	Retired gardener and florist
John	owner-occupied	Yes	Self-employed garage owner
Stephanie	owner-occupied	Yes	Employee at husband's garage business (above)
Doris	rented	No	Widowed housewife
Nancie	owner-occupied	No	Retired carpet factory setter

Every gardener had some kind of relationship with another or others in the sample: they were either friends, neighbours, work colleagues or they knew each other through the *Spen Valley Flower Club*. This community of gardeners shared similar reference points: they often used the same garden centres, they attended the same events and, in some cases – though I argue that the following practices among the gardeners I categorise as working-class – they gardened for each other, gave plants to one another and swapped cuttings and seeds. Since this study is based on a group of men and women who have at least a partial sense of shared community, I visited the garden centres my respondents referred to and I participated in the lunches, flower arranging events and occasional visits to local gardens of historic interest. I was also invited to the July Charity Fete, hosted by Maud the principal organiser of *Spen Valley Flower Club* and her daughter Rosemary.

Appendix 2

Respondent Biographies

Maud

Retired school teacher. Aged 96. Lives with her daughter Rosemary (below). She jointly owns her detached modern bungalow with her daughter. The flower garden constitutes half an acre. Maud is a principal organiser of the *Spen Valley Flower Club*.

Rosemary

Retired University Lecturer. Aged 61. Lives with her mother Maud (above). She jointly owns her detached modern bungalow with her mother. The flower garden constitutes half an acre. Rosemary is a flower arranger who first trained at the Constance Sprye School in the mid-1960s. She plays a key organisational role at the *Spen Valley Flower Club*.

David

Retired grammar school biology teacher. Aged 68. Lives alone in the house his parents bought in the 1930s. David's flower and vegetable garden constitutes three quarters of an acre. He is especially interested in the reproductive function of plants and in chrysanthemums.

Hugo

Retired chemical dye-house technician. Aged 78. Lives with his wife Margaret (below). He and his wife own their modern bungalow. They have a small modern garden which surrounds the house. Hugo is especially interested in composting.

Margaret

Housewife. Aged 68. Lives with her husband Hugo. Margaret and her husband own their modern bungalow. They have a small modern garden which surrounds the house. Margaret used to work part-time for the Conservative Party.

Anne

Part-time set builder and sales worker at Ikea. Aged 54. Separated from her husband Richard who used to work as a television set designer until he was made redundant. Anne and Richard jointly own their large Victorian semi-detached house, which has a number of outbuildings. Anne now lives with her daughter Phoebe (below) aged 26. Anne graduated from University four years ago with a BA (Hons) degree in Fine Art. They have a tiny front garden and a small back garden.

Phoebe

Unemployed. Aged 26. Lives with her mother Anne (above) in their large Victorian semi-detached house, which has a number of outbuildings. Phoebe graduated from University two years ago with a BA (Hons) degree in Textile Design. They have a tiny front garden and a small back garden. Phoebe is especially interested in herbs and poisonous plants.

Thomas

Retired sales executive. Aged 68. Lives with his wife Lena (below). They jointly own a large 1930s semi-detached house. They have a medium sized garden which surrounds the house.

Lena

Housewife. Aged 72. Lives with her husband Thomas (above). They jointly own a large semi-detached house. They have a medium sized garden which surrounds the house.

Jack

Retired 'securities' bank manager. Aged 57. Lives with his wife Millie (below). They jointly own a house in a shared complex which overlooks a communal garden. Jack and Millie are the most active gardeners in the complex.

Millie

Retired deputy bank manager. Aged 56. Lives with her husband Jack (above). They jointly own a house in a shared complex which overlooks a communal garden. Millie and Jack are the most active gardeners in the complex.

Keith

Production foreman at a fibreglass factory. Aged 46. Lives with his wife Joy and his two stepsons. They jointly own a corner Victorian terraced house. Keith is the main gardener and tends a medium sized flower garden. Keith is especially interested in summer bedding plants and new plant varieties.

Geoff

Laytex plant operator at a carpet factory. Aged 48. Lives with his wife Kate (below) and their son in a small terraced house. They own a tiny front garden. They have recently purchased some land at the back of the house previously owned by their neighbour. They were devising new plans for their back garden at the time of interview.

Kate

Part-time supermarket worker. Aged 46. Lives with her husband Geoff (above) and their son in a small terraced house. They own a tiny front garden. They have recently purchased some land at the back previously owned by their neighbour. They were devising new plans for their back garden at the time of interview.

Philip

Production planner at a carpet factory. Aged 55. Lives with his wife Catherine (below). They own a semi-detached 1960s bungalow. They own a modern surrounding garden.

Catherine

Winder at a carpet factory. Aged 56. Lives with her husband Philip (above). They own a semi-detached 1960s bungalow. They own a modern surrounding garden.

James

Retired professional gardener and florist. Aged 72. Lives with his wife Joyce. He owns a modern 1970s bungalow and half an acre of surrounding garden. James began work in private service in the 1930s. He held post as head gardener for two mill owners in the region. He went on to run a local floristry business.

John

Owns his own garage business and works as an engineer. Aged 41. Lives with his wife Stephanie (below) and their son and daughter in a small semi-detached modern house. They have a tiny front garden. The back garden has been a working vegetable garden, but is now used to store garage overspill and is a children's play area.

Stephanie

Works as an employee for her husband's garage business. Aged 38. Lives with her husband John (above) and their son and daughter in a small semi-detached modern house. They have a tiny front garden. The back garden has been a working vegetable garden, but is now used to store garage overspill and is a children's play area.

Doris

Widowed housewife. Aged 86. Was married to Bert who worked as a salesman. She has three sons. Owns a small 1930s semi-detached house and a modest surrounding garden. Doris is a member of the *Spen Valley Flower Club*.

Nancie

Worked as a setter at a carpet factory. Aged 66. Married to James, a retired quality control manager at a carpet factory. They own a small semi-detached 1930s house and a surrounding garden.

Appendix 3

1. Please describe your garden for me. For example, its size and shape and detail the plants it contains and any features of special interest.

2. Would you say that your garden has a particular ethos? Would you say, for example, that your garden could be described as an 'English country garden'?

For co-habiting couples and mother daughter households:

3. Who does what in the garden?

Alternatively:

3. What tasks do you do in the garden?

4. Do you have any special features of interest in your garden, for example, a sculpture, a water-feature, a pergola?

5. Is there anything that you would specifically not choose for your garden?

6. Do you have any dreams or aspirations for the future of your garden?

7. What aspects of the garden media do you consume?

8. Has your gardening ever been influenced by these aspects of the media?

Bibliography

Adkins, L. and Skeggs, B. (eds.) (2004), *Feminism After Bourdieu* (Oxford: Blackwell Publishing).

Ahmed, S. (2004), *The Cultural Politics of Emotion* (Edinburgh: Edinburgh University Press).

Arnold, M. (1993), *Culture and Anarchy and Other Writings* Stefan Collini (ed.) (Cambridge: Cambridge University Press).

Aslama, M. and Pantti, M. (2006), 'Talking Alone: Reality TV, emotions and authenticity', *European Journal of Cultural Studies,* 9:2, 167-184.

Atkinson, P. et al. (eds.) (2001), *Handbook of Ethnography* (London: Sage).

Attfield, J. (1995), 'Inside Pram Town: A Case Study of Harlow House Interiors, 1951-61', in Attfield, J. and Kirkham, P. (eds.).

Attfield, J. and Kirkham, P. (eds.) (1995), *A View from the Interior: Women and Design* (London: Women's Press).

Attfield, J. (1999), 'Bringing Modernity Home: Open Plan in the British Domestic Interior', in Cieraad, I. (ed.).

Austin, J. L. (1962), *How To Do Things With Words* (Cambridge, Massachusetts: Harvard University Press).

Bailey, P. (1978), *Leisure and class in Victorian England: rational recreation and the contest for control 1830-1885* (London: Routledge and Kegan Paul).

Ball, M. and Smith, G. (2001), 'Technologies of Realism? Ethnographic Uses of Photography and Film', in Atkinson, P. et al. (eds.)

Balmori, D. and Morton, M. (1993), *Transitory Gardens: Uprooted Lives* (New Haven and London: Yale University Press).

Barker, M. and Beezer, A. (1992), *Reading into Cultural Studies* (London: Routledge).

Bassnett, S. (ed.) (1997), *Studying British Cultures* (London: Routledge).

Bauman, Z. (1987), *Legislators and Interpreters: On Modernity, Postmodernity and Intellectuals* (Cambridge: Polity Press).

Bausinger, H. (1984), 'Media, Technology and Daily Life', *Media, Culture and Society* 6, 343-51.

Beauvoir, S. de (1988), *The Second Sex* (London: Pan Books).

Beck, U. (1992), *The Risk Society: Towards a New Modernity* (London: Sage).

Bedarida, F. (1990), *A Social History of England, 1815-1990* (London: Routledge).

Bell, D. and Hollows, J. (eds.) (2005), *Ordinary Lifestyles: Popular Media, Consumption and Taste* (Maidenhead: Open University Press).

Bell, D. and Hollows, J. (eds.) (2006), *Historicizing Lifestyles: Mediating Taste, Consumption and Identity from the 1900s to 1970s* (Aldershot: Ashgate).

Bennett, T. et al. (1999), *Accounting for Tastes: Australian Everyday Cultures* (Cambridge: Cambridge University Press).

Bhatti, M. (1999), 'The Meaning of Gardens in an Age of Risk' in Chapman, T. and Hockey, J. (eds.).

Bhatti, M. (2000), '"I never promised you a rose garden": gender, leisure and home-making', *Leisure Studies* 19:3, 183-197.

Bhatti, M. and Church, A. (2001), 'Cultivating Natures: Homes and Gardens in Late Modernity', *Sociology* 35: 2, 365-383.

Bhatti, M. (2006), '"When I'm in the garden I can create my own paradise": Homes and gardens in later life', *The Sociological Review*, 54: 2, 309-341.

Bondebjerg, I. (1996), 'Public Discourse/Private Fascination: Hybridisation in "True-Life-Story" Genres', *Media, Culture and Society,* 18, 2-45.

Bonner, F. (2003), *Ordinary Television: Analysing Popular TV* (London: Sage).

Bourdieu, P. (1977), *An Outline of a Theory of Practice* (Cambridge: Cambridge University Press).

Bourdieu, P. (1986), *Distinction: A Social Critique of the Judgement of Taste* (London: Routledge).

Bourdieu, P. and Passeron, J. C. (1990a), *Reproduction in Education, Society and Culture* (London: Sage).

Bourdieu, P. (1990b), *Photography: a middle-brow art?* (Cambridge: Polity).

Bourdieu, P. and Waquant, L. (1992), *An Invitation to Reflexive Sociology* (Chicago: University of Chicago Press).

Bourke, J. (1994), *Working-Class Culture in Britain 1890-1960: gender, class and ethnicity* (London: Routledge).

Boys, J. (1995), 'From Alcatraz to the OK Corral: Images of Class and Gender in Housing Design', in Attfield, J. and Kirkham, P. (eds.).

Brown, J. (1999), *The Pursuit of Paradise: A Social History of Gardens and Gardening* (London: HarperCollinsPublishers).

Brunsdon, C. (1996), 'A Thief in the Night: Stories of Feminism in the 1970s at CCCS' in Morley, D. and Chen, K. H. (eds.).

Brunsdon, C. (1997), *Screen Tastes: Soap Opera to Satellite Dishes* (London: Routledge).

Brunsdon, C. et al. (2001), 'Factual entertainment on British television: The Midlands TV Research Group's "8-9 Project"', *European Journal of Cultural Studies* 4:1, 29-62.

Brunsdon, C. (2003), 'Lifestyling Britain: The 8-9 Slot on British Television', *International Journal of Cultural Studies* 6:1, 5-23.

Bulos, M. and Teymur, N. (eds.) (1993), *Housing: Design, Research, Education* (Aldershot: Avebury).

Butler, J. (1990), *Gender Trouble: Feminism and the Subversion of Identity* (London: Routledge).

Butler, J. (1997), *Excitable Speech: A Politics of the Performative* (London: Routledge).

Campbell, C. (1995), *The Romantic Ethic and the Spirit of Modern Consumerism* (Oxford: Basil Blackwell).

Carrabine, E. and Longhurst, B. (1999), 'Mosaics of Omnivorousness: Suburban Youth and Popular Music', *New Formations*, 38, 125-140.

Cieraad, I. (ed.) (1999), *At Home: An Anthropology of Domestic Space.* (Syracuse: Syracuse University Press).

Chaney, D. (1996), *Lifestyles* (London: Routledge).

Chaney, D. (2001), 'From Ways of Life to Lifestyle: Rethinking culture as ideology and sensibility', in Lull, J. (ed.).

Chaney, D. (2002), *Cultural Change and Everyday Life* (Basingstoke: Palgrave).

Chapman, T. and Hockey, J. (eds.) (1999), *Ideal Homes? Social Change and Domestic Life* (London: Routledge).

Chevalier, S. (1998), 'From woollen carpet to grass carpet: bridging house and garden in the English suburb', in Miller, D. (ed.).

Clapson, M. (2000), 'The Suburban Aspiration in England since 1919', *Contemporary British History* 14:1, 151-174.

Clifford, D. (1962), *A History of Garden Design* (London: Faber and Faber).

Cobbett, W. (1996), *The English Gardener* (London: Bloomsbury).

Cockburn, C. (1985), *Machinery of Dominance: Women, Men and Technical Know-How* (London: Pluto Press).

Coffey, A. (2002), 'Ethnography and Self: Reflections and Representations', in May, T. (ed.).

Constantine, S. (1981), 'Amateur Gardening and Popular Recreation in the 19th and 20th Centuries', *Journal of Social History* 14: 3, 387-406.

Coward, R. (1984), *Female Desire* (London: Paladin).

Clapson, M. (2000), 'The Suburban Aspiration in England since 1919', *Contemporary British History* 14:1, 151-174.

Clarke, J. et al. (eds.) (1979), *Working-Class Culture: Studies in history and theory* (London: Hutchinson).

Critcher, C. (1979), 'Sociology, cultural studies and the post-war working-class', in Clarke, J. et al. (eds.).

Crouch, D. and Ward, C. (1999), *The Allotment: Its Landscape and Culture* (Nottingham: Five Leaves Publications).

Dann, C. (1992), 'Sweet William and Sticky Nellie: Sex Differences in New Zealand Gardening and Garden Writing', *Women's Studies International Forum* 15: 2, 233-249.

Davis, J. (1993), *The Wartime Kitchen Garden.* (London: BBC Books).

Davidoff, L. and Hall, C. (1994), *Family Fortunes: men and women of the English middle-class 1780-1850* (London: Hutchinson).

Don, Monty (1997), 'Cider with the Roses', *Observer Life*, October 19th : 56-57.

Don, Monty (1998), 'Cartoon Characters', *Observer Life*, September 6th: 38-39.

Douglas, M. and Isherwood, B. (1996), *The World of Goods: Towards an Anthropology of Consumption* (London: Routledge).

Dworkin, A. (1981), *Pornography: Men Possessing Women* (London: The Women's Press).

Dyck, I. et al. (1995), 'Women Talking: Creating Knowledge Through Difference in Cross-Cultural Research', *Women's Studies International Forum,* 18:5/6, 611-626.

Dyer, R. (1997), *White* (London: Routledge).

Eagleton, T. (ed.) (1989), *Raymond Williams: critical perspectives* (Oxford: Polity Press).

Easthope, A. (1997), 'But what *is* Cultural Studies?, in Bassnett, S. (ed.).

Edgell, S. et al. (eds.) (1996), *Consumption Matters: the production and experience of consumption* (Oxford: Blackwell Publishing).

Edwards, A.M. (1981), *The Design of Suburbia* (London: Pembridge).

Eliot, T.S. (1948), *Notes Towards a Definition of Culture* (London: Faber and Faber).

Ellis, J. (2000), 'Scheduling: The Last Creative Act in Television?', *Media, Culture and Society*, 22:1, 25-38.

Ellis, J. (1982), *Visible Fictions: Cinema: Television: Video* (London: Routledge and Kegan Paul).

Epstein, C.F. and Coser, R.L. (eds.) (1981), *Access to Power: Cross-National Studies of Women and Elites* (London: George Allen and Unwin).

Featherstone, M. (1991), *Consumer Culture and Postmodernism* (London: Sage).

Featherstone, M. (1995), *Undoing Cultures: Globalization, Postmodernism and Identity* (London: Sage).

Felski, R. (2000), 'The Invention of Everyday Life', *New Formations* 39, 15-31.

Fort, T. (2001), *The Grass is Greener: Our Love Affair with The Lawn* (London: Harper Collins).

Foucault, M. (1977), *Discipline and Punish: The Birth of the Prison* (London: Penguin).

Fowler, B. (1994), 'The Hegemonic Work of Art in the Age of Electronic Reproduction: An Assessment of Pierre Bourdieu', *Theory, Culture and Society*, 11:1, 129-154.

Fowler, B. (ed.) (2000), *Reading Bourdieu on Society and Culture* (Oxford: Blackwell).

Francis, M. and Hestor, R.T. (eds.) (1993), *The Meaning of Gardens: Idea, Place and Action* (Cambridge, Massachusetts: MIT Press).

Frankenberg, R. (1993), *White Women, Race Matters: The Social Construction of Whiteness* (London: Routledge).

Frow, J. (1995), *Cultural Studies and Cultural Value* (Oxford: Oxford University Press).

Gabb, J. (1999), 'Consuming the Garden: Locating a Feminine Narrative Within Popular Cultural Texts and Gendered Genres' in Stokes, J. and Reading, A. (eds.).

Garfinkel, H. (1987), *Studies in Ethnomethodology* (Cambridge: Polity).

Garnham, N. and Williams, R. (1980), 'Pierre Bourdieu and the Sociology of Culture: An Introduction', *Media, Culture and Society,* 2:3, 297-312.

Geraghty, C. and Lusted, D. (eds.) (1998), *The Television Studies Book* (London: Arnold).

Giddens, A. (1990), *The Consequences of Modernity* (Cambridge: Polity Press).

Gillespie, M. (1995), *Television, Ethnicity and Cultural Change* (London: Routledge).

Gorton, K. (2006), 'A Sentimental Journey: Television, Meaning and Emotion', *Journal of British Cinema and Television*, 3:1, 72-81.

Gorton, K. (2008), 'There's No Place Like Home: emotional exposure, excess and empathy on tv', *Critical Studies in Television* 3:1, 1-16.

Grampp, C. (1993), 'Social Meanings and Residential Gardens' in Francis, M. and Hester, R. T. (eds.).

Gray, A. (1992), *Video playtime: the gendering of a leisure technology* (London: Routledge).

Gray, A. (1997), 'Learning from Experience: Cultural Studies and Feminism' in Jim McGuigan (ed.).

Griffin, S. (1981), *Pornography and Silence: Culture's Revenge Against Nature* (London: The Women's Press).

Griffiths, M. and Tronya, B. (eds.) (1994), *Antiracism, Culture and Social Justice in Education* (London: Trentham Books).

Gripsrud, J. (1989), '"High Culture" revisited', *Cultural Studies* 3:2, 194-207.

Gripsrud, J. (2004), 'Broadcast Television: The Chances of Its Survival in a Digital Age' in Spigel, L. and Olsson, J. (eds.).

Groag-Bell, S. (1990), 'Women Create Gardens in Male Landscapes: A revisionist approach to eighteenth century English garden history', *Feminist Studies* 16:3, 471-491.

Gronow, J. and Warde, A. (eds.) (1999), *Ordinary Consumption* (London: Routledge).

Grossberg, L. (1987), 'The In-Difference of Television', *Screen* 28:2, 28-45.

Hadfield, M. (1979), *A History of British Gardening* (London: John Murray).

Hall, S. and Jefferson, T. (eds.) (1976), *Resistance Through Rituals: Youth Subcultures in Post-war Britain* (London: Hutchinson).

Hall, S. et al. (eds.) (1990), *Culture, Media, Language* (London: Routledge).

Hammersley, M. and Atkinson, P. (1995), *Ethnography: Principles in Practice* (London: Routledge).

Harkness, J. (1978), *Roses* (London: J. M. Dent & Sons Ltd).

Harvey, D. (1989), *The Condition of Postmodernity* (Oxford: Blackwell).

Hebdige, D. (1979), *Subculture: The Meaning of Style* (London: Methuen).

Hebdige, D. (1994), 'Postmodernism and "The Other Side"' in Storey, J (ed.).

Heller, D. (ed.) (2007), *Makeover Television: Realities Remodelled* (London: I. B. Taurus).

Helphand, K. (1997), 'Defiant Gardens', *Journal of Design History,* 17:2, 101-121.

Hermes, J. (1995), *Reading Women's Magazines*: *An Analysis of Everyday Media Use* (Oxford: Polity Press).

Hetherington, K. (1998), *Expressions of Identity* (London: Sage).

Heward, C. (1996), 'Masculinities and Families', in Mac An Ghaill, M. (ed.).

Hobson, D. (1982), *Crossroads: the drama of a soap opera* (London: Methuen).

Hoggart, R. (1957), *The Uses of Literacy* (London: Chatto & Windus).

Hoggart, R. (1958), 'Speaking to each other', in Mackenzie, N. (ed.).

Hollows, J. (2000), *Feminism, Femininity and Popular Culture* (Manchester: Manchester University Press).

Hollows, J. and Gillis, S. (eds.) (2008), *Homefires: Domesticity, Feminism and Popular Culture* (London: Routledge).

Holmes, S. and Jermyn, D. (eds.) (2004), *Understanding Reality Television* (London: Routledge).

Hoyles, M. (1991), *The Story of Gardening* (London: Pluto Journeyman).

Jameson, F. (1991), *Postmodernism; or, the Cultural Logic of Late Capitalism* (London: Verso).

Jardine, L. and Swindells, J. (1989), 'Homage to Orwell: the dream of a common culture, and other minefields' in Eagleton, T. (ed.).

Jellicoe, G. (1995), *The Landscape of Man: shaping the environment from prehistory to the present* (London: Thames and Hudson).

Jenkins, H. (1992), *Textual Poachers* (London: Routledge).

Jenkins, R. (1996), *Social Identity* (London: Routledge).

Jenkins, R. (2002), *Pierre Bourdieu* (London: Routledge).

Jordan, G. and Weedon, C. (1997), *Cultural Politics: race, class and gender in the postmodern world* (Oxford: Blackwell).

Kimber, C. (1973), 'Spatial patterning in the dooryard gardens of Puerto Rico', *Geographical Review* 63, 6-29.

Kirkham, P. (1995), 'The Personal, the Professional and the Partner(ship): the husband/wife collaboration of Charles and Ray Eames', in Skeggs, B. (ed.).

Kirkham, P. (ed.) (1997), *The Gendered Object* (Manchester: Manchester University Press).

Knight, D. (1999), 'Why We Enjoy Condemning Sentimentality: A Meta-Aesthetic Perspective', *Journal of Aesthetics and Art Criticism* 57:4, 411-420.

Lash, S. (1990), *The Sociology of Post-Modernism* (London: Routledge).

Leal, O. F. (1990), 'Popular taste and erudite repertoire: the place and space of television in Brazil', *Cultural Studies* 4:1, 19-29.

Lebeau, V. (1997), 'The Worst of All Possible Worlds?', in Silverstone, R (ed.).

Lefebvre, H. (1984), *Everyday Life in the Modern World* (New York: Transaction).

Lefebvre, H. (1987), 'The Everyday and Everydayness', *Yale French Studies* 73, 7-11.

Lloyd, C. (1984), *The Well-Chosen Garden* (London: Elm Tree Books).

Longhurst, B. and Savage, M. (1996), 'Social class, consumption and the influence of Bourdieu: some critical issues' in Edgell, S. et al. (eds.).

Lovell, T. (2000), 'Thinking Feminism with and against Bourdieu', *Feminist Theory* 1:1, 11-32.

Lull, J. (ed.) (2001), *Culture in the Communication Age* (London: Routledge).

Lusted, D. (1998), 'The Popular Culture Debate and Light Entertainment on Television', in Geraghty, C. and Lusted, D. (eds.).

Mac An Ghaill, M. (ed.) (1996), *Understanding Masculinities* (Buckingham: Open University Press).

MacDonald, S. and Porter, P. (1990), *Putting on the Style: Setting up Home in the 1950s* (London: The Geffrye Museum).

MacKenzie, N. (ed.) (1958), *Conviction* (London: MacGibbon and Kee).

MacLeod, D. (1982), *Down-to-Earth Women: those who care for the soil* (Edinburgh: William Blackwood).

Madigan, R. and Munro, M. (1990), 'Ideal Homes: Gender and Domestic Architecture', in Putnam, T. and Newton, C. (eds.).

Mahoney, P. and Zmroczek, C. (eds.) (1997), *Class Matters: 'Working-Class' Women's Perspectives on Social Class* (London: Taylor & Francis).

Mahoney, P. and Zmroczek, C. (1997), 'Why class matters', in P. Mahoney and C. Zmroczek (eds).

Matless, D. (1998), *Landscape and Englishness* (London: Reaktion Books).

May, T. (ed.) (2002), *Qualitative Research in Action* (London: Sage).

McCall, L. (1992), 'Does gender *fit*? Bourdieu, feminism, and conceptions of social order', *Theory and Society* 21, 837-67.

McGuigan, J. (1997), *Cultural Methodologies* (London: Sage).

McGuigan, J. (1999), *Modernity and Postmodern Culture* (Buckingham: Open University Press).

Meehan, E. (1991), 'Holy Commodity Fetish Batman!', in Pearson, R. E. and Uricchio, W. (eds.).

Medhurst, A. (1999), 'Day for Night', *Sight and Sound* 9:6, 26-7.

Medhurst, A. (2000), 'If Anywhere: Class, Identifications and Cultural Studies Academics', in Munt, S. R. (ed.).

Miles, S. et al (eds.) (2002), *The Changing Consumer: Markets and Meanings.* (London: Routledge).

Milner, A. (1999), *Class* (London: Sage).

Miller, D. (ed.) (1998), *Material Culture: Why some things matter* (London: UCL Press).

MINTEL (2000), *Home Interest and Gardening Magazines* (London: MINTEL International Group).

MINTEL (2001a), *Gardening Products Retailing* (London: MINTEL International Group).

MINTEL (2001b), *Gardening Review* (London: MINTEL International Group).

MINTEL (2007), *Gardening Review* (London: MINTEL International Group).

Moi, T. (1991), 'Appropriating Bourdieu: Feminist Theory and Pierre Bourdieu's Sociology of Culture', *New Literary History* 22, 1017-1049.

Moores, S. (1994), *Interpreting Audiences: The Ethnography of Media Consumption* (London: Sage).

Moores, S. (1996), *Satellite Television and Everyday Life: Articulating Technology.* (Luton: John Libbey Media).

Morley, D. (1986), *Family Television: Cultural Power and Domestic Television* (London: Comedia).

Morley, D. and Chen, K. H. (eds.) (1996), *Critical Dialogues in Cultural Studies* (London: Routledge).

Morris, M. S. (1995), '"Tha'lt be like a blush-rose when tha' grows up, my little lass": English cultural and gendered identity in *The Secret Garden*', *Environment and Planning D: Society and Space*, 14, 59-78.

Morris, M. S. (1997), 'Gardens "for ever England": Landscape, Identity and the First World War British Cemeteries on the Western Front', *Ecumene* 4:4, 410-434.

Moseley, R. (2000), 'Makeover Takeover on British Television', *Screen* 41:3, 299-314.

Mukerji, C. (1990), 'Reading and Writing with Nature: Social claims and the French formal garden', *Theory and Society* 19, 651-79.

Munt, S. R. (ed.) (2000), *Cultural Studies and the Working-class: Subject to change* (London: Cassell).

Murdock, G. (1997), 'Thin Description: Questions of Method in Cultural Analysis' in McGuigan, J. (ed.). *Cultural Methodologies* (London: Sage).

Nava, M. (1992), *Changing Cultures* (London: Sage).

Nava, M. and Nava, O. (1992), 'Discriminating or Duped? Young People as consumers of advertising/art', in Nava, M.

Nightingale, V. (1993), 'What's Ethnographic about Ethnographic Audience Research?' in Turner, G. (ed.).

Nowotny, H. (1981), 'Women in Public Life in Austria', in Epstein, C. F. and Coser, R. L. (eds.)

Olechnowicz, A. (1997), *Working-Class Housing in England Between the Wars: The Beacontree Estate* (Oxford: Clarendon Press).

Opie, A. (1992), 'Qualitative Research, Appropriation of the "Other" and Empowerment', *Feminist Review* 40, 52-69.

Palmer, G. (2004), 'The New You: Class and Transformation in lifestyle television', in Holmes, S. and Jermyn, D. (eds.).

Patemen, C. and Gross, E. (eds.) (1986), *Feminist Challenges: Social and Political Theory* (Boston: Northeastern University Press).

Pearson, R.E. and Uricchio, W. (eds.) (1990), *The Many Lives of Batman: Critical Approaches to a Superhero and his Media* (London: Routledge).

Peterson, R.A. and Kern, R.M. (1996), 'Changing Highbrow Taste: from Snob to Omnivore', *American Sociological Review* 61, 900-907.

Press, A. (1991), *Women Watching Television: Gender, Class and Generation in the American Television Experience* (Philadelphia: University of Pennsylvania Press).

Preston, R. (1995), 'Little English Landscapes: Developing suburban gardens between the wars', *Things* 2, 69-87.

Putnam, T. and Newton, C. (eds.) (1990), *Household Choices* (London: Middlesex Polytechnic and Future Publications).

Radway, J. (1987), *Reading the Romance: Women, Patriarchy and Popular Literature* (London: Verso).

Ravetz, A. and Turkington, R. (1995), *The Place of Home* (London: E and FN Spon).

Reay, D. (1995), 'Using habitus to look at 'race' and class in primary school classrooms' in Griffiths, M. and Tronya, B. (eds.).

Reay, D. (1996), 'Insider Perspectives or Stealing the Words out of Women's Mouths: Interpretation in the Research Process', *Feminist Review* 53, 57-73.

Reay, D. (2000), 'A useful extension of Bourdieu's conceptual framework?: emotional capital as a way of understanding mothers' involvement in their children's education?', *Sociological Review* 48:4, 568-585.

Rojek, C. (1995), *Decentring Leisure: Rethinking Leisure Theory* (London: Sage).

Savage, M. et al. (1992), *Property, Bureaucracy and Culture: Middle-Class Formation in Contemporary Britain* (London: Routledge).

Savage, M. and Miles, A. (1994), *The Re-making of the British Working-Class 1840-1940* (London: Routledge).

Savage, M. et al. (1999), 'Ordinary consumption and personal identity: radio and the middle-classes in the north west of England' in Gronow, J. and Warde, A. (eds.).

Savage, M. (2000a), *Class Analysis and Social Transformation* (Buckingham: Open University Press).

Savage, M. (2005), 'Working-Class Identities in the 1960s: Revisiting the Affluent Worker Study', *Sociology* 39:5, 929-946.

Savage, M. et al. (2000b), 'Individualization and cultural distinction' in Savage, M. (2000a).

Scheper-Hughes, N. (1982), *Saints, Scholars and Schizophrenics: Mental Illness in Rural Ireland* (London: University of California Press).

Scheper-Hughes, N. (2000), 'Ire in Ireland', *Ethnography* 1:1, 117-140.

Scott-James, A. (1981), *The Cottage Garden* (London: Allen Lane).

Scott Jenkins, V. (1994), *The Lawn: A History of an American Obsession* (Washington and London: Smithsonian Institution Press).

Scott-James, A. and Lancaster, O. (1977), *The Pleasure Garden* (Harmondsworth: Penguin).

Search, G. (1995), *Instant Gardening* (London: BBC books).

Seiter, E. et al. (eds.) (1989), *Remote Control: Television, Audiences and Cultural Power* (London: Routledge).

Seiter, E. et al. (1989), '"Don't treat us like we're so stupid and naïve": Towards an ethnography of soap opera viewers', in Seiter, E. et al. (eds.).

Seiter, E. (1990), 'Making Distinctions in TV Audience Research: Case Study of a Troubling Interview', *Cultural Studies* 4:1, 61-84.

Severson, R. (1990), 'United we Sprout: A Chicago Community Garden Story' in Francis, M. and Hester, H. J. (eds.).

Silverstone, R. (1994), *Television and Everyday Life* (London: Routledge).

Silverstone, R. (ed.) (1997), *Visions of Suburbia* (London: Routledge).

Sime, J. (1993), 'What makes a house a home: The garden?' in Bulos, M. and Teymur, N. (eds.).

Skeggs, B. (ed.) (1995), *Feminist Cultural Theory: process and production* (Manchester: Manchester University Press).

Skeggs, B. (1995), 'Theorising, ethics and representation in feminist ethnography', in Skeggs, B. (ed.).

Skeggs, B. (1997), *Formations of Class and Gender: Becoming Respectable* (London: Sage).

Skeggs, B. (2001), 'Feminist Ethnography' in Atkinson, P. et al. (eds.).

Skeggs, B. (2004a), *Class, Self, Culture* (London: Routledge).

Skeggs, B. (2004b), 'Exchange, value and affect: Bourdieu and 'the self'' in Adkins, L. and Skeggs, B. (eds.).

Southerton, D. (2002), 'Boundaries of 'Us' and 'Them': Class, Mobility and Identification in a New Town', *Sociology,* 36:1, 171-193.

Sparke, P. (1995), *As Long as it's Pink: The Sexual Politics of Taste* (London: Pandora).

Spigel, L. and Olsson, J. (eds.) (2004), *Television After TV: Essays on a Medium in Transition* (Durham and London: Duke University Press).

Spittle, S. (2002), 'Producing TV: Consuming TV', in Miles, S. et al. (eds.).

Stacey, J. (1994), *Star Gazing: Hollywood Cinema and Female Spectatorship* (London: Routledge).

Stacey, J. (1988), *Brave New Families*: *stories of domestic upheaval in the late twentieth century* (New York: Basic Books).

Stokes, J. and Reading, A. (eds.) (1999), *The Media in Britain: Current Debates and Developments.* (Basingstoke: Macmillan).

Storey, J. (ed.) (1994), *Cultural Theory and Popular Culture: A Reader* (Hemel Hempstead: Prentice Hall).

Strange, N. (1998), 'Perform, educate, entertain: ingredients of the cookery programme genre', in Geraghty, C. and Lusted, D. (eds.).

Taylor, B. (1987), *Modernism, Postmodernism, Realism: a critical perspective for art* (Winchester: Winchester School of Art Press).

Taylor, L. (2002), 'From Ways of Life to Lifestyle: The 'Ordinari-ization' of British Gardening Lifestyle Television', *European Journal of Communication* 17: 4, 479-493.

Taylor, L. (2005), 'It was beautiful before you changed it all: Class, taste and the transformative aesthetics of the garden lifestyle media', in Bell, D. and Hollows, J. (eds.).

Thacker, C. (1979), *The History of Gardens* (London: Croom Helm).

Thomas, K (1983), *Man in the Natural World* (London: Allen and Unwin).

Tilley, C. (2004), 'The Sensory Dimensions of Gardening', *Senses and Society* 1:3, 311-330.

Tulloch, J. (1989), 'Approaching the audience: The elderly', in Seiter, E. et al. (eds.).

Turner, G. (1990), *British Cultural Studies: An Introduction* (London: Routledge).

Turner, G. (1999), 'Tabloidization, journalism and the possibility of the critique', *International Journal of Cultural Studies* 2:1, 59-76.

Turner, G. (ed.) (1993), *Nation, Culture, Text: Australian Cultural and Media Studies*. London: Routledge.

Van Loon, J. (2001), 'Ethnography: A Critical Turn in Cultural Studies' in Atkinson, P. et al.(eds.).

Walkerdine, V. (1997), *Daddy's Girl: Young Girls and Popular Culture* (London: Macmillan Press).

Walkerdine, V. et al. (2001), *Growing Up Girl: Psychosocial Explorations of Gender and Class* (Basingstoke: Palgrave).

Warde, A. (2002), 'Setting the Scene: Changing conceptions of consumption', in Miles, S. et al. (eds.).

Warde, A. et al. (1999), 'Consumption and the problem of variety: cultural omnivorousness, social distinction and dining out', *Sociology* 33:1, 105-127.

Warhol, R. (2003), *Having a Good Cry: Effeminate Feelings and Pop-culture Forms* (Ohio: Ohio State University Press).

Weedon, C. (1987), *Feminist Practice and Poststructuralist Theory* (Oxford: Blackwell).

Weedon, C. (1999), *Feminism, Theory and the Politics of Difference* (Blackwell: Oxford).

Wilhelm, G. (1975), 'Dooryard gardens and gardening in the black community of Brushy, Texas', *Geographical Review* 65, 73-93.

Williams, R. (1993), *Culture and Society: 1780-1950* (London: The Hogarth Press).

Williams, R. (1979), *Politics and Letters: interviews with 'New Left review'* (London: New Left Books).

Williams, R. (1989), *Resources of Hope* (London: Verso).

Willis, P. (1977), *Learning to Labour: How Working-class Kids Get Working-class Jobs* (London: Saxon House).

Willis, P. (1996), 'Notes on method' in Hall, S. et al. (eds.).

Willis, P. (1990), *Common Culture* (Milton Keynes: Open University Press).

Willis, P. and Trondman, M. (2000), 'Manifesto for *Ethnography*', *Ethnography* 1:1, 5-16.

Wilson, A. (1991), *The Culture of Nature: North American Landscapes from Disney to the Exxon Valdez* (Oxford: Blackwell).

Wood, H. and Skeggs, B. (2004), 'Notes on Ethical Scenarios of Self on British Reality TV', *Feminist Media Studies* 4:2, 205-8.

Wood, H. (2008), *Talking With Television* (Urbana and Champagne: University of Illinois Press).

Wood, H. et al. (2008), '"It's Just Sad": the Mediation of Intimacy and the Emotional Labour of Reality TV Viewing' in Hollows, J. and Gillis, S. (eds.).

Wolschke-Bulmahn, J. and Groening, G. (1992), 'The ideology of the nature garden: Nationalistic trends in garden design in Germany during the early twentieth century', *Journal of Garden History* 12:1, 73-80.

Wynne, D. (1998), *Leisure, Lifestyle and the new middle-class: a case study* (London: Routledge).

Wynne, D. (1990), 'Leisure, Lifestyle and the Construction of Social Position', *Leisure Studies* 9:1, 21-34.

Wynne, D. and O'Connor, J. (1995), City Cultures and the New Cultural Intermediaries, paper presented to BSA Annual Conference, Leicester.

Yeatman, A. (1986), 'Women, Domestic Life and Sociology' in Pateman, C. and Gross, E. (eds.)

Yeo, E. and Yeo, S. (1981), *Popular Culture and Class Conflict 1590-1914* (Brighton: Harvester).

Index

Note: Bold page numbers indicate illustrations; Numbers in brackets preceded by *n* are footnote numbers.